THE McNAMARA STRATEGY

The McNamara Strategy

WILLIAM W. KAUFMANN

HARPER & ROW, PUBLISHERS
NEW YORK, EVANSTON,
AND LONDON

FIRST EDITION

LIBRARY OF CONGRESS CATALOG CARD NUMBER: 64–12672

D-O

In memory of
JOHN FITZGERALD KENNEDY
Thirty-fifth President of the United States
of America

Contents

Foreword   ix

1 : Prelude to Revolution   1

2 : The Search for Options   47

3 : Dialogue with NATO   102

4 : The Long View   135

5 : Cost and Effectiveness   168

6 : Capitol Controversies   204

7 : Tests of Effectiveness   251

8 : Agenda for Action   275

Epilogue   300

Notes   320

Index   335

Foreword

One of President Kennedy's most fascinating attributes was his ability to attract able men and women to the service of his Administration. How much impact they would have had on the life of the nation and the world, granted a normal span of office, we may never know. That is part of the great tragedy of John Kennedy's death. But there is one area in which some quite remarkable changes did occur, even in the short space of thirty-four months. It is the area of national security affairs. This book attempts to describe the nature of the changes.

The President himself played a vital role in sponsoring major adjustments in the style and substance of the nation's defense effort. At his side, and deeply committed to his service, stood Robert S. McNamara. If Kennedy was the patron of new departures in the realm of national security, McNamara has been their architect and engineer. As such, he is the central figure in the narrative that follows.

Another reason for the book's special focus lies in its origins, some months before the President's murder. Joseph Kraft of Harper's has long interested himself in the growing civilian contribution to the resolution of major defense issues, and it was he who first proposed an account of the changes directed by McNamara in the Pentagon. I have largely followed Mr. Kraft's original suggestion. One part of his proposal I have particularly taken to heart. That is to let McNamara describe what he has been doing in his own words wherever possible. There is good reason for adopting such a device: McNamara is well able to speak for himself.

In addition to the encouragement and advice of Mr. Kraft, it is a pleasure to acknowledge the sympathetic assistance of many officers and civilians in the Department of Defense. Theodore H. White has described the Pentagon as "one of the most bleakly depressing anthills in the world." But its inhabitants are friendly as well as industrious, and I have benefited greatly from their counsel, direction, and criticism. An understanding of the McNamara measures would have been impossible without them.

The Center for International Studies at the Massachusetts Institute of Technology and its director, Max F. Millikan, not only facilitated my research in a number of ways; they also freed me of other obligations so that I might undertake this work. In a very real sense, then, this is a publication of the Center. It is also the product of the tireless competence of Miss Emmalyn Heed, who saw the manuscript through several drafts.

An author is fortunate in his friends. A number of them, both in Washington and in Cambridge, have read and commented on the manuscript, including John M. Deutch, David L. Evans, Julia A. Kaufmann, Joseph Kraft, Wesley W. Posvar, and Eugene B. Skolnikoff. I am deeply grateful for their help even as I assume responsibility for the book as it now stands.

WILLIAM W. KAUFMANN

Cambridge, Massachusetts

THE McNAMARA STRATEGY

CHAPTER 1

Prelude to Revolution

THE ADMINISTRATION of John F. Kennedy held a powerful grip on many imaginations during its brief and brilliant career. Part of the fascination no doubt sprang from the glitter and elegance of the White House, the youth and spirits of its inhabitants, the endless appeal surrounding great affairs of state, and the power of the Presidency. But the President himself furnished the motive force to this magnetic field. There was an inexorable pull and attraction about his curiosity, the thirst for ideas, his allegiance to the rule of reason, the lack of dogma, his promise of action in pursuit of high ideals. Indeed, so strong still is their hold that memory is tempted, in the aftermath of tragedy, to recall only the light and luster surrounding the White House during the thirty-four swift months of the Kennedy Administration. Yet dark and bitter controversy also marked those same short months, and high among its subjects stood Robert S. McNamara, eighth Secretary of Defense.

President Kennedy had no reservations about his Secretary; he reportedly told visitors that McNamara was the most satisfactory member of his Cabinet.[1]* Senator Richard B. Russell, Chairman of the Senate Armed Services Committee, apparently shared this view. As early as 1961, he announced:

* Superior numbers refer to a section of notes beginning on page 320.

I have been listening to statements from officials of the Department of Defense now for almost thirty years . . . and I have never heard one that was clearer, more definitive, and yet more comprehensive than the statement that you have given to this committee.[2]

And this exchange took place in a committee of the House of Representatives in February of 1963 during testimony by McNamara:

MR. FLOOD. Mr. Andrews and I had the impression that if we would ask the Secretary for the number of nuts and bolts in warehouse No. 1, drawer 7, Fort Dix, he most probably could tell us.

MR. MAHON. I believe so, but——

MR. FLOOD. It is after 4 o'clock now, anyway, so there is no sense asking him.

MR. ANDREWS. I said in a note to Mr. Flood which I wrote him an hour ago that the Secretary can tell you the number of nuts and bolts in drawer 5, Fort Dix, July 17, 1962. Here is what Mr. Flood wrote in reply—"including the color of the paint on the warehouse and the box."[3]

Other commentary was highly critical. McNamara was accused of being concerned with slide rules, not soldiers. The *Army, Navy, Air Force Journal* claimed that "the professional military leadership of the nation is being short-circuited in the current decision-making process at the Pentagon."[4] One journalist has even questioned darkly whether McNamara was setting up a monarchy in the Pentagon. Some writers decried what they called his computer logic and lack of warmth, his supposed tendency to rely on civilian analysts (whiz kids) rather than generals, and his reputed determination to undermine NATO.

The personality of the Secretary may have given grounds for some of these strong and diverse feelings. He has been called the kindly computer. Stewart Alsop sees "something teacherish in his appearance. You might mistake him for a mathematics professor in a small college—it is easy to imagine him at the blackboard, patiently pointing out the errors of his duller students." But personality alone is an insufficient explanation for

the controversy; it is hard to stay angry at "a friendly and un-
pretentious man with a mild, slightly acid sense of humor."[5]
Presumably it is what McNamara has done as much as what he
is that has called forth such a volume of high praise, sarcasm,
and bitter denunciation. Yet what is it that he has accomplished?

It is probably not too much to say that in less than three
years, McNamara brought about two major revolutions within
the Department of Defense. He redesigned the military strategy and forces of the United States. At the same time, he installed an entirely new method of making decisions within the
Pentagon. In a world of revolutions, this may not seem a particularly startling accomplishment. But to veterans of the
Pentagon these and other changes are very large indeed. Any
appreciation of their magnitude requires an understanding
not only of the details of what took place during the thirty-four
months of the Kennedy Administration but also of the background against which the changes occurred.

The strength of the American defense establishment on June
30, 1938, stood at 322,932 men and women. That same establishment emerged victoriously from the Second World War
with a total of 12,123,455 men and women. In less than seven
years, the Armed Forces had increased by a factor of nearly
forty, spanned two great oceans, and played a vital role in the
defeat of Germany and Japan. Once the Japanese Empire had
surrendered, the nation proceeded to scatter this great combat
force to the four winds. By 1947, the size of the defense establishment had fallen to less than 1,600,000 men and women.
Never before had a country divested itself so fast of so great
a power. There remained, however, the seasoned generals and
admirals who had led the United States to its greatest military
triumphs. Their wisdom and experience remained at hand for
any emergencies that the nation might confront. But here, too,
there was a major problem. Just as they completed their work
and began to assimilate the lessons of their experience, they
found themselves plunged into a new and alien environment.

After eighteen years of the cold war it is easy to forget how
rapidly the postwar world diverged from wartime expectations.
The Grand Alliance quickly flew apart. First the Soviet Union,
then Communist China, showed a deeply hostile visage to the
West. Germany and Japan, on the other hand, gave promise of
becoming valued partners. Such a reversal of relationships was
by itself enough to strain credulity. It was by no means all. Of
the other wartime allies, Britain and France had had their
strength sorely depleted. The first line of defense in Europe,
behind which the United States had mobilized during two
great wars, no longer existed. The situation and prospects in
the Middle East and Asia were equally bleak. Here the great em-
pires of the past were in the process of disintegration. In their
place were arising inexperienced governments with strong anti-
Western feelings, strange ideological leanings, and serious vulnerabilities which communism would proceed to exploit. And
overshadowing all these other changes was the accelerating
revolution in the technology of war. Radar, jet engines, prox-
imity fuses, even ballistic missiles could be absorbed into the
traditional methods and culture of conflict. But the atomic
bomb inevitably brought into question both the relevance of
wartime experience to the conduct of future military operations
and the utility of maximum force as an instrument of foreign
policy. Clearly, a new and revolutionary era was at hand.

The responses of American foreign policy to this unprecedented situation are well known. Outstanding among them
have been the Marshall Plan, the Point Four Program, and the
extraordinary network of alliances by which the United States
has attempted to guarantee, and increase the strength of, the
non-Communist world. It is characteristic of nations that they
design their postwar policies to correct the mistakes that led
up to the last war. To this general rule the United States has
proved at least a partial exception. In a relatively short time it
surrendered the dream of a peaceful international society gov-
erned by the institutions of the United Nations. In their place
it substituted American leadership and, in less than ten years,

commitments to the security of forty-two nations. In effect, the
United States now provided the first line of defense against the
incursions and depredations of the Communist world.

This new role placed a heavy and unfamiliar burden upon
the American defense establishment. Heretofore, the tasks of
the Armed Forces in peacetime had been primarily to maintain
cadres of trained officers and men, to engage in mobilization
planning, develop prototypes of the weapons they would like
to order in quantity, and try to foresee the circumstances and
places in which they would be called upon to fight. Each Service had had a capability in being, especially the Navy, but
these forces were rarely expected to become involved in major
military operations until after America's friends had been pre-
cipitated into a war. This meant not only that American mobilization plans could be put into effect after the outbreak of conflict, but also that the Services could study and adopt the
weapons, strategy, and tactics of friend and enemy alike. It
meant, further, that they could correct many of their own mistakes before they went into combat. Now all this had changed.
Contingency plans might have to be executed, forces in being
might have to be used without a period of grace for mobilization. And weapons in the inventory were certain to be the ones
that would be fired in anger. The old days, in which the United
States could act as the second line of Western defense, seemingly had gone forever.

The burdens which the Armed Forces would be called upon
to bear under the new dispensation received definition as early
as 1946. *The United States Strategic Bombing Survey,* an extraordinarily perceptive analysis of the war in Europe and the
Far East, concluded one of its reports with this advice:

The Survey's report on the European war stated that the great
lesson to be learned in the battered cities of England and the ruined
cities of Germany is that the best way to win a war is to prevent it
from occurring. This is fully supported by the example of the
devastated cities of Japan and their unhappy and hungry surviving
inhabitants. The prevention of war must be the ultimate end to

which our best efforts are devoted. It has been suggested, and wisely so, that this objective is well served by insuring the strength and the security of the United States. . . . Prevention of war will not be furthered by neglect of strength or lack of foresight or alertness on our part.[6]

The President's Air Policy Commission, reporting its findings on January 1, 1948, was of a similar mind.

Reluctantly this commission has come to the conclusion that . . . relative security is to be found only in a policy of arming the United States so strongly (1) that other nations will hesitate to attack us or our vital interests because of the violence of the counterattack they would have to face, and (2) that if we are attacked we will be able to smash the assault at the earliest possible moment. The alternative policy—of having inadequate arms in a world in which war must be reckoned with as the final solution of international differences—would be foolhardy. Nothing would be more likely to provoke aggression than the spectacle of an unarmed or inadequately armed United States. This country, therefore, if it is to have even relative security, must be ready for war.[7]

The implication of these words could not be mistaken: to the defense establishment would now fall the responsibility for the deterrence and conduct of war all around the globe. The fulfillment of that responsibility immediately entailed, and has continued to require, the performance of four major functions. The first of these may best be described as the formation of strategic concepts: how forces of a given type should be selected and employed to attain desired security objectives. The distinguished American military theorist, Admiral Mahan, writing toward the end of the nineteenth century, had found the task difficult enough with centuries of experience upon which to draw. To see clearly the role of sea power, its potential and limitations, to determine what forces might be required—how they could be most profitably used and supported —was a major intellectual achievement. It took a long time in coming. The task facing the postwar military planner was substantially more difficult. As the new weapon systems developed, it became evident that the familiar ways of conducting a war no longer were wholly valid. Given the sharp distinction between nuclear and conventional explosives, considering the many possible fronts upon which the United States might be called to act, the need arose to understand and characterize a number of possible wars—all of them in one way or another outside the range of experience. Admiral Mahan, pondering the lessons of Trafalgar, would have found nothing there to inform him about the outcome of a conventional engagement between two major nuclear powers. Nor would he have discovered how a conventional war might escalate, or shift, into a nuclear conflict. Least of all would he have learned much about the conduct of a nuclear campaign, especially one fought with long-range bombers and intercontinental ballistic missiles. Yet this, in effect, was the situation of the postwar planners. The formation of strategic concepts had to take place in what was close to a historical void.

The second function, intimately related to the first, has to do with the allocation of resources to the development and deployment of forces designed to implement the chosen strategic concepts. Within the constraints set by national resources, difficult choices have to be made about men and weapons for the Army, Navy, and Air Force—and for the branches of each Service. Admiral Mahan and his immediate successors had to worry about coaling stations and home ports, about the best balance between battleships, cruisers, and destroyers required to gain and maintain command of the seas. The modern-day planner must distribute his resources among three Services and two major categories of weapons. He must do so, moreover, in the face of grave uncertainties about the kind of war he may be called upon to fight. His work is complicated still further by the fact that he must maintain a diversified research and development program which will continually replenish his arsenal with up-to-date and tested weapons. A modern planner's life is not a simple one.

A third major function has been a direct outgrowth of American overseas commitments. When the United States first developed its system of alliances, the treaties constituted much more a guarantee of American support than they did a pooling of military power to assure the containment of Communist imperialism. There was no allied power to pool. But as Europe in particular regained its economic and political health, there developed the need to coordinate American defense plans and programs with those of the other members of the North Atlantic Treaty Organization. Under the conditions of modern weaponry and their very high costs, this has meant far more than the traditional alliance in which each signatory might pledge the commitment of certain of its forces to the common defense under specified circumstances. It has involved the hammering out of agreed strategic concepts, the force levels for their support, and the division of costs among the allies. To perform this complex function the planner has found himself cast as economist and statesman as well as strategist.

The last function is the most complex of all: the actual operation of the military establishment. The United States, in its short history, has experienced a great deal of war. But the postwar period is unprecedented in the demands it makes on the management of military power. Forces must be maintained in being armed with constantly changing weapons. They must be prepared to stand on high alert, deploy overseas, face crises, make demonstrations, and engage in instant combat. All this they must do, moreover, in the shadow of the nuclear holocaust. The wise application of military power in support of American foreign policy is as difficult as it is novel in these circumstances. How well the civilian and military planners and commanders actually provide this support is the ultimate measure of the effectiveness of the military establishment.

The functions themselves, however strange to American traditions, are easy enough to describe. Their actual performance under the exacting conditions of the postwar environment has proved difficult indeed. In particular, the process of forming workable strategic concepts has turned out to be extraordinarily complex. The new Admiral Mahan has as yet to emerge from his study. In one vital respect, however, the planners have shown a high degree of ingenuity. That has been in coming to grips with the advent of nuclear weapons. This new explosive force not only promised to increase the destructiveness of combat; it also permitted a radical departure from traditional modes of warfare. Conventional conflict still remained a possibility. But now, with the swift march of technology, it seemed feasible to invent types of combat that had no historical parallels. High on the list of such prospects was strategic nuclear warfare.

The first atomic bombs were of such great weight, seemingly so scarce, and so closely identified with the strategic bombing mission of World War II, that the Air Force—with its heavy, long-range bombers—naturally fell heir to the responsibility for their delivery. Air Force planners initially saw the bomb as a vastly more economical means than high explosives for the destruction of industrial targets, and they concentrated their early efforts on the creation of a force that could get to the enemy's territory, penetrate his defenses, and destroy a carefully selected system of targets associated with the opponent's warmaking capacity. Out of these efforts came the Strategic Air Command and a growing complex of overseas bases from which the bombers would strike at the enemy's industrial heart. When the Air Force first adopted this mission, it hoped, but did not believe, that it could win a war by itself. Strategic bombing with atomic weapons still remained an adjunct, though a vital one, to a major land battle. Strategic bombing would ensure that the force of an enemy's ground attack would dissipate rapidly, or that the crust of his resistance would collapse with great speed. Or so it was hoped.

The detonation of a nuclear device by the Soviet Union in August, 1949, instituted a major change in the planners' thought. As the problem of countering an enemy's nuclear capability came to the forefront of their calculations, strategic warfare began to be regarded as an independent and decisive

type of conflict—an engagement of such overwhelming significance that action on land or at sea would seem irrelevant. The
growing power of atomic bombs, the expansion of the stockpile of weapons, and the development of the thermonuclear
weapon all contributed to that conclusion.

Henceforward, concepts about the deterrence and conduct
of strategic nuclear warfare developed at a rapid pace. So did
the weapon systems designed to implement the concepts. In
trying to design a deterrent to a hostile nuclear power, the
planners first visualized a Soviet attack as being directed
against the industrial strength of the United States. In effect,
they attributed to the Red planner the same strategy that they
themselves proposed to use. Their counter to this strategy was
twofold: the construction of early warning systems and air defenses to reduce the impact of such an attack, and of an overwhelming capability for a counteroffensive against Soviet society. The combination, it was thought, would probably deter
the Soviets or, if deterrence failed—and this was a possibility
that the planners had to take into account—would enable the
United States to prevail. After several years of thinking in
these terms, it occurred to the planners that the Soviets might
attempt to disrupt or even suppress the counteroffensive by attacking the bases from which it would be launched. If they
could do this successfully, American retaliatory power would
vanish, and so would deterrence. It became necessary, therefore, to reduce the vulnerability of the offensive forces in order
to have a capability for surviving an enemy first strike and retaliating effectively against him.

The task of reducing the vulnerability of the American offensive forces was a difficult and absorbing one. The first step,
which longer-range bombers and air-refueling techniques made
possible, was the gradual withdrawal of the offensive forces to
the North American continent. This was followed by the development of increasingly sophisticated systems of continental
warning and air defense. But as Soviet capabilities improved
and the intercontinental ballistic missile became a reality, even

these costly measures appeared unsatisfactory. The planners worried increasingly about the possibility of a surprise attack— one which would either elude the American warning system or arrive at the targets so rapidly that warning would not be effective. Distance, warning, and air defenses no longer sufficed in the face of these possibilities. The maintenance of a secure, second-strike, retaliatory capability required forces that could survive even a surprise attack. This meant bombers on airborne alert, mobile missiles, and even missiles in highly protected silos which could withstand the great blast effects of near misses by thermonuclear weapons. It also meant larger and more dispersed forces, the actual deployment of nuclear weapons from stockpiles to bombers and missiles, and the maintenance of the retaliatory capability on a high state of alert.

While the search for survivability was going on, and the deadly game of measures, countermeasures, and counter-countermeasures proceeded, the planners came increasingly to question their original assumptions about the uses to which the strategic forces would be put. The threat to destroy all or some portion of an enemy's society wore the appearance of a powerful deterrent. But what if the strategic exchange started accidentally? Indeed, what if the enemy's first strike were confined to military targets, or the United States itself were required to retaliate with its strategic forces for an attack on Western Europe? Did it remain desirable, in all these circumstances, to launch the offensive capabilities against the urban-industrial targets of the enemy, or would the United States really be interested in destroying the hostile nuclear forces, striving to limit damage to itself and its allies, and attempting to end the war on terms acceptable to the West? Gradually a number of different answers developed. One school of thought argued for only a small, well-protected offensive force that would retaliate against an enemy's cities. Another school maintained that the United States should have the capability and the plan simultaneously to destroy both the enemy's civil society and his strategic offensive forces, and, regardless of the damage, to "prevail" in one great blow. A third school noted that the number of casualties in a thermonuclear war could vary significantly as a function of many factors, including the number of weapons actually detonated, their yields and heights of burst, and the types of targets attacked. This school therefore argued for a capability large enough to perform the counterforce, damage-limiting, and war-termination missions and yet be able to destroy the enemy's civil society, if that should become necessary. As the debate developed, it stimulated a whole new series of interests. If the offensive forces were to respond at all, and certainly if they were to react in other than a reflex manner, a directing brain composed of high civilian and military leaders, known as command-and-control, must also survive to operate them. If the damage from a nuclear attack were to be limited, offensive forces would have to be supplemented with passive as well as active defenses. And if the offensive forces were to reach and destroy their appointed targets, new measures must be devised to get them through enemy defenses and identify their targets. By the end of the 1950's, even though the school of massive retaliation dominated official thinking, the possibilities and perplexities of strategic nuclear warfare seemed endless.

Several features of this strange evolution require emphasis. To begin with, in the short space of little more than ten years, the planners and their technical collaborators had invented an essentially new mode of warfare. It was, of course, a paper war that they had devised. No nation had detonated a nuclear weapon in combat since Hiroshima and Nagasaki in 1945, and then the bombs yielded fifteen and twenty kilotons respectively, in contrast to the multimegaton monsters of the late 1950's. Yet the United States and the Soviet Union had arrayed against one another major nuclear forces ready on short notice to attempt the delivery of the equivalent of billions of tons of high explosives. That in itself necessitated taking strategic nuclear warfare very seriously indeed. In the United States, the primary responsibility for this awesome mission rested with the

Air Force, although the Navy had equipped its aircraft carriers with nuclear weapons, and in the summer of 1956, by conceiving of a solid-fueled ballistic missile married to a nuclear-powered submarine, had found a way of playing a major role in the mission. The Army had not had such good luck. The best it could do was to capture a part of the air defense task with short-range surface-to-air missiles and enter into a vigorous pursuit of the antimissile missile. By the 1950's the cost of maintaining and modernizing all the interlocking elements of a strategic nuclear system had risen to more than $10 billion per annum. Not only was this a new and vital form of warfare in which all the Services aspired to play a part; it was also a major competitor for the defense resources of the nation. Indeed, senior Air Force officers and many civilians considered it the only capability in which an investment was worthwhile. As General Curtis E. LeMay once put it: "I do not understand why a force that will deter a big war will not deter a small one too, if we want it to and say it will. . . . I think we are going to have to build for the worst cases and then use that for all the others."[8]

The United States Army did not see the matter quite that way. It was not that Army officers were necessarily against nuclear weapons. Like their colleagues in the other Services they had decided to embrace rather than reject the new technology; the horse cavalry and polo had lost their allure. But Army planners did not quite believe that the Air Force could win a nuclear war all by itself. Nor did they really see a future for the Army if they failed to find an important nuclear mission for it. Their position, so they felt, was comparable to that of a large and competent carriage manufacturer who suddenly discovers his competitor selling automobiles. They had to find a way of adapting nuclear weapons to ground warfare.

Help came from an influential source. Many nuclear physicists were concerned about the single-minded dedication of the Air Force to strategic nuclear systems; they feared that these capabilities would become neutralized as the Soviets developed their own strategic forces. At the same time they were learning to create atomic weapons in sizes, shapes, and weights that might serve the Army's purposes. It thus was possible to visualize what has come to be known as tactical nuclear warfare. The immediate advantages of this kind of warfare seemed substantial. The atomic stockpile of the United States was expanding rapidly; the Soviet stockpile had only just begun. And it would have to be devoted, so went the assumption, to countering American strategic capabilities. Consequently the United States would enjoy a monopoly in the tactical use of nuclear weapons and thus could compensate for its presumed inferiority to the Soviet Union in military manpower. As General Omar Bradley somewhat cautiously put the argument in 1949: "The A-bomb, in its tactical aspect, may well contribute toward a stable equilibrium of forces, since it tends to strengthen a defensive army." Project Vista, established at the California Institute of Technology to study the tactical use of nuclear weapons, waxed more enthusiastic in its final report. It recommended "bringing the battle back to the battlefield," and recommended diverting a large portion of the nation's nuclear resources to the production of tactical weapons.[9]

When it became evident that the Soviets could develop a sufficient stockpile of nuclear weapons for both strategic and tactical purposes—and were apparently interested in doing so—Army planners found it necessary to change somewhat their rationale for tactical nuclear capabilities. They could, and did, point to the need for such capabilities as a deterrent to the initiation by the Soviets of local nuclear warfare. They also argued, though with declining conviction, that tactical nuclear weapons would favor the defense and compensate for any inferiority in Western divisional strength, even in a two-sided atomic war. But they staked their case primarily on two other arguments. The first was that the Army would still have a role to play during a strategic nuclear exchange. This might be the defense of Europe against the massed armies of the Soviet Union, in which event, according to the argument, tactical nu-

clear weapons would have to be used while SAC destroyed
Russia; or it might be a counteroffensive into Eastern Europe
for the purpose of liberating the satellite countries and helping
to end the war. The second argument postulated the feasibility
of a local land battle fought with low-yield nuclear weapons.
It contended that such a battle could be kept from developing
into a larger nuclear exchange and that the United States would
achieve a better outcome under such circumstances than by
trying to resist superior Communist manpower by conventional
means. Whatever the merits of these two arguments, the Army
foresaw the need for a large arsenal of nuclear weapons, ranging from the relatively high-yield, four-hundred-mile Pershing,
down to the very low-yield, battlefield Davy Crockett. The Air
Force, not to be outdone, claimed a share in these missions for
its tactical air forces and proceeded to arm them with nuclear
weapons. The Navy, for its part, demanded nuclear weapons
for antisubmarine warfare and tactical strikes from its aircraft
carriers.

Although tactical nuclear war as a concept lacked the con-
creteness of detail and plausibility that the Air Force planners
managed to give to the concept of strategic nuclear warfare,
the case for it seemed sufficiently persuasive so that policy-
makers had to take its occurrence and deterrence seriously.
Thus a second new form of conflict entered the lists and laid
claim on the resources of the country.

The policy-makers themselves were responsible for still another competitor. When, on June 25, 1950, the North Koreans
plunged across the thirty-eighth parallel, the United States—
despite its nuclear capabilities—embarked upon a local, conventional campaign in conjunction with the forces of the Republic
of Korea. In so doing, a nuclear power invented and proved
the feasibility of a limited non-nuclear war. The circumstances
admittedly were special: the war took place in a relatively narrow peninsula, and the United States, with its virtual monopoly
of nuclear weapons, exercised most of the restraint. Nevertheless, three years and eight divisions later, the United States had

emerged from a local conventional war and had achieved the bulk of its objectives in the process.

Thereafter, a great deal of debate centered upon the desirability and feasibility of another such limited war. Some argued that the United States would do better to use nuclear weapons in a similar situation in the future. Others maintained that the circumstances of the Korean war were unique and that another comparable confrontation would result sooner or later in the use of nuclear weapons. Still others expressed the fear that if the example of Korea were followed, the United States would become engaged in a whole host of local wars. They worried that to concede the feasibility of local conventional war would sap the deterrent effect of America's nuclear arsenal. They deplored in particular any tendency to apply the lessons of Korea to the situation in Europe. To them, the notion that Soviet and American forces might clash in Central Europe without nuclear weapons being immediately used was tantamount to inviting attack and guaranteeing the defeat of the United States. Wherever Russians fought Americans, they argued, general nuclear war must ensue.

Still, the concept of local conventional war hung on. The Korean conflict had, after all, occurred, and some of its students even maintained that, without it, someone would have had to invent it. They recognized the possibility of escalation, which meant to them the process by which such an engagement might expand into a nuclear conflict. But, in their view, a conventional war would be easier to control than any tactical nuclear exchange. And they remained persuaded that, on balance, it would prove more advantageous to the United States.

The outcome of the debate remains inconclusive. The dynamics of escalation are hardly better understood today than they were a decade ago. Nor is it at all clear what is meant by the term limited non-nuclear war. Under modern conditions, the Second World War, if it were to be refought, would qualify as a limited non-nuclear conflict. Whether anyone contemplates such a repetition seems doubtful. Nevertheless, what constitutes the allowable magnitude and duration of a local non-nuclear war continues to be clouded in obscurity. But the Korean war, like Mount Everest, is there. And since art—even the military art—tends to imitate nature, the policy-makers find themselves obliged to face yet another contingency for which they must contemplate preparations.

As if the problem of strategy and forces were not complicated enough, the communists revived the ancient technique of guerrilla warfare in order to exploit the vulnerabilities of those areas which had been thrown into turmoil by the ravages of World War II. Within six years after the surrender of Japan, the United States experienced this kind of aggression three times: in the Philippines, Greece, and parts of Korea. The British suffered from it in Malaya, and the French encountered it in Indochina. There occurred, in addition, other types of insurgency in Kenya, Cyprus, Algeria, and Indonesia with which the West was obliged to contend. Despite all this, the problem of guerrilla warfare and counterinsurgency received the least attention in the calculations of the planners during the early postwar years. True, it came under a measure of scrutiny and a variety of theories began to emerge on how to deter or defeat guerrilla action; but the subject lacked a powerful backer. It therefore stood in the wings, a fourth candidate for defense dollars, awaiting recognition. Not until 1961 would Khrushchev give it the necessary sponsorship with his endorsement of "wars of national liberation." Then, of course, counterinsurgency became very fashionable indeed.

The types of possible wars thus had increased substantially since 1945. So had the range of capabilities available for the deterrence or conduct of most of them. But what was lacking still was an over-all concept for the use of force by the United States and a plan for a force structure capable of covering some or all of these contingencies at what looked like an acceptable cost. Secretary of State John Foster Dulles succinctly expressed the difficulty of arriving at such a posture in his notable speech of January 12, 1954. In his view, if the enemy "could pick his

time and his place and his method of warfare—and if our policy
was to remain the traditional one of meeting aggression by direct and local opposition—then we had to be ready to fight in
the Arctic and in the tropics, in Asia, in the Near East, and in
Europe; by sea, by land and by air; by old weapons and by new
weapons."[10] To Dulles such a prospect was appalling. Yet only
five years before, the Truman Administration had embarked
upon precisely this kind of program. NSC-68, the document
which laid down the approach, was substantially to the credit
of Paul H. Nitze, then head of the policy planning staff in the
State Department. Nitze and his colleagues foresaw a number
of dangers: general nuclear war, piecemeal aggression, subversion, disunity in the Western alliance, and possibly even a
loss of American will unless the military posture of the United
States and its allies was substantially changed and strengthened. As Nitze later explained, NSC-68 advocated "an immediate and large-scale build-up in our military and general
strength and that of our allies with the intention of righting
the power balance and in the hope that through means other
than all-out war we could induce a change in the nature of the
Soviet system."[11] By 1954, this approach would have involved
about 21 Army divisions, a Navy of 408 major combat vessels,
and an Air Force of 143 wings.

For its time, NSC-68 was an extraordinarily sophisticated
document. At a very early date it filled an important gap in
American strategic thought. Yet for some years to come, it was
to remain almost unique in the annals of planning papers. And
it was soon to be cast aside as a basis for the military policy
of the United States. That it should meet this fate was hardly
surprising. The problem of choosing among the many alternative weapon systems and strategies, and deciding how to or-
chestrate them, would have been an imposing one even if there
had been no other complications. But there were. Soviet as well
as American capabilities were rapidly changing under the impact of the new military technology. And since the Soviets possessed the initiative to commit aggression, they could upset

even the best-laid plans. Whatever strategic concept was designed in the face of these uncertainties was bound to be tentative and subject to early change.

There were other complications as well. Although the Services
had managed to fight the Second World War more or less in har-
ness, they found it impossible to agree upon postwar strategic
plans and force structures. The National Security Act of 1947,
in recognition of this difficulty, had established the Joint Chiefs
of Staff as a permanent peacetime planning agency and created
the office of Secretary of Defense to coordinate the activities of
the three Services. But Service rivalries for the budget were
such that the Chiefs, even with a strong Chairman added, could
not really develop a coherent set of strategic plans. At best,
they could engage in compromise solutions—like dividing the
expected budget into three equal shares and letting each Service spend its money as it saw fit—or agree on a budget and program of such major proportions that the political leadership
was bound to reject or reduce them. Admiral Denfeld, who, as
Chief of Naval Operations, had been a member of the JCS,
claimed that "on nine-tenths of the matters that come before
them, the Joint Chiefs reach agreement among themselves.
Normally the *only* disputes are on strategic concepts, the size
and composition of forces, and budget matters."[12] That, unfortunately, was the point. On the critical 10 percent of their
business, the Chiefs could not agree.

Under the postwar organization of the military establishment
the Secretary of Defense presumably had the authority to
establish a strategic concept and require agreement on force
size and composition. But he labored under several severe
handicaps. He lacked any independent basis on which to assess
what the Services were demanding. And, in the American tradition, he tended to assume that it was impossible for him to understand, much less learn, the art of military planning. That was
a mystery that could only be performed by the military staffs
themselves. To argue with veteran commanders in these circumstances seemed presumptuous and dangerous. Military

judgment was sacrosanct. Moreover, the Chiefs had access to the President and, more importantly, to the Congress. They might accept a ruling by the Secretary and even obey it; but in their role as advisers, they had a disconcerting habit of making it known on occasion that a given decision had been made in spite of their advice rather than because of it. No Secretary relished the thought of risking this kind of embarrassment. Nor could any Secretary grow enthusiastic over the prospect of making a decision with potentially immense military consequences without the support of his principal military advisers. For those who might even contemplate such an enormity, there was the example of Secretary Louis Johnson, whose political head had rolled at the outset of the Korean war. His worst crime was simple. He had reduced Service expenditures and whittled away at favored Service projects. And he had done so in the teeth of military opposition.

James V. Forrestal, first Secretary of Defense, attempted to achieve a measure of coherence in planning, control over expenditures, and rationality of force structure by getting the Chiefs to sign a treaty on roles and missions. Forrestal hoped that by allocating major combat functions among the Services he could persuade them to work together. Changing technology, lack of an agreed strategic concept, and the absence of any budgetary guidance doomed the effort from the outset. Secretary and Chiefs met at Key West and Newport in 1948; eventually they produced a treaty. Major combat functions were in fact distributed by Service. But each of the Services received collateral as well as primary missions, so that their jurisdictions continued to overlap. Critical questions such as who would have responsibility for ballistic missiles were left unanswered, and at no point did the agreement indicate what magnitudes of resources would be applied to the major combat functions. In an era of rapid technological change when new weapon systems were unlikely to respect traditional Service boundaries, such an agreement was bound, at best, to contain many ambiguities. At worst, it could and would become another bone of contention among the Services. The wonder, in the circumstances, is not that NSC-68 had a very short life; it is that it was ever adopted at all.

When President Eisenhower took office in 1953, the need for a disciplined approach to the military establishment seemed particularly acute. As a result of the Korean war, the Armed Forces had burgeoned from 1.4 million to 3.6 million men and women. Defense expenditures had also shot up; they stood at $49.3 billion as against $14.3 billion in 1950 and were now consuming 13.5 percent of the Gross National Product compared with 5 percent in 1950. As a result of these expenditures, the Army commanded 20 divisions and 18 regimental combat teams, the Navy possessed 1,130 ships together with 3 Marine divisions and their 3 supporting air wings, and the Air Force had reached its interim goal of 95 wings. Although this was a balanced force, there seemed no end to its possible growth. To the new President such a prospect was intolerable. In his view, "the foundation of military strength is economic strength. A bankrupt America is more the Soviet goal than an America conquered on the field of battle."[13] With the Korean war drawing to its end, moreover, he could see no point to the retention of so large a ground force. The Soviets were credited with an active army of 175 divisions and were believed capable of expanding it to 300 divisions in the first month or so of a war. On this assumption, whether the United States Army stood at 20 or 10 divisions did not make a great deal of difference. The security of the United States in future would have to rest primarily on nuclear weapons. As the President was to say later: "Where these things are used on strictly military targets and for strictly military purposes, I see no reason why they shouldn't be used just exactly as you would use a bullet or anything else."[14] Starting with this premise, it seemed entirely feasible to bring the Pentagon under close control.

The President used four major instruments in his campaign. The first was a National Security Council document called *Basic National Security Policy* (and known more familiarly to veterans of its drafting as BNSP). Issued annually, and purporting to set forth the basic strategic concept for the United States, BNSP has been described by General Maxwell D. Taylor as "a broad outline of the aims of U.S. national strategy and a more detailed discussion of the military, political, economic elements to support the over-all national strategy."[15] In it, the Eisenhower Administration announced that the United States henceforward would place main but not sole reliance on nuclear weapons. With this guidance, the Joint Chiefs of Staff were expected to prepare a Joint Strategic Objectives Plan (JSOP) which would project force requirements five years into the future.

BNSP and JSOP obviously were not enough. General Taylor, testifying in 1960, threw further light on the Eisenhower approach:

> The NSC members hear the debate on the language of the "Basic National Security Policy," which is in general language which only the experts really understand. That debate takes place usually about May. Then the budget guidelines are issued which should produce military forces compatible with the strategic concept of that basic document.[16]

The technique of the budget ceiling was, of course, the most powerful tool at the disposal of the Administration. President Truman had used it regularly between 1945 and the Korean war and purportedly had decreed that, after the fixed charges on the budget were met, military activities would receive one-third of the remaining revenues. President Eisenhower followed a similar practice. According to one reporter, there was "only one hard-and-fast restriction that the President . . . imposed upon the Pentagon in its development of forces: that the cost of the forces be financed on a pay-as-you-go basis—that is, within a balanced budget."[17] In fact, once defense expenditures had been brought down from their Korean war heights, they remained remarkably constant as a percentage of the Gross National Product. For the six-year period between 1955 and 1960, the amount varied between 9 and 10 percent. Moreover, the

New Look, as it became known, stabilized the allocation of funds among the three Services. The Air Force received about 47 percent of the budget, the Navy approximately 29 percent, and the Army about 22 percent.

Although BNSP and budget ceilings were powerful weapons, the President was not content to stop there. Twice during his eight years of office, he reorganized the Department of Defense. The intent of the changes in both 1953 and 1958 was to end the interservice disputes without going so far as unification. Toward this end, the Secretary of Defense received full legal authority to control his department. His principal military advisers were to be the Chairman of the Joint Chiefs, whose powers were increased, and the Chiefs themselves, who were to delegate their Service responsibilities to their respective Vice-Chiefs. The great unified and specified commands in North America, Europe, and the Far East were now to be responsible for the conduct of military operations. The Services, for their part, were reduced in principle to the organization, training, and equipping of forces for employment by the unified and specified commands. Presumably the potential now existed for objectivity of thought and unity of effort within the Pentagon.

As one last measure of insurance against failure of this system, the President turned increasingly to the *ad hoc* committee, made up of prominent citizens from outside the government, who in a few months would try to make sense and recommendations out of those issues of defense which the Pentagon proved incapable of resolving for itself. Indeed, this was perhaps the most unusual feature of the Administration's entire system of policy-making. The *ad hoc* committees had originally developed as a device for mobilizing specialized technical advice to help in the increasingly complex decisions about future weapons and weapon systems. Under the Eisenhower Administration they became increasingly a board of review—a gallery of wise men with the task of blessing existing policies or charting their way through controversies to new but fiscally acceptable courses of action. During the course of the years there appeared, among others, the Kelly, Sprague, Killian, Gaither, and Coolidge Committees—all charged with the examination of some important aspect of defense policy. And at the center of this process stood the President himself, Commander-in-Chief, architect of victory in World War II, and wise in the ways of the Pentagon. Presumably the system could not fail to achieve its objectives.

Fail, however, it did. BNSP proved quite inadequate as a statement of the strategic concept. This was not for any lack of consistency from year to year. For eight years the document remained remarkably constant to the notion that the United States would place main but not sole reliance on nuclear weapons. The trouble lay elsewhere. General Taylor, testifying in 1960, described one of the difficulties this way:

> . . . there was always enough language in the National Security Council paper to give grounds for argument which my predecessor, General Ridgway, used very strongly and ably in opposition. I took generally the same position because I agreed with the soundness of his views.

> The paper was often ambiguous. For example, it would say we will depend upon these weapons of massive retaliation, but at the same time will maintain flexible mobile forces capable of coping with lesser situations in the world. Paragraph (a) would support the need for general war forces and paragraph (b) the need for limited war forces but the budget would not provide for both. The ground for argument was there all the time.[18]

During the four years he was Army Chief of Staff, Taylor explained:

> . . . we had a division over massive retaliation versus what we call now a strategy of flexible response. It slowly built up. By 1958 it was a clear split right down the middle of the Joint Chiefs of Staff, crying for decision. It was never laid before the National Security Council as such but appeared indirectly twice annually. Once, when the revision of the basic national security policy was considered, where the general language was debated. Second, when the budget came up, which . . . was presumably based on the

thought that inspires this particular paper. So at least twice a year the existence of this kind of split was apparent.

We had formal presentations of the two points of view before the NSC at the time of the consideration of the Defense budget. But in spite of this evidence of division, the next year the basic national security document was not rewritten to decide the issue one way or another so we would not continue this particular kind of argumentation. In that sense I think I would be justified in saying we were not getting clear guidance in this area.[19]

Clear guidance was not forthcoming to the Chiefs for the simple reason that the Administration remained of several minds about what its strategic concept really was. Secretary of State Dulles, in his speech of January 12, 1954, maintained that "there is no local defense which alone will contain the mighty land power of the Communist world. Local defense must be reinforced by the further deterrent of massive retaliatory power." Thus, the President and the National Security Council had taken a basic decision, namely "to depend primarily upon a great capacity to retaliate instantly by means and at places of our own choosing."[20] That seemed clear enough; and President Eisenhower echoed the thought toward the end of the year when he said: "If you could win a big one, you would certainly win a little one."[21] By early 1957, however, the Secretary of Defense, Charles E. Wilson, had somewhat modified the concept of massive retaliation. American defense policy, he told the Congress,

is based on the use of atomic weapons in a major war and is based on the use of such atomic weapons as would be militarily feasible and usable in a smaller war, if such a war should be forced upon us.

In other words, the smaller atomic weapons, the tactical weapons, in a sense have now become the conventional weapons.[22]

Dulles explained the change of concept in an article for *Foreign Affairs* in October of 1957. He paid homage to the strategy of massive retaliation as the great deterrent of the middle 1950's. Then he shifted his ground.

However, the United States has not been content to rely upon a peace which could be preserved only by a capacity to destroy vast segments of the human race. Such a concept is acceptable only as a last alternative. In recent years there has been no other. But the resourcefulness of those who serve our nation in the field of science and weapon engineering now shows that it is possible to alter the character of nuclear weapons. It now seems that their use need not involve vast destruction and widespread harm to humanity. Recent tests point to the possibility of possessing nuclear weapons the destructiveness and radiation effects of which can be substantially confined to predetermined targets.

In the future it may thus be feasible to place less reliance upon deterrence of vast retaliatory power. It may be possible to defend countries by nuclear weapons so mobile, or so placed, as to make military invasion with conventional forces a hazardous attempt.[23]

President Eisenhower appeared to modify even this view when, in 1959, at a press conference held during the Berlin crisis of that year, he expressed doubt that "you could free anything with nuclear weapons." However, he went on to say that "we are certainly not going to fight a ground war in Europe," and added that "I didn't say that nuclear war is a complete impossibility."[24] Shortly thereafter, Under Secretary of State Herter informed the Senate that he could not "conceive of the President involving us in an all-out nuclear war unless the facts showed clearly that we are in danger of devastation ourselves or that actual moves have been made toward devastating ourselves."[25]

To compound the confusion, the President supported the Reserve Forces Act of 1955 which had as its goal a ready reserve of 2.9 million men by 1960. And when it came to sponsoring the military assistance program, his views seemed substantially in contradiction to the dictates of BNSP. Thus, in recommending funds for mutual security in 1958, he argued to the Congress that:

Our defensive power must be directed as well toward deterring local aggressions which could lead to global war or to piecemeal absorption of the free world by Communist imperialism. It is imperative that the free world maintain strong conventional forces capable of dealing effectively with such aggressions whenever and wherever they may occur. America alone cannot maintain such forces on the scale required. They must be developed by the threatened nations themselves.[26]

To complete the uncertainty, there was the evidence of the Administration's behavior in the crises which marked its eight years of office. As war threatened over Indochina, Lebanon, the offshore islands of Quemoy and Matsu, and Berlin, the Administration either refrained from action or desperately sought the conventional forces with which to manage the situation. In the circumstances, it is little wonder that the Joint Chiefs failed to make out exactly what was meant by BNSP. General Taylor delivered an appropriate valedictory on the document when he wrote:

The end product . . . has thus far been a document so broad in nature and so general in language as to provide limited guidance in practical application. In the course of its development, the sharp issues in national defense which confront our leaders have been blurred in conference and in negotiation. The final text thus permits many different interpretations. The protagonists of Massive Retaliation or of Flexible Response, the partisans of the importance of air power or of limited war, as well as the defenders of other shades of military opinion, are able to find language supporting their divergent points of view. The "Basic National Security Policy" document means all things to all people and settles nothing.[27]

The knife of budgetary controls proved somewhat sharper, but it cut in curious ways. Although military spending remained fairly constant measured as a percentage of the Gross National Product, in absolute terms it began to creep up in 1956. The low point occurred in 1955 with an outlay of $39.1 billion, compared with the Korean war peak of $49.3 billion. By 1960, expenditures had climbed back to a total of $45.1 billion. Although the increase did not meet with President Eisenhower's wholehearted approval, two major forces were running counter to his desires. One was the alliance between the Congress and the Services which frequently resulted in larger appropriations for expenditures than the President had requested. Pressure of this kind had to be firmly resisted. Much more difficult to ignore was the technical progress of the Soviet Union. In 1954, the Soviets demonstrated the capability to produce medium and heavy jet bombers of what appeared to be a sophisticated character. This led, in 1956, to the fear in the Air Force and the Congress that there would be a "bomber gap," and the Administration found itself under heavy fire for not accelerating the production of the B-52. Soviet announcement of an ICBM capability in August, 1957, followed by the successful orbiting of two large sputniks, produced even more serious repercussions. It appeared, in the wake of these developments, that the Soviets had indeed stolen a technological march on the United States, and the Administration found it necessary to increase its defense expenditures slightly in an effort to quiet apprehensions about a "missile gap." Although pressure of this kind proved irresistible, the technique of the budget ceiling nevertheless was reasonably successful in holding defense expenditures within ranges that the President found acceptable. In that sense it worked.

In another sense, however, it produced some very odd consequences. The budgetary tool can be a scalpel or a much blunter and less discriminating instrument. As General Taylor saw it in operation:

. . . economic and budgetary factors have come to play an overriding part in determining military posture. Each year the services receive rigid budget guidelines which control the growth, direction and evolution of the Armed Forces. These guidelines are often set with little knowledge of their strategic implications.

As a matter of fact [Taylor went on], it is very difficult to determine their implications because of the way in which the defense budget is constructed. In spite of the fact that modern war is no longer fought in terms of separate Army, Navy, and Air Force, nonetheless we still budget vertically in these service terms. Yet, if we are called upon to fight, we will not be interested in the services as such. We will be interested rather in task forces, these combinations of Army, Navy, and Air Force which are functional in nature such as the atomic retaliatory forces, overseas deployments, continental air defense forces, limited war expeditionary forces, and the like. But the point is that we do not keep our budget in these terms. Hence it is not an exaggeration to say that we do not know what kind and how much defense we are buying with any specific budget.

General Taylor's conclusion from these observations was somewhat startling.

As a result of the foregoing conditions [he said], we have the strange phenomenon of the partial loss of control of the military in a Government where all parties, including the military, are dedicated to the principle of civilian control.[28]

The difficulty was essentially twofold. BNSP was a remote and general document which really did not provide guidance on how the Administration wanted its defense dollars spent. Moreover, those dollars were appropriated directly to the Services, and neither the President nor the Secretary of Defense exercised very much control over what was being done with them. Despite BNSP and the budget ceiling, the Services enjoyed considerable latitude as to how they spent their funds. McNamara, when he came into office, was appalled.

. . . we found that the three military departments had been establishing their requirements independently of each other. I think the results can fairly be described as chaotic: the Army planning, for example was based, largely, on a long war of attrition, while the Air Force planning was based, largely, on a short war of nuclear bombardment. Consequently, the Army was stating a requirement for stocking months of fighting supplies against the event of a sizable conventional conflict, while the Air Force stock requirements for such a war had to be measured in days, and not very many days at that.[29]

In one instance, McNamara discovered that the Army, "while in general far short of its stated requirements, had 270% of its requirements for 105 mm. towed howitzers, 290% of the requirements for 4.2 inch mortars; we had ten times as many 2.75 inch rockets as were required."[30]

The field of research and development was particularly rich in examples of independent and frequently competitive Service initiatives. One of the most notable cases was the development of the Thor and Jupiter intermediate-range ballistic missiles. There was also the competition between the Nike and the Talos surface-to-air missiles. And duplication abounded in jet aircraft engine development. McNamara's favorite example of this prodigal development concerned fighter aircraft. As he informed a subcommittee of the Congressional Joint Economic Committee:

One of the most costly areas of duplication has been that of fighter aircraft. For example, in the 1955–58 period there were no less than four aircraft under development to perform the fighter mission—two in the Navy and two in the Air Force. The Navy aircraft were the F4H-1 and the F8U-3. The Air Force aircraft were the F-105 and the F-107. One might argue that there were special requirements associated with Air Force and Navy missions which necessitated basically different aircraft. Even so both the F4H-1 and the F8U-3 were, as the House Appropriations Committee noted in its report on the 1958 Defense Appropriation Bill, "all-weather fighters with approximately the same mission and operational characteristics." Accordingly, the Committee directed the Navy to "take prompt action to decide which of these aircraft it will place in production. This should be accomplished at an earlier date and with fewer test and evaluation aircraft than is presently scheduled." The Navy eventually chose the F4H-1 for production, but by the time the F8U-3 development was terminated, it had cost the Government over $136 million.

In the case of the Air Force, the F-107 was terminated at a cost of about $85 million. Even so, two of the four aircraft, the F4H and the F-105, were actually placed in production.[31]

As the House Appropriations Committee noted, as early as May, 1957: "Each service, it would seem, is striving to acquire an arsenal of weapons complete in itself to carry out any and all possible missions."[32]

Budget ceilings managed, in short, to keep expenditures under a degree of control. But by themselves they did not guarantee that the funds would be sensibly allocated. In fact, lacking firm strategic guidance, the Services became more competitive than ever. Since money was in relatively short supply, the battle for the budget intensified. In the field of research and development, each Service launched its own projects independently of the others in the hope of laying claim to some future mission and thereby increasing its share of available funds. Without sharper budgetary controls, the Administration found itself obliged either to increase its expenditures or to engage in a periodic but belated trimming of research and development projects. As in the case of the multiple fighters, the trimming usually occurred only after a great deal of money had already been spent.

Under the reorganization schemes instituted by the President, the Chiefs should have been able in theory to resolve some of these difficulties. But, as General Taylor noted, "in effect we put a sack worth $40 billion in front of four very earnest men and ask them to agree how to split it. That is asking almost the impossible whether the men are in or out of uniform."[33] There remained the Secretary of Defense who, by 1958, had had his authority to run the Department reaffirmed in no uncertain terms. But the lack of clearly defined strategic objectives and the unwillingness to challenge the judgment of the military lingered on. Wilson shied away from "all that military stuff" and concentrated on trying to introduce efficiencies into arms production and procurement. Neil H. McElroy, Wilson's successor, looked at the "stuff," but seemed unable to decide what to do about it. When Senator Stennis asked whether the Secretary would welcome a Congressional decision on a choice among overlapping air defense systems, McElroy replied:

This is one area where we have not done very well in making a decision. As far as I am concerned, it would not bother me if you held our feet to the fire and forced us in connection with this budget.[34]

Thomas S. Gates, when he became Secretary, revived the practice of sitting with the Chiefs when they disagreed on major
issues. During the first six months of 1960 he participated in
twenty-one such meetings and made decisions on six unresolved
issues. General Lemnitzer noted this as a "great advance . . .
in dealing with controversial problems and issues more quickly,
resolving them, providing a decision, and getting on with the
business."[35] Even so, the Secretary remained an arbitrator of
disputes rather than an initiator of policies.

The *ad hoc* committees undoubtedly performed important
services in these difficult circumstances. But rather than con-
form to the Administration's desire for a conservative approach
to defense problems, they tended to become advocates for new
and expensive programs. Indeed, members of the Gaither Committee became so agitated at the failure of the President to heed
their warnings that they seriously contemplated taking their
case for increased expenditures to the public. In the event, they
did not; nor did their report have a very large impact on the defense establishment. Like the other measures employed by the
President, the *ad hoc* committees managed only rarely to give a
sense of plausible direction and unity of effort to the defense
establishment.

In the wake of the sputniks, the President introduced still another device to help him bring order and economy into defense
policy. It took the form, initially, of a Special Assistant for Science and Technology. James R. Killian became the first holder
of the office, and, under his guidance, the President's Science
Advisory Committee (PSAC) found itself cast in a new and vital
role. It was now required to provide advice directly to the
White House on the difficult choices among competing weapons
and strategies. With Killian again providing the leadership, it
also inspired the establishment of the Directorate of Defense
Research and Engineering (DDR&E) in the Department of Defense to monitor and control Service expenditures on future
weapon systems. Both PSAC and DDR&E thus constituted an
important precedent for the kind of analysis that McNamara

would incorporate into the Pentagon with his famed and controversial "whiz kids."

Despite the promise of these last innovations, a coherent defense policy still seemed to elude the President. Something of his frustration expressed itself in his final address to the nation in January, 1961. As he saw the problem of defense, it was not a matter of leadership and hard choice but a need to keep the military and their industrial allies in some undefined position of subordination. Thus, he warned:

In the councils of government, we must guard against the acquisition of unwarranted influence, whether sought or unsought, by the military-industrial complex. The potential for the disastrous rise of misplaced power exists and will persist.

We must never let the weight of this combination endanger our liberties or democratic processes. We should take nothing for granted. Only an alert and knowledgeable citizenry can compel the proper meshing of the huge industrial and military machinery of defense with our peaceful methods and goals, so that security and liberty may prosper together.[36]

An academic observer of the scene arrived at a more philosophical but equally intriguing conclusion about what was actually happening. His finding was not that St. George was battling the military-industrial dragon, but rather that "strategic programs, like other major policies, are not the product of expert planners, who rationally determine the actions necessary to achieve desired goals. They are the result of controversy, negotiation, and bargaining among officials and groups with different interests and perspectives."[37] It remained to be seen, as an election year and a new Administration loomed, whether either the President or the professor had understood the puzzle or found the right key.

Meanwhile, there was the Eisenhower legacy in the field of defense to be counted. It was a mixed inheritance. To say that there was a coherent and detailed strategic concept to guide the military establishment would be an exaggeration. Basic National Security Policy persisted in saying that the United States would place main but not sole reliance upon nuclear weapons. But Secretary Gates, in his final report to the President, informed him that "the largest part of our armed forces" were trained and equipped for countering local aggression. The statement, while true, was not necessarily an encouraging one. Of the fourteen Army divisions, three were actually training divisions without sufficient manpower to engage in immediate combat. Seven of the remainder were already committed in Europe and Korea. The strategic reserve consisted of one division in Hawaii and three in the United States. Their equipment was aging; they lacked the supplies that would give them significant staying power; and the available air and sealift was sufficient to move only a fraction of them into a combat theater within a month. Exactly what these forces could do must remain uncertain. But an interesting measure of their capabilities lies in this statement of General Taylor's:

. . . I based the limited war requirement of the Army on being able to close a corps of three divisions in an overseas theater in 2 months, and to have the necessary logistic backup to fight these divisions until a supply pipeline was established. That was taken merely as a commonsense objective, something more than we could do, but a goal far enough in advance to give us something to strive for regardless of whether it was theoretically adequate or not.[38]

Presumably the existing reserves were not capable of approximating anything like that kind of an effort. Whether the ground forces at home and overseas could have operated effectively with nuclear weapons is even more difficult to say. Certainly they possessed a growing nuclear capability. But the Army did not have very well developed ideas on how it might use nuclear weapons in combat. Moreover, there remained grave doubts about using them unilaterally and considerable uncertainty about the course of a war in which the opponent started firing them as well. It was not clear, in short, that tactical air and ground forces armed with nuclear weapons represented an adequate substitute for major conventional capabilities. Certainly the Eisenhower Administration was unwilling to put the hypothesis to the test.

This left the strategic nuclear forces. Under the prodding of Soviet technical advances, Congressional urging, and a variety of analyses, the Administration had substantially improved these forces. By 1960, the Strategic Air Command was maintaining one-third of its bombers on a fifteen-minute ground alert and had begun testing a small airborne alert. The Distant Early Warning line to signal the approach of enemy bombers had been completed, and work had started on the Ballistic Missile Early Warning System in Alaska and Greenland. Operational Atlas ICBM's and Polaris submarines were also entering the combat inventory. But the backbone of the force—the bombers —still remained highly vulnerable to a surprise missile attack; so did the command-control system on which the entire force depended for its launching and direction. How effectively it could retaliate depended critically on whether or not its commander received adequate and reliable warning of an attack. That he could count on receiving such an ironclad notice seemed terribly uncertain.

There remained another problem about the strategic forces in addition to their vulnerability. Despite the talk of Secretary Dulles about massive retaliation, other Administration leaders retained doubts about the freedom with which this enormous power could be used. As early as August, 1956, the Secretary of the Air Force, Donald A. Quarles, went so far as to say:

Neither side can hope by a mere margin of superiority in airplanes or other means of delivery of atomic weapons to escape the catastrophe of such a war. Beyond a certain point, this prospect is not the result of *relative* strength of the two opposed forces. It is the *absolute* power in the hands of each, and in the substantial invulnerability of this power to interdiction.[39]

No one within the Administration or Congress thought it necessary to argue with Mr. Quarles when he said this, or even when he described "the military scheme of things in this air-atomic age" as one of "balanced terror." Indeed, the Air Force made certain that terror would be the outcome of a major nuclear exchange by insisting on a strategy of "optimum mix." What the strategy involved, according to Hanson Baldwin, was "a target list that includes Soviet cities as well as missile sites and air bases."[40] In adopting such a plan, the Administration simply increased the remoteness of the possibility that the strategic forces would ever be used except in the most desperate kind of retaliation.

This mixture of uncertain strengths and serious weaknesses found its counterpart in NATO where only the 7th Army and the tactical air forces of the United States represented combat-ready power. In recognition of its weaknesses, NATO had directed its Supreme Commander to plan on using nuclear weapons in the event of war in Europe. General Norstad chose to interpret this directive as authorizing him to attempt to enforce a "pause" on the attacker by conventional means before using nuclear weapons; and in doing so, no doubt, he understood correctly the wishes of both the United States and the European allies. At the same time, he involved himself in a somewhat contradictory position with respect to his plans and programs. The nuclear forces under his own command were exceedingly vulnerable and inadequate, by themselves, to conduct an effective campaign against the Soviet Union. Consequently, all of General Norstad's planning relied very heavily on the prompt intervention of the Strategic Air Command. At the same time he insisted with growing vehemence that he must replace his vulnerable tactical air with medium-range ballistic missiles on the ground in Europe. His reasoning tended to be that a theater commander should not have to rely for crucial operations on forces outside of his control. Nevertheless, General Norstad himself knew that even if he acquired the MRBM's, he would be helpless without SAC in a major nuclear war. His own war plans, in effect, conceded this point.

General Norstad's lapse of logic would not have mattered so much had he, as an American theater commander, been engaged

in a discussion with his superiors in Washington. But he was
also Supreme Allied Commander, Europe, and as such, his attitude was of considerable political consequence. The United
States had already encouraged its European allies to believe
that a nuclear defense was just as good as, if not better than, a
conventional defense. By 1958, it had revived its special nuclear
relationship with Great Britain, begun stockpiling nuclear
weapons in Europe, and started to furnish some of its allies with
a nuclear delivery capability. Secretary of State Herter went
further and suggested that the United States would be recep-
tive to the idea of a European strategic nuclear force, and the
President himself indicated that the time had come to revise the
Atomic Energy Act yet again so as to give direct nuclear assistance to the European allies. General Norstad's insistence on
the need for a European-based MRBM capability—even though
it would be under his control—thus gave still further impetus
to the idea that Europe must somehow achieve nuclear independence from the United States.

It was an odd situation, to say the least. SAC had been permitted to adopt a war plan which stood only the remotest
chance of ever being executed. Although General Norstad had
taken some steps to reduce the vulnerability of his own forces,
he continued to rely heavily on SAC, yet insisted that he have
under his own control a small fraction of the capability necessary to wage a comprehensive nuclear campaign. All the while,
European political and military leaders were told that their salvation lay in a nuclear defense. It is little wonder that, in this
welter of confusion, some allied politicians should have come to
believe that they must get into the nuclear business themselves.

An ambiguous strategic concept in which no one really believed except for purposes of deterrence, forces that were out
of balance and contained serious individual weaknesses, and an
anomalous situation within NATO were not the only legacies of
the Eisenhower Administration. Despite its talk of massive retaliation, crises were brewing on every hand: in Cuba, the
Congo, Berlin, Laos, and South Vietnam. Nor was that all. As a

result of successive reorganizations, the office of Secretary of Defense now contained the authority to run the Pentagon. By custom, however, it remained only a partially filled box on an organization chart. The Services still dominated the policy-making machinery in the areas that counted. Basic National Security Policy did not seriously inhibit independent action by the individual Services; it merely provided them with another basis for disagreement and encouraged a debate over words which was more conducive to legal skills than to careful military analysis. The budget ceilings were more constricting, but they did not by themselves ensure that resources would be efficiently allocated within and between the military departments. Each Service clung to the missions that it cherished, and funded them according to its own priorities. Nevertheless, the Eisenhower system left its marks. The Services remained more jealous than ever of their independence, and they had become addicted to nuclear weapons. The Air Force, having achieved its postwar pre-eminence on the basis of its nuclear delivery capabilities, looked with particular suspicion upon any suggestion that there might be complementary ways of guarding the nation's vital interests. The other Services, their missions somewhat less dependent on nuclear weapons, shared this same suspicion, though not to the same degree. Collectively, the attitudes of the Services meant that any effort to reduce the dependence of the United States, or of NATO, on a nuclear strategy would arouse their hostility and opposition.

Ironically enough, it was with respect to its nuclear policies that the Administration inspired the least confidence. Starting in 1957, with the Soviet ICBM announcement and the orbiting of the sputniks, the impression gained ground inside as well as outside the Administration that the United States might soon become vulnerable to a surprise missile attack which would eliminate the retaliatory power of SAC. The popular expression of this concern was that a "missile gap" was developing between the Soviet Union and the United States. The Administration was not particularly successful in allaying this concern. In fact, Secretary McElroy, testifying before the Senate Armed Services Committee in 1958, said:

We have no positive evidence that they are ahead of us in the long-range missile. We are conducting ourselves on the assumption that they are ahead of us, and I think we should so conduct ourselves. But we have no positive evidence that they are ahead of us in long-range missiles.[41]

Secretary Gates, in 1960, said that McElroy had been working on the assumption that the Soviets would achieve a three-to-one advantage in ICBM's over the United States. His own view, as expressed to the House Defense Appropriations Subcommittee, was different.

Heretofore we have been giving you intelligence figures that dealt with the theoretical Soviet capability. This is the first time we have had an intelligence estimate that says, "This is what the Soviet Union probably will do." Therefore, the great divergence, based on figures that have been testified to in years past, narrows because we talked before about a different set of comparisons—ones that were based on Soviet capabilities. This present one is an intelligence estimate on what we believe he will probably do, not what he is capable of doing.[42]

Despite the Secretary's assurances that the gap was not materializing, the doubts remained. General Taylor, only recently retired from the Army, repeated the widely shared concern six months later to a subcommittee of the Senate.

. . . I view the coming years, the next 5 years, let us say, with very great concern. I feel that we will have to do better than we have in order to close the missile gap. By the missile gap, I don't simply mean the deficiency in numbers of our operational missiles, but our entire missile system to include protective devices, particularly the antimissile missile requirement.[43]

The Administration, in bequeathing the controversy over the missile gap to its successor, did more than stir great public concern about the nation's vulnerability. It also concentrated at-

tention on American nuclear capabilities to the exclusion of almost everything else. Just as the Services had come to equate
the ability and willingness to use nuclear weapons with national
security, so the wider public tended to regard the nation's
strength primarily as a function of its nuclear forces. Breaking
away from this constricting habit of thought would prove to be
a difficult and time-consuming process.

One candidate for the Eisenhower succession was eager at
least to attempt the change. During the two years preceding the
election of 1960, Senator John F. Kennedy spoke frequently and
aggressively about the danger of relying almost exclusively on a
nuclear strategy, which in his view was what the President had
been doing. As he put it:

Under every military budget submitted by this administration,
we have been preparing primarily to fight the one kind of war we
least want to fight and are least likely to fight. We have been driv-
ing ourselves into a corner where the only choice is all or nothing at
all, world devastation or submission—a choice that necessarily causes
us to hesitate on the brink and leaves the initiative in the hands of
our enemies.[44]

The Administration might go out of office on a crest of "peace"
popularity, but Kennedy maintained that it would leave on the
next Administration's doorstep a whole host of crucial international problems. Worst of all,

they will not leave behind sufficient military power to enable us to
deal with these situations—Berlin, Quemoy-Matsu, and all the rest—
from a position of strength—not strength for war alone, but for
peace.[45]

Kennedy, in taking this stand, did not minimize the missile
gap. The issue was too rich politically to lay aside and he ex-
ploited it at length and in depth. Speaking to the Senate in
1958, he announced:

We are rapidly approaching that dangerous period which General
Gavin and others have called the "gap" or the "missile-lag period"—

a period, in the words of General Gavin, "in which our own offensive and defensive missile capabilities will lag so far behind those
of the Soviets as to place us in a position of great peril."

The most critical years of the gap would appear to be 1960–64.[46]

He foresaw the possibility that "the deterrent ratio might
well shift to the Soviets so heavily, during the years of the gap,
as to open to them a new shortcut to world domination." But
there were other dangers about which he expressed even greater
concern.

. . . the Soviets may be expected to use their superior striking
ability to achieve their objectives in ways which may not require
launching an actual attack. Their missile power will be the shield
from behind which they will slowly, but surely, advance—through
Sputnik diplomacy, limited brush-fire wars, indirect non-overt aggression, intimidation and subversion, internal revolution, increased
prestige or influence, and the vicious blackmail of our allies. The
periphery of the Free World will slowly be nibbled away. . . .
Each such Soviet move will weaken the West; but none will seem
sufficiently significant by itself to justify our initiating a nuclear war
which might destroy us.[47]

In these circumstances, "our threats of massive retaliation will
lose most of their impact" and "our exercises in brink-of-war
diplomacy will be infinitely less successful."[48]

What, according to Kennedy, had the Eisenhower Administration done in the face of these dangers?

We have steadily cut the numbers and strength of our ground
forces—our Army and Marines. We have steadily failed to provide
our conventional forces with modern conventional weapons, with
effective versatile firepower. And we have particularly failed to
provide the airlift and sealift capacity necessary to give these forces
the swift mobility they need to protect our commitments around
the world. Do you realize that some of our units entering the
Lebanon "pipeline," so to speak, at the time of the Iraqi revolt,
emerged at the other end only to find that by then the dust had
settled—we had already recognized the new regime—and it was
time to be evacuated?[49]

Meanwhile, the Soviets had "invalidated the original strategic conception of NATO, by outflanking its key element—the deterrent power of the U.S. Strategic Air Command." By virtue of their advances in the techniques of rockets and missiles, they had also "enlarged the military importance of Russia's vast conventionally equipped land army."[50] Such, in Kennedy's view, was the plight to which the Eisenhower Administration had brought the United States.

What was to be done? It would be an exaggeration to suggest that Kennedy foresaw in detail what would be needed in order to remedy the deficiencies he had described. But he held strong views about the areas in which action should be taken. First on his list of priorities was reduction of the missile or deterrent gap:

More air tankers to refuel our SAC bombers and more air-to-ground missiles to lessen the need for their deep penetration of Soviet territory are among the first steps to be taken while we expedite our longer-range ICBM and IRBM developments, and our progress on atomic submarines, solid fuels, the Polaris and the Minuteman. Our continental defense system . . . must be re-designed for the detection and interception of missile attacks as well as planes.[51]

Kennedy argued, however, that the process of change could not stop here. Nuclear retaliatory power by itself was not enough.

It cannot deter Communist aggression which is too limited to justify atomic war. It cannot protect uncommitted nations against a Communist takeover using local or guerrilla forces. It cannot be used in so-called "brush-fire" peripheral wars. It was not used in Korea, Indochina, Hungary, Suez, Lebanon, Quemoy, Tibet, or Laos.[52]

Since the limits on the utility of the strategic nuclear forces were so severe, other types of capability would be required. Tactical nuclear weapons, in the Senator's view, were not the answer. "Inevitably, the use of small nuclear armaments will lead to larger and larger nuclear armaments on both sides, until

the world-wide holocaust has begun."[53] This was not to say that
the country could do without a tactical nuclear capability. "We
need tactical atomic weapons—to deter their use by the Russians, to serve as a shield for our conventional forces on the
battlefront. But we still need those conventional forces on that
front."[54] Kennedy did not say what the size of the conventional
capability should be, but he indicated a need "to reverse what
General Gavin describes as the 'critical cut' in our military manpower begun in 1954." There was also the requirement for "sea
and airlift necessary to intervene in a limited war with the
speed, discrimination, and versatility which may well be needed
to keep it limited. . . ."[55] Only with such capabilities could
the Communists be contained, especially during the period of
the missile gap.

Kennedy thought it necessary to take two steps with respect
to NATO.

. . . we must consider whether it is wise to maintain a situation
in which information is denied to our friends which we know for
certain is available to our potential enemies, and which places a
premium on our allies developing at great expense nuclear capabilities which in themselves are of limited military significance.

Of more importance, he thought the time had come "for the
North Atlantic Alliance as a whole to consider whether its non-
nuclear forces are adequate either for the effective deterrence
of limited war or to provide an adequate security force should
a break-through be achieved in the international control of
nuclear weapons."[56]

That the control of nuclear weapons and steps toward disarmament were desirable, Kennedy did not doubt. That the
Eisenhower Administration had acted with sufficient energy, he
questioned. As a first step, more should be done, he felt, to obtain a ban on nuclear testing. He did not claim that an international agreement to end tests would solve all problems.

But it would place a major obstacle in the path of those nations
which have not yet successfully conducted tests, and which would

be unwilling to risk the tremendous investment necessary in weapons which could not be tested. And surely such an agreement would give reassurance to those of us who are concerned about the atmosphere we live in and the air our children breathe. . . .[57]

Such was the program that Kennedy put before the public between 1958 and 1960. It clearly represented a substantial departure from the policies of the Eisenhower Administration in its emphasis on closing the missile gap, its skepticism about the utility of tactical nuclear weapons except for the deterrence of their first use by the Soviets, and its heavy reliance upon conventional forces as the cutting edge of American power. Of equal certainty, it would require a great deal of refinement and operational detail before it could become the policy of the United States. When, on November 8, 1960, Kennedy became President-elect of the United States, he set out to find a Secretary of Defense who could execute this enormous task for him. His choice was McNamara.

On the face of it the choice was a conventional one. For the day after Kennedy's election, McNamara succeeded to the presidency of the Ford Motor Co. and thereby reached that pinnacle of big business from which Eisenhower had drawn Wilson, McElroy, and Gates. But appearances were deceptive. A native of San Francisco, born in 1916, McNamara had graduated from the University of California at Berkeley with a Phi Beta Kappa, acted briefly as a sailor's union organizer, and gone on to the Harvard Business School. Thereafter, he had married, spent a year as an accountant with the firm of Price, Waterhouse, and then returned to the Business School to serve as an assistant professor of accounting. His specialty, statistical control, brought him into contact with the Army Air Forces, and by 1943 he was in uniform and helping the AAF to keep track of what it had at any given moment in its world-wide inventories, what it was going to need next, and what supplies it could begin to discard. A senior Air Force officer recalls when McNamara came to India and, after days of absorbed calculation, determined the mixture of supplies that should be flown over the Himalayan Hump to China where the first B-29's were waiting for the logistic support necessary to attack Japan. Obviously, he was at home with numbers, and with the problems that plagued the military.

After the war, he and nine associates from the AAF moved as a package to the Ford Motor Co. His rise there was quick and unorthodox. He went to the top, not by way of engineering or sales, but through finance and product planning. Even his methods were unusual. He came to Detroit as a Quiz Kid and the eternal questioner he remained. When told that Detroit could not build a Volkswagen competitive with the German version, he had his staff buy a Volkswagen, dismantle it, determine the cost of each part, and compare it with the German cost. Planning of the compact Falcon automobile grew out of this questioning and analysis.

The passion for questions was accompanied by a capacious appetite for facts. Henry Ford II once claimed that McNamara had "in his head the facts and figures most of us have to go to the library to dig out."[58] He had another side as well. Ann Arbor rather than Detroit was where he chose to live. There he participated in discussion groups, acted as elder of the First Presbyterian Church, and contributed to the NAACP and the American Civil Liberties Union. On vacations he went mountain climbing and skiing. His politics were difficult to classify. Nominally a Republican, he contributed funds to candidates whose views he approved. In 1960, he reportedly voted for a Republican for Governor of Michigan, and John F. Kennedy for President of the United States. When, on the day after election, he succeeded to the presidency of Ford, he entered the stereotyped ranks of the great corporate executives; but he belonged to a new breed. As a friend remarked: "McNamara has all the best qualities of a professional manager. He has the ability to range over broad areas of interest. He is interested in ideas, has an analytical mind, and a capacity for action. He doesn't worry over details or the possibility of making mistakes. He doesn't nibble decisions to pieces. He won't be scared off from a decision by someone else's reservations."[59]

McNamara accepted the office of Secretary of Defense with a minimum of agonizing, despite his recent arrival at the seats of corporate power. He divested himself of his Ford stock, surrendered his stock options, and put his money in trust. Then he moved to the Pentagon.

CHAPTER 2

The Search for Options

THE TASK that awaited McNamara when he entered the office of Secretary in the deep snows of January, 1961, had two major dimensions. He needed to redeem the President's campaign pledges to reduce the missile gap. At the same time, he had to start providing a detailed blueprint of the Kennedy defense program. The President set him a rapid pace. He had already alluded to defense matters in his inaugural address when he said: "Only when our arms are sufficient beyond doubt can we be certain beyond doubt that they will never be employed."[1] Ten days later, in his State of the Union message, he made abundantly clear his expectations.

We are moving into a period of uncertain risk and great commitment in which both the military and diplomatic possibilities require a Free World force so powerful as to make any aggression clearly futile. Yet in the past, lack of a consistent, coherent military strategy, the absence of basic assumptions about our national requirements and the faulty estimates and duplication arising from inter-service rivalries have all made it difficult to assess accurately how adequate—or inadequate—our defenses really are.

I have, therefore, instructed the Secretary of Defense to reappraise our entire defense strategy—our ability to fulfill our commitments—the effectiveness, vulnerability, and dispersal of our strategic bases, forces, and warning systems—the efficiency and economy of our operation and organization—the elimination of obsolete bases and installations—and the adequacy, modernization and mobility of our present conventional and nuclear forces and weapons systems in the light of present and future dangers. I have asked for preliminary conclusions by the end of February. . . .[2]

In addition, McNamara received two other instructions: "Develop the force structure necessary to our military requirements without regard to arbitrary or predetermined budget ceilings. And secondly, having determined that force structure, . . . procure it at the lowest possible cost."[3] It was a tall order, but McNamara, facing his first press conference, seemed unperturbed. He said: "The President in the State of the Union message referred in one point to the American Eagle and the fact that in its talons it held an olive branch and a bundle of arrows. We propose to give equal attention to each."[4]

McNamara's apparent calm probably stemmed from several sources. The Eisenhower defense budget for fiscal year 1962 (running from July 1, 1961 to June 30, 1962) was already before the Congress, and it gave him a basis for determining what further action needed to be taken. At hand, in addition, were the staffs of the Services and of the Joint Chiefs to advise him about prospective changes; and he had already set in motion four task forces to explore for him the requirements for strategic nuclear war, limited war, research and development, and military installations. Furthermore, he was rapidly acquiring an understanding of the techniques by which military planning is done. There was good reason why he should be able to do so. Military planning deals with numbers: of dollars in the budget; of men and weapons; of ships sunk, aircraft and missiles destroyed, casualties suffered, prisoners taken, and so forth. Many of the numbers come from experience in previous wars. Others are derived from force exercises, maneuvers, and the hypothetical experience of detailed war games in which forces with known attributes are tested against an enemy in simulated combat. The costs of alternative forces can also be determined,

and the expected effectiveness of these alternatives can be measured to some degree in the laboratory of the war game. The best
buy for a given budget can thus be defined; or, what amounts
to the same thing, it is possible to find the force with the lowest
cost to achieve a given set of objectives. That, in essence, is
what peacetime military planning is all about. The practice of
it is, of course, extremely complex, and many subtleties enter
into it. Nevertheless, McNamara found in it much that was
similar to his own mode of thought and experience.

McNamara is notorious for his habit of immersing himself
in the details of staff reports, annotating them in his left-
handed script, and locking away the summaries in his personal
safe at the Pentagon. It is doubtful that he has in there a set of
rules for policy-making. But it is possible to surmise what are
major parts of his code. He likes to see objectives concretely
defined. He abhors the thought that there is only one way of
doing something; he is intensely interested in alternatives. And
he is a restless seeker of ways to measure the effectiveness of the
alternatives. Several of McNamara's operating principles are in
the highest tradition of military planning. He dislikes having
programs out of balance; he sees no point in calling up soldiers
when there is no ammunition for them to shoot. He is an econo-
mizer of resources, always on the alert for ways of determining
how much is enough to perform a given mission. He is an advo-
cate of taking out insurance against the failure of a program or
an action. And above all, he recognizes that the world is an uncertain place and believes in plans that take the uncertainty
specifically into account. One way to deal with uncertainty is to
buy options, and that is what he seeks. As he told a Congressional subcommittee, "I do not believe we should embark upon a
course of action that is almost certain to destroy our Nation
when that course of action can be avoided without substantial
penalty to us."[5] That spirit dominated his approach to his two
great tasks.

Among his first acts was to inform himself on the nature of
the missile gap. Whether or not a gap still existed, he found the

deterrent itself in working order, although in need of urgent repair in order to survive a future surprise attack. He was reported to have said as much at a press briefing. Two days later the President took the position that it would be premature to say whether the gap was still there. Judgment would have to be reserved until the Defense Department had completed its review of the problem. Some months later, a reporter twitted McNamara about the gap.

QUESTION: The [House Appropriations] Committee suggested that there might be, if you will pardon the expression, a gap in the Polaris program if you did not have long lead-time items.

SECRETARY MCNAMARA: Yes. We did not request funds for Polaris submarines beyond Boat 29. I will pass by without commenting on the gap. (Laughter.)[6]

Exactly why the gap did not materialize remains something of a mystery. Responsible officials in the Eisenhower Administration and other knowledgeable students of the problem were deeply concerned about the prospective state of the strategic nuclear balance. The reaction of the Eisenhower Administration, in strengthening SAC, reducing its vulnerability, and accelerating the missile program, goes part of the way toward explaining why the situation in 1961 looked less ominous than had been expected. Crying wolf for once had had a salutary effect. But the greater part of the explanation lies with what the Soviets had not done. In a word, they had not built as many ICBM's as they were thought to be capable of doing. Everyone had reason to be thankful.

McNamara, however, had the responsibility not only for the here-and-now, but also for the future. And if the present looked less gloomy than he had anticipated, the future remained uncertain and precarious. He owed it to the country to prevent the specter of the gap from arising again. But what precisely did that mean? The school of thought which was labeled minimum deterrence had already made its case to McNamara that numerical superiority, or even equality, was meaningless as a deterrent to strategic nuclear war. What the nation required, rather, was a small, well-protected force—perhaps several hundred Polaris missiles—aimed at Soviet cities. That would provide a sufficient deterrent. It would also contribute to a slowing down of the arms race, reduce the possibility of provoking the Soviets into an attack, and free resources for other purposes.

An alternative would have been to continue with the existing strategy and program of the optimum mix: buying the forces necessary to crush Soviet society and knock out enemy bombers and missiles on the ground in one great spasm. But it was not at all clear what one was buying with this kind of approach other than the terrifying ability to make sure that in a war more Russians than Americans ended up dead. The third major contender for McNamara's attention went variously under the war-fighting, flexible response, and counterforce label. It argued that deterrence was not the only function of the strategic nuclear forces and that, in any event, the best deterrent was the ability to establish military superiority in a war. Accordingly, the proponents of the strategy of the flexible response, led by General Thomas D. White, Air Force Chief of Staff, recommended a posture which would be so designed and controlled that it could attack enemy bomber and missile sites, retaliate with reserve forces against enemy cities, if that should prove necessary, and also exert pressure on the enemy to end the war on terms acceptable to the United States. The recommendations specifically stated that the posture should be designed, not for the case of a first strike against the Soviet Union, but for the retaliatory role, especially since important military targets would remain for attack in the second strike.

The strategy of the flexible response rested upon several premises. The first was that there were circumstances in which deterrence might not work. The second was that the number of lives lost in a thermonuclear war would vary significantly, depending, among other factors, on the types of targets attacked by the belligerents. The third was that limiting damage to the United States and its allies would constitute a major wartime objective, and that it could best be done by attacking the enemy's bombers and missiles, and providing active and civil defenses for American and allied populations. The fourth and related premise was that the combination of avoiding enemy cities and holding forces in reserve would provide the enemy with incentives to confine his own attacks to American and allied military targets and thus contribute further to the limitation of damage. Whether or not the incentives would prove powerful enough, it would be foolish, according to this argument, automatically to destroy cities at the outset of the war when they could always be taken under attack by reserve forces at some later stage, if that should seem necessary. Finally, there was the premise that even a thermonuclear conflict would not totally erase the interest of the United States in the postwar world; hence, sufficient forces should be available to eliminate or neutralize residual enemy capabilities, bring the war to a conclusion, and provide a measure of protection thereafter. Proponents of the flexible response answered the argument that a shift in strategy would weaken deterrence by asking whether the enemy would be any more willing to go to strategic nuclear war if he faced the prospect of being thwarted in his objectives and suffering substantial damage than if the outcome was likely to be mutual civil devastation. As for the arms race, they questioned whether unilateral American restraint would really slow it down, and pointed out that under the concept of the flexible response there were limits to the numbers of offensive forces that it would be necessary to procure, owing simply to the combination of high costs and the law of diminishing returns.

As McNamara surveyed these alternatives, several points became apparent. All three concepts possessed certain features in common: they stressed second-strike forces of high survivability and emphasized the importance of command-control to guard against unleashing the holocaust in the face of accidents and unauthorized acts. Where they differed was in the size and composition of the offensive forces, the role of active and passive defenses, and the targets to be attacked. The concept of minimum deterrence was the most extreme in these respects. It rested on the assumption that the Soviets could not find ways to counter a small offensive force by such measures as antisubmarine warfare, antimissile defenses, and the pressure of superior nuclear power; it also tended to ignore the overseas commitments of the United States and the role that strategic nuclear forces might have to play in their fulfillment. What was involved, therefore, was a choice between a deterrent capability of high quality with a range of options built into it, and a deterrent of lesser quality, greatly dependent on Soviet restraint for its effectiveness, with essentially one strategy open to its commander in the event that deterrence should fail. McNamara, naturally, was predisposed toward the alternative of the flexible response with the options that it contained. As early as February, 1961, therefore, he set in place a major building block in his strategic concept.

He made a typically cautious statement about it to the House Armed Services Committee. "So long as the adversaries of freedom continue to expand their stockpiles of mass destruction weapons," he explained,

the United States has no alternative but to ensure that at all times and under all circumstances it has the capability to deter their use. In this age of nuclear-armed intercontinental ballistic missiles, the ability to deter rests heavily on the existence of a force which can weather a massive nuclear attack, even with little or no warning, in sufficient strength to strike a decisive counterblow. This force must be of a character which will permit its use, in event of attack, in a cool and deliberate fashion and always under the complete control of the constituted authority.[7]

McNamara's first step toward implementing the new concept was to accelerate the existing Polaris program by nine or ten months. A month later he recommended a more elaborate program which would add ten more Polaris submarines to the number planned by the Eisenhower Administration, double the production capacity for the Minuteman ICBM, place one-half

of SAC's bombers on a quick-reaction ground alert (as against
the previous one-third), complete the capability for maintaining an eighth of SAC's B-52's on an airborne alert in a crisis,
strengthen the air defenses of the country against bomber attack, and improve the critically important command-control
and communications system for the strategic nuclear forces. As
McNamara was to explain later, "in the short term, that is to
say, between 1961 and 1962, we have simply taken the steps
that were within our capability to increase the megatonnage
as rapidly as possible in the alert force. And that involved ex-
pending the funds to raise the percentage of bombers in the
alert force, plus accelerating certain delivery schedules."[8]

This was the technique of the quick fix: doing those things
which would add measurably to combat strength in a relatively
short period of time. In what was to become a typical Mc-
Namara tactic, he recommended simultaneously a series of reductions in what appeared to be superfluous aspects of the Eisenhower program so as to hold down the costs of the proposed
improvements. Among the projects which suffered from this
economizing approach were two squadrons of heavy ballistic
missiles, the obsolete Snark air-breathing missiles which the
Air Force had installed in Maine, the mobile Minuteman program, the atomic-powered airplane, and the famed and controversial B-70. At the same time, McNamara put additional
funds into a number of major development projects, including
the Skybolt air-to-surface ballistic missile, the Midas early
warning satellite, and such esoteric programs as Dynasoar, Advent, Defender, and Discoverer—all concerned with military
activities in space. In total, the new changes required an addition of $1.5 billion to the proposed Eisenhower budget.

McNamara explained the rationale for the program to a Senate subcommittee in these words:

Today our strategic forces are fully adequate to carry out their
assigned tasks. But as our principal antagonists acquire a large and
ready force of ICBM's which could be launched with little or no
warning, the problem of preventing the destruction of our forces

on the ground becomes much more difficult. Essentially, there are two major approaches available to us: (1) develop forces which can be launched within the expected period of tactical warning; (2) develop forces which can ride out a massive ICBM attack.

The feasibility of the first approach is heavily dependent on timely and unambiguous warning. While we can be reasonably sure of timely warning, we cannot in the present state-of-the-art be wholly sure of unambiguous warning. In the case of the manned bomber, this uncertainty presents some serious, but not necessarily critical, problems. The bomber can be launched under positive control and then ordered to attack its target only after the evidence of an attack is unmistakable. But, a ballistic missile once launched cannot be recalled. Yet, unless it is deployed in a mode which gives it a good chance to survive an attack, it too must be launched before the attacker strikes home (i.e., within the relatively brief tactical warning time) or risk destruction on the ground. I need not elaborate on the dangers of this situation.

Accordingly, in re-evaluating our general war position, our major concern was to reduce our dependence on deterrent forces which are highly vulnerable to ballistic missile attack or which rely for their survival on a hair-trigger response to the first indications of such an attack. Conversely, we sought to place greater emphasis on the second approach—the kind of forces which could ride out a massive nuclear attack and which could be applied with deliberation and always under the complete control of the constituted authority.[9]

To make the strategy of the flexible response meaningful, it was clearly necessary to provide the kind of strategic offensive forces and active defense systems that McNamara was now advocating. But that, by itself, was not sufficient. If planning was to proceed on the basis that thermonuclear war might occur, and if it became a prime objective to limit damage to the United States and its allies, something had to be done about the problem of fallout. If the enemy confined his attack to military targets, the fallout from his bombs would still cause tremendous devastation. If he acted irrationally and struck cities, the damage would be more appalling still. But in both cases, large numbers of people could be saved from fallout if not from blast—provided they could find adequate shelter and stay protected for days or possibly even several weeks. Strategic offensive forces and active defenses could do only so much in destroying enemy weapons and limiting damage. Fallout shelters were an essential component of the flexible response.

Fallout shelters, however, had become the focus of attack by those citizens who were understandably concerned about the dangers of nuclear war and fearful that something might be done to drive one or the other of the great powers over the nuclear brink. Civil defense, they suggested, might be just such a measure, and they developed a number of arguments to support their case. A letter to the Harvard *Crimson* not only parodied the opposition to fallout shelters, but also provided one of the better arguments in favor of civil defense in the process. The letter went as follows:

It has been brought to our attention that certain elements among the passengers and crew favor the installation of "life" boats on this ship. These elements have advanced the excuse that such action would save lives in the event of a maritime disaster such as the ship striking an iceberg. Although we share their concern, we remain unalterably opposed to any consideration of their course of action for the following reasons.

1. This program would lull you into a false sense of security.
2. It would cause undue alarm and destroy your desire to continue your voyage in this ship.
3. It demonstrates a lack of faith in our Captain.
4. The apparent security which "life" boats offer will make our Navigators reckless.
5. These proposals will distract our attention from more important things, i.e., building unsinkable ships. They may even lead our builders to false economies and the building of ships that are actually unsafe.
6. In the event of being struck by an iceberg (we will never strike first) the "life" boats would certainly sink along with the ship.

7. If they do not sink, you will only be saved for a worse fate, inevitable death on the open sea.

8. If you should be washed ashore on a desert island, you will be unaccustomed to the hostile environment and will surely die of exposure.

9. If you should be rescued by a passing vessel, you would spend a life of remorse mourning over your lost loved ones.

10. The panic engendered by a collision with an iceberg would destroy all vestiges of civilized human behavior. We shudder at the vision of one man shooting another for the possession of a "life" boat.

11. Such a catastrophe is too horrible to contemplate. Anyone who does contemplate it obviously advocates it.

Committee for a Sane Navigational Policy[10]

The President, it turned out, also favored "life" boats, despite the arguments against them. In July, he transferred the bulk of the civil defense responsibility to the Defense Department and submitted a $207 million request to Congress for the first installment on a national civil defense program. McNamara's defense of the request was straightforward.

As the size and range of strategic weapons are multiplied, civil defense becomes an essential element to round out our over-all defense capabilities. The proper balance between active and passive defense is always open for discussion. By any standard, however, the present level of civil defense spending is not only inadequate but wasteful. It buys an organization but not a program.

What was needed to correct this major deficiency was a national system of fallout shelters, as recommended by the President. McNamara described the proposal this way.

The heart of the President's program is the identification, marking and stocking of available community shelter space in existing buildings throughout the United States. Our best estimate by extrapolation from pilot surveys made in the past is that this program will identify some 50 million usable shelter spaces, and will provide a minimum of shelter for approximately one-fourth of our population. This does not mean that the program will save 50 million lives.

Again, as the 1959 study [by the Special Committee on Radiation of the Joint Committee on Atomic Energy] pointed out, nearly 75 per cent of the deaths from the hypothetical attack would have resulted from blast and thermal effects combined with immediate radiation effects. Other patterns of attack might increase or decrease the proportion of the population exposed to fallout alone, and thus increase or decrease the number of lives that could be saved by fallout shelter. But it is probably a reasonable estimate that the identification and marking of existing fallout shelter space could, without additional effort, save at least 10 to 15 million lives in the event of a thermonuclear attack.[11]

With the introduction of the civil defense program, Mc-Namara's approach to the problem of strategic nuclear warfare was taking a definite but by no means final form. There remained, however, all the other threats: tactical nuclear war, local conventional war, and the deadly combination of subversion and guerrilla warfare. They raised a whole series of difficult issues including, particularly, the roles of conventional and tactical nuclear forces in countering conventional aggression, and the magnitudes of the different capabilities that the United States should acquire. McNamara's first reaction to these issues was to apply the technique of the quick fix to improve the effectiveness of existing forces. One way of doing this was to improve their mobility. Accordingly, he recommended the procurement of 129 new, longer-range, modern airlift aircraft. He also recommended increased funds for modern Army and Air Force non-nuclear munitions and equipment, expanded research on non-nuclear weapons, and modest additions to the conventional forces of the Army and Marine Corps. Perhaps the most spectacular change was in the size of the Army's Special Forces. These forces had been designed to act as guerrillas in a general nuclear war. McNamara reoriented them toward the counterinsurgency mission and more than doubled their numbers. Still, the cost of all the changes came to only $693 million. He clearly did not yet feel that he had the basis for proposing a more dramatic adjustment in the nation's capa-

bilities. Although existing conventional forces were adequate
to cope with only one small-scale local action at a time, the
specter of seemingly inexhaustible Communist manpower dis-
couraged a sharp break with the heavily nuclear-dependent
strategy of the past.

McNamara nevertheless made no particular secret of the direction in which he would prefer to go. As he told a Senate
hearing in April, 1961:

We must continue to provide for the forces required to deter an
all-out nuclear war. Only behind the shield of such forces can the
Free World hope to cope successfully with lesser military aggressions. But, having provided for these essential forces, we want to
see to it that this Nation, in cooperation with its friends and allies
abroad, has the kinds of forces needed to discourage more limited
military adventures by the enemies of freedom.

As recent events have again demonstrated, these adventures may
range from guerrilla and subversive activities involving small
scattered bands of men to organized aggression involving sizable
regular military forces. Our limited war forces should be properly
deployed, properly trained, and properly equipped to deal with
the entire spectrum of such actions; and they should have the means
to move quickly to wherever they may be needed on very short
notice. The ability to respond promptly to limited aggressions, possibly in more than one place at the same time, can serve both to
deter them and to prevent them from spreading into larger conflicts.[12]

That was the desired goal. For the time being, however, a
somewhat different statement of intentions had to stand in its
place.

There has been a tendency since the end of the Korean War to
emphasize the nuclear capabilities of these forces. These capabilities are, of course, essential to our over-all national strategy, since all
of our forces have a role in general nuclear war. Even in limited
war situations, we should not preclude the use of tactical nuclear
weapons, for no one can foreshadow how such situations might
develop. But the decision to employ tactical nuclear weapons in

limited conflicts should not be forced upon us simply because we
have no other means to cope with them. There are many possible
situations in which it would not be advisable or feasible to use
such weapons. What is being proposed at this time is not a reversal
of our existing national policy but an increase in our non-nuclear
capabilities to provide a greater degree of versatility to our limited
war forces.[13]

Despite this apparent adherence to existing national policy,
there was one area, in addition to strategic nuclear deterrence,
where McNamara, following the President's lead, had determined to institute a major change. That was with respect to the
defense of the underdeveloped countries. In justification of the
change, he cited two sources. The first was a major declaration
of policy by Khrushchev on January 6, 1961, just before the
Kennedy Administration had come into office. McNamara
quoted the declaration at some length.

With respect to world wars, Mr. Khrushchev maintains that:
"Communists are the most resolute opponents of world wars, as
they are of wars among states in general." He then goes on to
describe the terrible death and destruction such a war would wreak
on all mankind, and concludes that world wars are not needed for
the victory of Communism. Local wars are also rejected since a
small war "might develop into a world thermonuclear rocket war."
Communists, Mr. Khrushchev proclaims, ". . . must wage a struggle
both against world wars and against local wars." There is, however,
a third type of conflict, which we know as subversion and covert
aggression, but which he calls "wars of national liberation" or
"popular uprisings." "What attitude do Marxists have toward such
uprisings?" he asks; "The most favorable," he replies. Such conflicts,
"Communists fully and unreservedly support. . . ."

McNamara's second source was the President himself. Kennedy, upon his return from a somber meeting with Khrushchev
in Vienna at the beginning of June, 1961, told the nation:

In the 1940's and early '50's the great danger was from Communist armies marching across free borders. . . . Now we face a
new and different threat. We no longer have a nuclear monopoly.

Their missiles, they believe, will hold off our missiles, and their troops can match our troops should we intervene in these so-called wars of liberation.

Thus the local conflict they support can turn in their favor through guerrillas or insurgents or subversion. A small group of disciplined Communists could exploit discontent and misery in a country where the average income may be $60 or $70 a year and seize control, therefore, of an entire country without Communist troops ever crossing any international frontier.

Castro had already taken power in Cuba in this manner, and both Laos and South Vietnam stood in imminent danger of being reduced to complete chaos by guerrilla attacks. The answer to the threat, in these circumstances, lay not in nuclear weapons or even in large conventional forces, but in a battery of political, economic, and military measures. To fulfill the responsibility of the Defense Department for counterinsurgency, McNamara repeated the request of the previous Administration for over $1.8 billion in military assistance funds. In doing so, he spelled out to the Senate Foreign Relations Committee the approach he proposed to take.

From the President's messages to Congress you will have noted the new emphasis on strategic forces which can ride out a nuclear attack, on command and control of nuclear weapons, on increased and more mobile non-nuclear forces, and on the problem of how best to assist those jeopardized by internal aggression. Our projected military assistance programs are a necessary, integral part of this conceptual framework. Through the assistance planned we anticipate an improvement in our ability to deal with aggression in its incipient phases, to furnish help for friends and allies which will be more consistent with the kind of threat they face, and to maintain the facilities abroad required for the quick and effective deployment of appropriate U.S. forces.

McNamara divided the threatened countries into two major categories.

In the first category, which may be called the single-threat countries, belong the underdeveloped nations of Asia, the Middle East,

Africa and Latin America that are not contiguous to the Sino-Soviet Bloc but which Communist words and actions have shown to be targets for indirect aggression. In these areas we recognize as the primary requirement the need for economic and social progress and the cooperation of governments and peoples in striving for a better life. Through economic programs we seek to contribute to this development. An essential component of their progress, however, is the maintenance of internal stability, and in this function the role of the military establishment and other security forces is essential. Military aid to such countries involves primarily the provision of small arms, transport, communications and training. Our objective here is to provide the means for local military establishments, with the support and cooperation of local populations, to guard against external covert intrusion and internal subversion designed to create dissidence and insurrection.

McNamara also pointed out, in the President's words, that military assistance to these countries could, "in addition to its military purposes, make a contribution to economic progress. The domestic works of our own Army Engineers are an example of the role which military forces in the emerging countries can play in village development, sanitation and road building."

The problem in the countries of the first category was complicated enough. It was still worse elsewhere.

In the second category, which may be called the double-threat countries, belong those nations contiguous to or near the Sino-Soviet Bloc that face a direct threat from without and an indirect threat from within. Vietnam today is a classic example of how these threats feed on and reinforce each other. The two-fold threat requires dual-purpose forces in terms of arms, equipment and personnel. Our military assistance programs play an essential role in furnishing arms and equipment and in teaching troops to operate, maintain and use them. Because of this two-fold threat the military aid we plan to give them is proportionally high. We recognize the inadequacy of their forces to cope with an outright Communist invasion, yet with our assistance we count on their courage and ability to deal with large-scale guerrilla warfare. Should they suffer an open attack across their borders, we look for local forces to resist the initial thrust until such time as Free World forces may come to their support. In these areas the capability of our own forces to deploy quickly against aggression is heavily dependent upon the development and maintenance of base facilities or military infrastructure on the spot or in the vicinity. Military assistance is a key factor in constructing new facilities, improving existing facilities and ensuring their availability when required.[14]

McNamara's objective here was to create a system of defense for what used to be called the gray areas—the Far East, South Asia, and Latin America—that would be responsive to the threats without having to depend on nuclear weapons. The military assistance program was one way of fostering this development. Another way was to give American ground and air forces stationed in the United States, Hawaii, and Okinawa the mobility necessary to move them rapidly into an area threatened by overt attack. Increased airlift and sealift were intended to do that. But problems still remained. The American strategic reserve consisted on paper of six Army and two Marine divisions. But three of the Army divisions lacked combat capability. This meant that if the United States committed only a few divisions to a conflict in South Asia, for example, it would be without reserves for another conflagration of approximately equal magnitude. Should such a situation arise, the choice would be between nuclear weapons and doing nothing. As a way out of the dilemma, McNamara turned to the National Guard and the Army Reserve.

Over a year later, he described the situation that he had found.

Today's 700,000 authorized drill strength is made up of 400,000 men authorized for the National Guard and 300,000 for the Army Reserve. Both the total strength and the division between Guard and Reserve were set in the winter of 1956–57. At that time the previous Administration was building the size of the reserve components in accordance with a 1954 plan, scheduled to be fully implemented by 1960. Two years later, in 1958, the entire plan was dropped. For Fiscal Year 1959, and for each of the next three Fiscal Years, the previous Administration recommended a cut in paid drill strength which would have brought it to 630,000. Congress just as persistently appropriated the funds for 700,000.

It is clear from the record that neither the Congress' 700,000 figure, nor the Administration's 630,000 was the product of military planning. Both figures were based on pure happenstance. The first one being a half-way figure in an abandoned plan, and the second being simply ten per cent less than the first.[15]

Not only did the reserve structure make very little sense in terms of size; its mission was obscure to say the least. Its major combat units would have taken on the order of four to nine months to reach a state of readiness, which meant that they had virtually no capability for responding rapidly to an emergency. This was a very small benefit to accrue for an expenditure of nearly $2 billion a year. What McNamara wanted from them was the ability to replenish the strategic reserve, and to do so in a timely fashion. If he could use the reserves in this fashion, it would enable him to commit the active forces to a local conflict and still have in hand a sufficient capability to meet other local commitments that might arise. With this goal in mind he proposed reorganizing the ready reserves so as to have them combat ready on the following schedule:

Two divisions and supporting forces with 3 weeks' notice; two more divisions and supporting forces with 5 weeks' notice; and six additional divisions and their supporting forces with 8 weeks' notice. This gave a total of 10 divisions deployable within 8 weeks.[16]

The ability to nearly double the size of the combat-ready Army in a period of less than two months would obviously increase the country's options with respect to conflict in the gray areas. Forces of the proposed magnitude would enable the President to meet a wide range of contingencies without resort to nuclear weapons—something the Chiefs had advised him he could not do in April of 1961, when he faced simultaneous crises in Cuba and Laos. But there remained the difficult problem of what to do about Europe.

The crises in the Congo, Cuba, Laos, and South Vietnam had stimulated the Administration to improve its ability to handle a variety of situations by non-nuclear means. Khrushchev's revival of the Berlin crisis raised in the most immediate form the issue of strategy and forces for Europe. As the President reported to the nation after his meeting with Khrushchev in Vienna:

Our most somber talks were on the subject of Germany and Berlin. I made it clear . . . that the security of Western Europe and therefore our own security are deeply involved in our presence and our access rights to West Berlin, and that these rights are based on law not on sufferance; and that we are determined to maintain these rights at any risk and thus our obligation to the people of West Berlin and their right to choose their own future.[17]

Exactly how American rights were to be protected, however, was not at all clear. Khrushchev announced that "the conclusion of a peace treaty with Germany cannot be postponed any longer. A peaceful settlement in Europe must be attained this year."[18] On the assumption that he was serious, that did not leave much time. As matters stood, NATO had fewer than twenty divisions on the Central Front facing Berlin. The Soviets, for their part, reportedly had twenty-two divisions in East Germany alone, and supposedly could reinforce them at a rate of two to four divisions a day from their large armies in the western USSR. If they chose to sever the West's access to Berlin, NATO would be hard put to do anything about it by conventional means; and it would run the risk of leaving large holes in its defenses if it attempted to do so.

An alternative would have been to rely exclusively on the nuclear deterrent, as the Eisenhower Administration had seemed to do. It was becoming evident at this juncture not only that the missile gap had evaporated, but also that the United States had a far greater strategic nuclear power at its disposal than the Soviet Union. Indeed, in October, Deputy Secretary of Defense Gilpatric was to be quite explicit on that score. He advised his audience that "the total number of our nuclear delivery vehi-

cles, tactical as well as strategic, is in the tens of thousands; and
of course, we have more than one warhead for each vehicle."
American nuclear retaliatory power, in his estimation, had "such
lethal power that an enemy move which brought it into play
would be an act of self-destruction on his part."[19] Despite this,
however, the President was determined "to have a wider choice
than humiliation or all-out nuclear war." McNamara, for his
part, was skeptical that the strategic nuclear deterrent would be
any more effective in this kind of situation than it had been in
the past. And he was more than doubtful that anyone would
actually be willing to use nuclear weapons at the outset of a
conflict over Berlin. In fact, he informed the Senate Armed
Services Committee precisely to this effect.

Believing that the Western World will be very reluctant to invoke
the use of nuclear weapons in response to anything short of a direct
threat to its survival, the Kremlin leaders hope to create divisive
influences within the Alliance by carefully measured military threats
in connection with the Berlin situation. In order to meet such
threats with firmness and confidence and to provide us with a
greater range of military alternatives, we will need more non-nuclear
strength than we have today.[20]

Non-nuclear strength, however, in the quantities that were
likely to become available during the critical period, would not
necessarily suffice to overcome the supposed Soviet advantage
in conventional capabilities. Therefore, the question remained
as to what purpose any additional non-nuclear forces would
serve. The answer came in the form of the strategy of escalation.
The idea here bore some similarity to a poker game. Presumably, the non-nuclear chips were the easiest ones to play; NATO
therefore should have a sufficient supply of them to make a substantial ante in the event that the Soviets started the game. Not
only would this be a believable step; it would also commit the
United States irrevocably to the play. As such, it might well act
as a deterrent to Soviet action. If not, it might suffice to cause a
Soviet withdrawal from the game. However, if the Soviets per-

sisted, the United States would then have to resort to nuclear weapons, at first on the tactical level; and if that did not work, on the strategic level. The threat of a graduated use of force, in which non-nuclear capabilities would be the leading elements, thus was the only technique that seemed applicable to the threat in Europe.

McNamara never subscribed explicitly to the strategy of escalation. Rather he talked around and about it as he advocated still another increment to the defense budget in the summer of 1961.

We feel very strongly that the U.S. defense establishment must have a greater degree of flexibility in responding to particular situations. We need to expand the range of military alternatives available to the President in meeting the kind of situation which may confront us in maintaining our position in Berlin.

I want to make it clear, however, that this does not mean we are lessening the effectiveness of our tactical nuclear capabilities. As I pointed out . . . earlier this year, "Even in limited war situations we should not preclude the use of tactical nuclear weapons, for no one can foresee how such situations might develop."[21]

The additional measures proposed by McNamara were designed to strengthen the totality of American capabilities—at a cost of nearly $3.5 billion. But most of the recommendations were directed toward increasing the number of non-nuclear chips. All three Services were authorized increases in manpower, but the Army received the lion's share. Its strength was to go from 875,000 to about 1,000,000 men. To fill out existing units and add new strength, authority to call up reserve units was requested. And as the summer progressed, two National Guard divisions were ordered to active duty and two more were put on notice for possible call-up. The three training divisions in the active Army were filled out and made into combat-ready units, and a further large procurement of non-nuclear equipment and ordnance was instituted. Gradually, the Army expanded to sixteen combat-ready divisions, of which five stood at full strength in Europe and two more could reinforce them

on short notice. At the same time, the Navy added forty destroyers and destroyer-escorts to the Fleet, and strengthened its
antisubmarine capability by eighteen air reserve squadrons. The
Air Force dispatched eleven of its Air National Guard fighter
squadrons to Europe and called up six Air Force Reserve transport squadrons for airlift duty. It was an impressive surge of
power.

Looking back at the build-up in the spring of 1962, McNamara remarked:

It became clear last spring that the existing forces were quite
inadequate to cope with the many threats confronting us around the
world. The Berlin crisis later in the year was convincing evidence
that the total combat-ready non-nuclear forces then available to us
and our allies severely limited the range of our possible response
to a Soviet aggression in Europe. We recognized from the beginning
that we must always be prepared to use our nuclear weapons. But
it was also evident that our position throughout the world would
be greatly strengthened if we were not forced to choose between
doing nothing or deliberately initiating nuclear war.[22]

The partial mobilization that proceeded in the autumn of
1961 was intended to get around that dilemma. It did not, and
could not, increase the President's range of choice by a very
great deal—at least if the Soviets were as strong in conventional
capabilities as the intelligence estimates proclaimed them to be.
But in a world of great uncertainties, even a modest increase in
the range of conventional options no doubt struck McNamara
as eminently worthwhile. Senator Margaret Chase Smith
thought otherwise. She charged in the Senate that the emphasis
on limited war and the conventional build-up had "practically
told" Khrushchev that "we do not have the will to use that one
power with which we can stop him; in short, we have the nuclear capability but not the nuclear credibility." McNamara replied that the charges were unwarranted and declared:

We have spent $2 billion to strengthen our nuclear deterrent
and to strengthen it in a way that would enable us to use it im-

mediately. It is absurd to think that we would have unbalanced the budget simply to strengthen a weapon that we had decided never to use under any circumstances.[23]

In November, 1961, McNamara went to Atlanta to attend a dinner honoring Senator Russell and Congressman Vinson. He took the opportunity to review the accomplishments of the past ten months.

The core of our deterrent power is our nuclear strike force. Our intercontinental bombers number nearly 1,700, including 630 B-52's, 55 B-58's, and 1,000 B-47's. We can count 80 Polaris missiles, deployed beneath the oceans in nuclear-powered submarines, and several dozen operational Atlas intercontinental ballistic missiles in the United States.

During the past six months we have taken significant steps to strengthen and protect our nuclear strength, further increasing our ability to survive a surprise attack and to launch an effective counter-strike. Of the $6 billion added to the military budget by President Kennedy this year, more than $2 billion was added for the purpose of increasing and protecting our nuclear capability.

Here are some of the more significant actions we have taken:

We are increasing the number of Polaris submarines, so that by 1964 we will have half again as many as were originally planned for.

We have increased the portion of our strategic bomber force on 15-minute ground alert, so that the number of bombers in our alert force is 50 per cent greater.

We have retained in operational readiness 270 B-47 bombers, making up six wings that were about to be phased out of our nuclear delivery force.

We are increasing by 100 per cent our capacity to produce Minuteman missiles, against the day when that capacity may be needed.

We have increased our procurement objectives for the current fiscal year by 200 Polaris and Minuteman missiles.

Our tactical land-based air forces number more than 2,000 combat aircraft. These include more than 1,000 supersonic jet fighters, a majority of which are armed with nuclear weapons. A wide variety of penetration devices enable both strategic and tactical aircraft to neutralize opposing air defenses—unless we direct our bombers to stand off beyond the range of these defenses and fire their Hound Dog air-to-ground missiles several hundred miles toward their targets. Against our intercontinental missiles themselves, no effective countermeasures have yet been developed.

Equally great improvements had occurred in the capability for deterring or fighting local aggression.

Steps have been taken in recent months to augment the strength of our non-nuclear forces, which provide a significant increase in the military options and responses available to us.

On land, we have doubled the number of combat divisions held in the strategic reserve in this country, increasing that number from 5 to 10 divisions. Three of our Army divisions previously engaged in training missions are being converted to combat readiness. Two National Guard divisions have been called to active duty. Two additional National Guard divisions have been placed in a high state of readiness for possible rapid call-up.

During the second half of this year, our over-all military personnel strength will have been increased by more than 300,000 men, most of whom will augment our ground forces and their support. We have increased our military personnel strength in Europe alone by more than 40,000.

We have also increased the size of our anti-guerrilla forces by 150 per cent. Our amphibious lift capability has been increased by one third. Forty-five combat air squadrons have been called to active duty. We are substantially increasing the modern, long-range airlift capability of the Military Air Transport Service.

We have established a new Unified Command to combine the combat units of the Strategic Army Corps and the Tactical Air Command located in the United States. This action will further improve the mobility and flexibility of our ground strength.

At sea, we have marshaled the most massive seapower ever assembled under one flag. The active fleet, which has been increased by more than 70 vessels, includes nearly 900 ships, ranging from attack carriers, guided missile cruisers, and nuclear-powered submarines, to patrol and auxiliary ships. From the decks of a single carrier of the Forrestal class, fifty attack aircraft can be launched, armed with megaton nuclear weapons. Six carriers of this class, as well as nine other attack carriers, are deployed throughout the world's oceans, and two other attack carriers are currently in maintenance.

Twelve carrier air groups and nearly 1,000 aircraft are available for the mission of hunting down and killing enemy submarines wherever they may be operating.[24]

It was an imposing force, and more in balance than had been the case since the Korean war. Yet it was not a force with which McNamara could be entirely satisfied. The most immediate difficulty was that the call-up of the reserves had produced a certain amount of discontent and, with it, a flurry of Congressional protest. Not only was the reserve system in evident need of reform; it seemingly was not as available an instrument for emergencies as McNamara had hoped. For crises of a scale that did not require a major mobilization, an alternative would have to be found. But beyond this immediate difficulty was the immensely more complicated problem of relating forces and budgets to an over-all strategic concept. This was partly a matter of determining the role that each of the major types of forces—strategic nuclear, tactical nuclear, and conventional—would play in the face of existing and potential threats. But it was also a delicate balancing of the desirable against the feasible, a careful allocation of scarce resources to those areas where they would do the most good, and a strenuous effort to reduce waste and duplication so as to obtain the utmost in useful combat power from available funds.

In 1961, McNamara had applied the quick fix to the existing force structure; he had removed major imbalances and accelerated programs of obvious importance. He had also put the Armed Forces into the business of counterinsurgency with a vengeance. As a result of the improvements in airlift and sealift, and the expansion of the Army, Marine Corps, and tactical air forces, he was approaching a position from which the nation could handle one medium-sized local conflict with conventional means and still have the reserves to meet the full American commitment to NATO or deal with another small-scale local threat. Although the character of a tactical nuclear engagement remained obscure, and the question mark of escalation loomed over it, McNamara commanded a powerful and still growing tactical nuclear capability. And contrary to the expectations of 1960, he had acquired a strategic nuclear capability which was superior to that of the Soviet Union in numbers, in quality, and in survivability. All in all, the country was obtaining a greater number of options—achieving more flexibility—in its military posture. Nevertheless, if estimates of Soviet conventional capabilities were correct, situations could still arise—particularly in Europe—where the United States could be forced into a strategy of nuclear escalation if it wanted to stay in the conflict.

To McNamara, this was a thoroughly undesirable state of affairs on several grounds. He had no doubts about the importance of maintaining powerful nuclear capabilities. But the record was replete with instances where, despite the direst threats of massive or limited nuclear retaliation, forbidden actions of one kind or another had taken place. And no one could question the paralyzing effect that heavy reliance on nuclear weapons exerted on political and military action before and after the breakdown of deterrence. That was one drawback. Another deficiency was that the strategy of escalation virtually surrendered the destiny of the United States into the hands of a tenacious opponent. For if an enemy with a powerful conventional capability refused to cease and desist at an early stage in a conflict, the United States would be forced to climb inexorably up the ladder of nuclear escalation. Commitment to so automatic an approach was completely repugnant to McNamara. To the extent that it lay within his power, he wanted, not rigidity, but a considerable range of choice. There was, moreover, a technical problem about the strategy of escalation that was bound to make McNamara uncomfortable. It gave him no real measure of sufficiency. Who could say whether twenty divisions were really any better than fifteen, or ten, or that one set of tactical nuclear capabilities was better than some other? The strategy, in short, provided no solid basis for determining a force structure.

The struggle to get on sounder ground and to achieve a satisfactory relationship between strategy, forces, and budgets occupied a great deal of McNamara's time during the next two years. It was bound to since his longer-range responsibility for the military posture was coming increasingly to dominate the crisis-ridden considerations of 1961. The problems now had much less to do with courses of action with respect to Berlin tomorrow than they did with major programs over the next five years. Strategy, forces, and budgets thus had to be concerned explicitly with the problem of uncertainty. Actually, there were a number of different types of uncertainty: about the fruits of technology, the kinds of forces that possible enemies might develop, which types they might choose to employ in any given contingency, how they might elect to use them, and how the United States and its allies might decide to act or react. All of these uncertainties had to be taken into account in the design of a long-range force structure. Irrevocable commitment to the concept of nuclear escalation was not, in McNamara's view, the best way of going about it. Rather, he sought a force structure permitting the country sufficient options so that the President would not be obliged to choose in advance which he would have to exercise. But perhaps even more, he wanted to deter most forms of warfare, and, to the extent that that was impossible, he sought to limit conflict to non-nuclear means.

The architecture of McNamara's thought began to emerge in the first full defense budget of the Kennedy Administration in January of 1962. McNamara accompanied the request with a statement of unprecedented length and detail about the military plans and programs of the United States. A month later, in Chicago, he gave an equally striking exposition of his views on the roles and requirements of the major types of forces. In the Chicago speech, he started by referring to Khrushchev's declaration, "For New Victories of the World Communist Movement," the statement of January 6, 1961, in which the Chairman had given his support to "wars of national liberation." McNamara proceeded from there.

Our response to this new Soviet threat cannot be a simple one. Clearly the new Soviet posture, as announced by Khrushchev, gives us no cause to relax our nuclear guard. The Soviet decision to concentrate on wars of covert aggression was not taken in a power vacuum. It rests on the fact of U.S. nuclear power, which is able to survive a nuclear surprise attack and strike back with sufficient power to destroy the enemy target system. We have such power today, and we are continuing to devote to it the energies and the resources necessary to keep it up-to-date under conditions of accelerated technological advance. But our superior nuclear power may not be a credible deterrent for the kind of conflict proposed by Khrushchev.

In other words, a wide range of threats had to be taken into account and multiple capabilities maintained.

The first requirement for such a policy is clearly to maintain our nuclear strike power as a realistic, effective deterrent against Soviet initiation of major wars. We can no longer hope to have such a deterrent merely by maintaining a larger stockpile of nuclear weapons. Our weapons must be hardened, dispersed, and mobile so that they can survive an enemy attack, and they must be equipped with the most sophisticated devices necessary to penetrate enemy defenses. This kind of nuclear capability is expensive. To achieve it, we have over the last 12 months added a total of almost $4 billion to the previously planned level of the military budgets for the current and the following fiscal years.

McNamara recited the improvements that he had instituted, and then went on.

It is not enough, however, for us to have weapons that can survive an enemy attack and that can penetrate enemy defenses. In a world in which both sides may be capable of inflicting severe damage on each other, we must have machinery for the command and control of our forces, which is itself able to survive an attack and to apply the surviving forces in consonance with national security objectives. To this end we are providing alternate command posts at sea and in the air, with communications links to all elements of our strategic force.

With this protected command and control system, our forces can be used in several different ways. We may have to retaliate with a single massive attack. Or, we may be able to use our retaliatory forces to limit damage done to ourselves, and our allies, by knocking out the enemy's bases before he has had time to launch his second salvos. We may seek to terminate a war on favorable terms by using our forces as a bargaining weapon—by threatening further attack. In any case, our large reserve of protected firepower would give an enemy an incentive to avoid our cities and to stop a war. Our new policy gives us the flexibility to choose among several operational plans, but does not require that we make any advance commitment with respect to doctrine or targets. We shall be committed only to a system that gives us the ability to use our forces in a controlled and deliberate way, so as best to pursue the interests of the United States, our Allies, and the rest of the Free World.

In light of all the measures undertaken to improve our strategic striking forces—with respect to their survivability, strength and control—it is clear that we have upgraded rather than downgraded our thermonuclear power. That power is essential to our strategy and tactics, indeed to our survival as a nation.

But it is equally clear that we require a wide range of practical alternatives to meet the kind of military challenges that Khrushchev has announced he has in store for us. Unless the Free World has sufficient forces organized and equipped to deal with these challenges at what appears to be the highest appropriate levels of conflict, we could be put into difficult situations by the Communists. In such situations we could lose by default; or we could lose by limiting our response to what appears to be the highest appropriate level—but a level at which we may be inferior; or we could resort to thermonuclear war—the level at which we are superior—but at a cost which could be out of proportion to the issues and dangers involved.

McNamara was clear about the limitations of the nuclear deterrent in the face of what he called the "salami-slice" technique.

In areas where the nuclear deterrent is the only deterrent, and where the political or other issue is such that the nuclear deterrent does not appear to be fully persuasive to the Soviets, our friends ultimately could come to believe in the sincerity of Soviet threats.

They could be inclined to succumb to Soviet blackmail if we had available no suitably scaled and obviously credible countermeasures.

The only satisfactory answer to this kind of threat was a conventional build-up.

An adequate level of non-nuclear military strength will provide us with the means to meet a limited challenge with limited forces. We will then be in a position of being able to choose, coolly and deliberately, the level and kind of response we feel most appropriate in our own best interests, and both our enemies and our friends will know it.

The non-nuclear build-up will increase our capacity to tailor our responses to a particular military challenge to that level of force which is both appropriate to the issue involved and militarily favorable to our side. Not only will it avoid complete dependence on nuclear weapons, but it will also enhance the credibility to the Soviets of our determination to use nuclear weapons, should this prove necessary. If we have shown ourselves able and ready to engage in large-scale non-nuclear warfare in response to a Communist provocation, the Soviets can hardly misconstrue two things: first, that we regard this provocation as a challenge to our vital interests; and second, that we will use nuclear weapons to prevail, if this becomes necessary.

There were echoes here still of the strategy of escalation, but now McNamara was talking about large-scale non-nuclear warfare. He was also stressing the need for a balanced defense.

Nuclear and non-nuclear power complement each other, in our own military forces and within the NATO alliance, just as together they complement the non-military instruments of policy. Either without the other is, over-all, not fully effective. If we strengthen one and not the other, part of the effort is wasted. Our policy is aimed at achieving the best balance of military capabilities—over the entire range of potential conflict, in the various areas of the globe where the Free World has vital interests, and over the years as far ahead as we can reasonably plan. I firmly believe that the non-nuclear build-up will—by improving and expanding the alternatives open to the Free World—reduce the pressures to make concessions in the face of Soviet threats.

McNamara, in conclusion, returned to the theme of guerrilla warfare with which he had begun.

It is tempting to conclude that our conventional forces will leave us free to compete with communism in the peaceful sphere of economic and social development, where we can compete most effectively.

But we shall have to deal with the problems of "wars of liberation." These wars are often not wars at all. In these conflicts, the force of world communism operates in the twilight zone between political subversion and quasi-military action. Their military tactics are those of the sniper, the ambush, and the raid. Their political tactics are terror, extortion, and assassination. We must help the people of threatened nations to resist these tactics by appropriate means. You cannot carry out a land reform program if the local peasant leaders are being systematically murdered.

To deal with the Communist guerrilla threat requires some shift in our military thinking. We have been used to developing big weapons and mounting large forces. Here we must work with companies and squads, and individual soldiers, rather than with battle groups and divisions. In all three Services we are training fighters who can, in turn, teach the people of free nations how to fight for their freedom. At the same time that our strategic weapons are becoming more and more sophisticated, we must learn to simplify our tactical weapons, so that they can be used and maintained by men who have never seen a machine more complicated than a well sweep.

Combating guerrilla warfare demands more in ingenuity than in money or manpower. But to meet the range of Communist military challenges calls for unprecedented efforts in men, money and organization.[25]

To finance this strategic concept required still another increase in military expenditures. The defense budget of the Eisenhower Administration for the previous fiscal year had been $43,685,000,000. Kennedy, in three successive amendments, had raised the amount to $49,878,000,000. Now, for fiscal year 1963, McNamara was asking for $51,640,000,000. There was much that was new, as well as the continuation of previous programs, that had to be paid for from this enormous sum. A year later, McNamara was to summarize what this budget had accomplished.

We have a total of about 650 manned bombers on 15-minute ground alert and over 200 operational Atlas, Titan, and Minuteman missiles on launchers and about 144 Polaris missiles in submarines. And this force is rapidly expanding as additional Minuteman and Polaris enter our operational inventory. . . .

There has been no change in the Atlas program during the last year and all 13 Atlas squadrons, aggregating 126 operational missiles on launchers, are now in place. . . .

All six squadrons of Titan I, aggregating 54 missiles, are now in place. We expect all 12 squadrons of Titan, aggregating 108 missiles on launchers, to be in place by the end of the current calendar year, . . .

A total of 800 Minuteman missiles have been programmed through fiscal year 1963. These should all be in place by the end of fiscal year 1965. The program is on schedule, the first 30 operational missiles are already in place, and the first three squadrons totaling 150 missiles should be operational by the end of the current fiscal year [1963]. . . .

Thirty-five Polaris submarines were fully funded through fiscal year 1963 and the long lead-time equipment for six additional ships was provided for. . . .

The number of combat-ready divisions today is roughly 45 per cent greater than it was 18 months ago. At that time there were 11 combat-ready divisions; today there are 16.

The number of tactical fighter wings today is roughly 30 per cent greater than it was 18 months ago. At that time there were 16. Today there are 21.

The logistical foundation of all the services is substantially improved versus 18 months ago, this because of the expenditure of literally billions of dollars on the procurement of equipment and combat consumables for each of the three services.

In total, the conventional forces today are substantially superior to what they were 18 months ago. . . .

. . . we are planning on a total active force of about 836 ships [in the Navy]. That excludes certain supplementary vessels, and it excludes about 57 that you will see . . . in the reserve forces. There are other ships in mothballs not, however, as ready for use as those 57 shown in the reserve forces . . . you see very few changes in the size or composition of the fleet. The attack carriers are kept at 15, the ASW carriers—anti-submarine warfare carriers—at 9. The cruisers roughly at the present level. The frigates increase, this being a new type that the Navy is emphasizing. The destroyers and escorts decrease slightly because the frigates pick up some of their job as do some of the smaller patrol boats.

The attack submarines remain relatively constant but there is a shift in the mix, nuclear increasing very substantially in number as the conventional submarines decrease in number. . . .

The present Marine Corps force of three divisions and three air wings and supporting units manned by 190,000 active duty military personnel will be maintained throughout the programmed period. Within this force are personnel being trained to constitute a nucleus of a 4th division/air wing. This team could be formed very quickly by calling up the Organized Marine Corps Reserves, which has recently been realigned to fulfill better this requirement. . . .

I have not referred to the tremendous increases, percentagewise, that have taken place in our counterinsurgency forces. These are sometimes thought of as a special category separate from the conventional forces. Both the counterinsurgency forces of the Army and of the Air Force have been substantially increased in the last 18 months. Those of the Army have been trebled, and I would say those in the Air Force have been increased by a comparable amount.[26]

The growing power and flexibility of the strategic nuclear forces no doubt was McNamara's most dramatic revelation in his presentation of the budget for fiscal year 1963. But equally important was the increase in strength of the Active Army. The change here, from 11 to 16 combat-ready divisions, combined with the 21 tactical air wings, and the 3 Marine divisions with their air wings, now gave him something like a 10-division strategic reserve. With it, he could handle a Korean-sized engagement and still have several divisions left over for another emergency. Alternatively, he could triple the size of the American forces in Europe, and do so in fairly short order, since he had prepositioned in Europe the equipment for two divisions and was continuing to expand the airlift and sealift to move the strategic reserve. Moreover, he could now meet an emergency of rather severe proportions without engaging in the desperate scramble for reserves that had characterized the onset of the Berlin crisis. His conventional options were expanding steadily.

That did not mean that McNamara had lost interest in the reserves. Although he might not want to risk another call-up except in the most extreme circumstances, he still regarded them as a resource of great value. And he still wanted a significant fraction of them to be able to reach a state of combat readiness on short notice. The objective, in other words, remained the same as it had been in 1961; only the numbers needed changing. As McNamara told the Governors' Conference at Hershey, Pennsylvania:

The recent changes in the active Army have themselves dictated changes in the reserve structure. Furthermore, our studies showed, and last Fall's call-up confirmed, that the reserve components are geared to a gradual mobilization, whereas today's need is more for a highly ready group of forces to round out and strengthen the active Army in a hurry. The era of leisurely mobilization is past.[27]

He was not prepared to say that the Berlin call-up had been a mistake; quite the contrary.

We are convinced that the rapid buildup in our conventional forces made possible by the call-up of the Reserves has done much to stabilize the Berlin situation. But improvisation is not a substitute for a sound long-term policy. It is not a practical policy to rely on the Reserve Forces to meet the repeated crises which inevitably lie ahead. We must maintain an adequate level of Active Forces to meet these crises, relying on the Reserve Forces only when armed conflict is imminent. . . .

Plainly, if we could bring at least selected units of the Reserve components to a high level of combat readiness, we would not need to call them to active duty until the situation had reached the point where conflict had started or was clearly imminent.[28]

With this consideration in mind, McNamara set forth two key objectives for the reserve program:

a. Provide a Reserve Component structure which will produce at the right time the numbers and kinds of units in the state of readiness required by current contingency defense plans. This requires organizing new units to meet modern demands and converting or eliminating units that are no longer essential.

b. Provide the Active Army with the quick reinforcement it needs to meet sudden crises while retaining the present capability to support a general mobilization. This requires the development of a high-priority force of strongly manned, well-trained, and adequately equipped units.

Under this plan, the United States Army Reserve would consist of 6 combat divisions, 13 training divisions, 4 brigades, 2 maneuver area commands, and 2,155 other units. The Army National Guard would be made up of 23 combat divisions, 7 brigades, and approximately 1,743 other units. Total manpower would be on the order of 670,000 men. As McNamara explained the concept:

Two types of high-priority forces are included in the reorganization plan. One type consists of units required to provide support for Active Army divisions in sustained combat. The other consists of six self-sufficient division forces required to perform missions in the early stages of a war. The readiness objective of both types of forces is to be capable of deployment in 8 weeks, with some of the units to support the Active Army scheduled to be ready for deployment in 4 weeks.

To assure an advanced degree of combat readiness, the personnel strength of these high-priority forces will be raised to 75–80% of full war strength, a substantial increase. Savings in strength effected through elimination of non-essential units will make this higher manning level possible.

After the reorganization is completed, approximately two-thirds of the Reserve Component personnel will be assigned to priority units, a marked increase above the percentage of the present force in a high readiness category. . . . Complete equipment for the 16

Active Army divisions and their support forces and for the six priority reserve component divisions and their support forces is being
budgeted.[29]

With such a system, the strategic reserve could be increased
by 60 percent over a period of eight weeks. Among the options
thereby opened up to the country would be the ability, simultaneously, to conduct two rather large local wars, or, at a minimum, a twenty-one-division effort in Western Europe. To
support such an effort, the United States would also have
twenty-one active and about seven reserve tactical air wings.
All in all, it was an impressive capability. But despite its magnitude, it apparently would not allow McNamara to escape from
the strategy of escalation. According to General Decker, at the
time Army Chief of Staff:

I think you can be assured that the Communists will put pressure
on us not only in one place but several places at the same time if
they really intend to apply pressure at all.
So consequently, we have to be able to react in several different
directions at the same time.
Previously, our Reserve in the United States has been inadequate
to enable us to do it. But once we have these eight divisions in good
shape, I think we will have enough to take care of these contingencies that can happen anywhere in the world.
I would not create the impression that these eight divisions will
give us the capability to take on the Russians in a land war in Europe or the Chinese Communists in a land war in Asia. Not at all.

Presumably twenty-one divisions operating in conjunction
with allied forces in Europe would not be able to deal with the
Soviets on a conventional basis either; for as General Decker
went on to explain:

We believe the USSR has about 150 divisions within an Army
strength of about 2.2 million. I think the strategic situation of the
two armies is somewhat different, and different in its uses of manpower.
For instance, the USSR is going to fight on its own continent,

with interior lines of communication. They won't have the long oversea pipeline that we have to support.

Eighty percent of the forces of the USSR are concentrated in their own country with the balance in the nearby satellites.

The Soviets can initiate hostilities at any time and place they choose. To that extent they have what you might say is an initiative that we don't possess. We are smaller, but we have to be able to respond to any threat at any point on the globe. . . .

Now, we don't have quite the same support for our forces in many ways that the Soviets do, or conversely, they don't provide many of the things that we do. . . .

They train differently. They train their recruits in their divisions generally, whereas we have a training establishment to provide for that training before they actually are put into divisions.[30]

It was for these reasons, according to General Decker, that the Soviets could produce 150 divisions out of 2.2 million men, whereas the United States could muster only 16 divisions out of an Active Army of close to 1 million men. Granting even the points that General Decker had made, the Soviets somehow or other were getting better than four times the number of divisions that the United States was obtaining out of every million men. Either something was wrong with the comparison, or the Soviets were simply more efficient than the United States. It was a puzzling situation. More than that, unless it could be resolved, McNamara would remain a prisoner of nuclear escalation.

The effort to solve the riddle had already begun in the summer of 1961, when members of the Secretary's staff started to question the prevailing assumptions about Soviet tactical air power as well as its ground strength. It was found, in the air-power case, not only that the number of Soviet tactical fighters had been inflated, but also that their performance had been greatly exaggerated. In fact, as the analysis proceeded, it became evident that the United States in conjunction with its NATO allies had more and better aircraft in its tactical inventory than did the Soviet Union, and that NATO's air defenses were superior to those in Eastern Europe.

The questioning with respect to the strength of the Soviet ground forces intensified. At first, the interrogators centered their attention on the number of men in uniform. They pointed out that the Soviets purportedly possessed a much more heavily mechanized and armored force than had been the case in 1945, and that they would have supply lines stretching over seven hundred miles if they were to launch an attack on Western Europe. Was anyone prepared to say, in these circumstances, that the Soviets could actually obtain something like 150 American-style divisions from 2.2 million men? Nobody, it turned out, really was; and as second and third looks were taken at the Soviet order of battle, the number of divisions underwent a steady decline.

Paul H. Nitze, then Assistant Secretary of Defense for International Security Affairs, reflected the changed nature of the estimates in a speech early in 1963. He pointed out:

Active army units of the Soviet Union (not counting the satellites) total about 2 million men, which, under Western standards of ground force organization and not their own, would suffice to man between 40 and 60 divisions.

Today, in a conflict along Western Europe's central front, the Communist side could not count on having clear superiority. There are 22 understrength but probably "combat-ready" Soviet divisions in East Germany and Poland, supported by about 35 satellite divisions in lesser states of readiness and of doubtful reliability under many circumstances. NATO has about 25 M-day divisions available for the central front, with additional divisions in France which should be available in an emergency. NATO has more and better tactical aircraft and more air defense missiles, and of course superior sea power. Most of NATO's aircraft, for example, can carry twice the payload twice as far as their Soviet counterparts. In short, NATO is more powerful and the Soviets less overwhelming than generally realized.[31]

While this view of the problem was encouraging, the case for believing that a conventional defense of Europe was manageable still had several obstacles to overcome. Adherents to the more customary view of Soviet ground strength pointed out

that, despite the Nitze calculation, there were more than
sixty divisions in the Soviet order of battle; they also argued
that the Soviet capability for generating reinforcements from
their reserves was larger and quicker than the West's. Accordingly, the West would still be overwhelmed by the Red hordes.
Again the skeptics raised questions: about the Sino-Soviet dispute and its effect on Soviet deployments; about the Soviet reserve system and its ability to produce combat-ready troops on
short order; about the availability of manpower of appropriate
age, considering the population losses suffered by the Soviet
Union during World War II; about the effectiveness of a Soviet
division compared with a standard American division. Above
all, they asked about the equipment and supplies for this massive army. Men springing up out of the ground without weapons are not particularly useful in combat against modern firepower. Had the Soviets stockpiled the necessary matériel; had
the troops exercised with it? Here again, a paradox presented
itself. The United States was now spending around $2.4 billion
each year to maintain and modernize the equipment and
supplies for 16 Active Army and 6 reserve divisions. By this
measure, it would cost the Soviets over $16 billion a year to
maintain adequate stocks for 150 divisions. It seemed an im-
plausibly large sum in view of the other military and civil
programs to which the Soviets were committed. What, then,
was the situation?

The Economist of London arrived at one interesting estimate.

Even if the Red Army maintained the same proportion between
fighting men and supply columns as, say, the South Korean Army,
its divisional strength could not be more than about 125; if the comparison were with the Bundeswehr, the figure would drop to about
80. But in fact both these armies get the benefit of a good many
rear-echelon services provided by other people, which nobody provides for the Russians. On the contrary: one of the calls on Russian
military manpower, which does not afflict the Americans to anything like the same extent, is the need to keep an avuncular eye on
the markedly reluctant heroes manning the east European armies.
If one adds all these factors up, it seems quite possible that the

Red Army cannot deploy much more than, say, 60 to 80 ready-for-battle divisions of its own. And Marshal Malinovskii, sticking this number of coloured pins into his wall maps, may now be looking almost as hard at those 5,000-odd miles of border with China as he is at his western front. . . .

The one major qualification to this analysis is that the Russians possess an unknown number of "cadre divisions"—that is, skeleton formations that can be covered fairly rapidly in case of crisis with the flesh of infantry, gunners and tankmen from the supplies of recently released conscripts. But western experience suggests that, the more modern an army gets (and the Red Army is now very modern), the longer it takes to bring these reserves up to scratch.[32]

An even more authoritative view of the situation was that of Cyrus R. Vance, then Secretary of the Army. By his estimate:

Today, in a conflict along Western Europe's central front, the Warsaw Pact could not muster that clear superiority—generally taken as three-to-one—prerequisite to a successful ground offensive. Moreover, many of the satellite units are of doubtful ability and reliability. . . .

This does not mean there are no problems. NATO is vulnerable to a sudden attack—the inevitable vulnerability of a non-aggressive power—and the Communist divisions now facing it could be reinforced from the Soviet Union. Unless NATO reinforced too, the balance would alter unfavorably.

It is sometimes suggested that the Soviets, with an army of 2 million men, can manage to field about 150 divisions within several weeks of the time they are called up. This would be ten times the number of divisions we have manned, with only twice as many men in active duty. In my view, the Soviets could not field an effective force of this strength in less than several months' time, [and it would be] limited even then as to first-line equipment.

Moreover, there is a practical limit to the number of divisions which can be supported from the Communist logistic base in Russia, so that the problem posed by Soviet reinforcements is finite and not, as it is so often put, infinite. The forces a Communist planner can count on are limited by the same constraints as limit us, by the inherent capabilities of the transportation net leading into the theater, by the damage he can expect Allied interdiction to wreak on that net, and by the adequacy of his home supply base. As an aside, it will do him no good to substitute satellite forces for Soviet ones. The latter are utterly dependent on the Russian logistic system.

He is further circumscribed by the competing demands of other areas. Even if combat is limited to NATO's center, there are the Manchurian, Mongolian and Sinkiang borders to be watched; there are certain internal security minimums to be met; and there are the NATO forces on the northern and southern flanks. All these will strike divisions from the "available" list. And, if the Soviets are going to engage in any major adventure, they cannot accept parity; they must attain enough superiority to insure a decisive victory.

In short, the ready conventional forces which can be brought to bear against NATO are significant, but far from overwhelming, and the Soviet mobilization capability, though great, is no more capable of conjuring up first-rate armies overnight than the Free World's.[33]

By all the evidence, then, the Soviet conventional threat was of much more modest proportions than General Decker had estimated. It looked as though McNamara might find a way to increase his options after all.

While McNamara no doubt saw the creation of multiple options as the answer to the President's demand for a choice between humiliation and holocaust, he also regarded it as the only appropriate method of dealing with the uncertainties of the future. But multiple options said very little about how the United States would actually fight in the event of aggression. The Eisenhower Administration had provided a measure of guidance on this score by announcing a policy of main but not sole reliance on nuclear weapons. The military establishment looked eagerly to McNamara to furnish comparable direction. Stubbornly, he refused to do so. Instead, he immersed himself in the details of future force structure. There could be no question, in these circumstances, about the nature of the capabilities that he wanted to have at the disposal of the country; to that degree he removed the ambiguities that accompanied the BNSP and budget ceilings of the Eisenhower era. But could satisfactory contingency planning proceed on the basis of clear directives about force structure and the concept of multiple

options? The Joint Chiefs and the Services thought not; they
wanted further guidance. McNamara remained unpersuaded.
He disliked being tied down to any rigid doctrine about when
and how the different types of forces should be employed. There
was something dangerous and ridiculous about the dogma, for
example, that any direct Soviet-American confrontation meant
general nuclear war. His experience with the Berlin crisis, and
more recently with the Soviet missiles in Cuba, convinced him
—if he needed any convincing—that the best strategy was to let
the circumstances determine the choice of weapons and make
sure that there was a plentiful supply in each major category.
Despite this wariness, he made no secret about his preferences.
He wanted to have the capabilities for all the modern types of
warfare and, if forced to commit himself, he wanted to place
main but not sole reliance on non-nuclear weapons.

The full range of McNamara's thinking became evident in
his statements and testimony to the Congress in support of the
defense budget for fiscal year 1964. He started by giving his
estimate of the threat.

Although Communist China is the more reckless and belligerent
of the two, the Soviet Union has by far the greater capability to
cause us injury or otherwise damage the interests of the Free
World. There is no gainsaying that Soviet resources, industry and
technology have given that country the potential to challenge the
primacy of U.S. military power in the world. While the size, variety
and power of our strategic retaliatory forces still greatly exceed
those of the Soviets, the Kremlin leaders have at their command the
resources, production capacity, and technology to produce strong
forces of their own. We believe they will continue to make great
efforts to do so. The Soviet Union can also be expected to maintain
large and well-equipped conventional forces to ensure the internal
security of the Soviet Union, to control its Eastern frontiers and
to threaten Western Europe.

But, in McNamara's view, the Soviets could not excel in everything.

In other words, the Soviet leadership is confronted with a very severe resources allocation problem and must strike a balance among its various objectives: military, space, foreign aid, civilian housing, agriculture, improvement of the standard of living of the Soviet people, and so forth. The Soviets could, over the next few years, build a large force of hardened second-generation ICBM's; they could develop and deploy an ICBM delivery system for the large-yield nuclear warheads they have been testing since 1961; they could expand and improve their MRBM/IRBM systems; they could continue to maintain and improve their active defenses against manned bomber attack; they could maintain a large and modernly equipped army; they could develop and deploy some sort of system of active defense against ballistic missile attack; they could modernize and improve their large fleet of submarines including ballistic missile-firing types; they could continue the space race; they could expand both military and economic aid to the non-aligned nations; they could make the great investment needed to create an efficient agricultural economy; they could continue to push the development of heavy industry; or they could increase the standard of living of the Soviet people—but they cannot do them all at the same time.

What could the United States expect in these circumstances? McNamara's estimate was:

a strategy in which their military forces are designed to permit the Soviet Union to:

    a. Confront us with continuing political pressure, subversion, and various forms of unconventional warfare under the umbrella of their growing nuclear power.
    b. Capitalize on their conventional military power by the threat of bringing it to bear in situations where they have local conventional superiority.
    c. Deter the West from military action.

Communist China will most likely follow an independent policy designed to expand its own influence in the Communist Camp and among the unaligned nations, resorting to armed aggression to satisfy its ambitions only where this can be done without a direct confrontation of U.S. military forces. . . .

Communist China's economic difficulties and the strain of the recent campaign against India should tend to limit her ability to engage in large-scale aggression against other of her neighbors. . . . A large-scale overt attack elsewhere in Southeast Asia, or against Taiwan or South Korea, is not very likely under present circumstances. However, an intensification of lesser efforts to cause trouble for the Free World should be anticipated, particularly in terms of psychological warfare and political intrigue. And we have no reason to doubt that Communist China will continue to fuel the guerrilla war in South Vietnam, at least at the present scale, or support the position of the Communist elements in Laos.

McNamara proceeded on a *tour d'horizon* in the light of these threats. His first concern was for Latin America.

Although the Cuban crisis has greatly solidified the unity and cohesion of the American states, the threat of Communism has by no means abated, and a Communist government still rules in Cuba. Our forceful response to the threat of armed aggression from Cuba no doubt has diminished for the present the military aspect of the threat. But this simply means that Communist efforts will be shifted to other areas, and the Castroist Communist sabotage last fall in Venezuela is but one of the more violent examples of this danger. More important from the longer term point of view is the fundamental instability engendered by the widespread lack of adequate economic progress. So long as hunger and economic instability persist in Latin America, the danger of Communism will be ever present. . . .

Africa is another area in which the Communists will try to take advantage of any political and economic instability. Although overt Communist military aggression against Africa is conceivable, it is not very probable because of the logistic difficulties involved. The real danger here is quite similar to that in Latin America, namely, that the Communists could gain a foothold by subverting and overthrowing an existing government. . . .

In the Near East we face quite a different kind of situation. . . . In general, our interest in this area is to help create an environment in which each of the nations can maintain internal stability and develop in its own way without fear of attack from its neighbors or from the Communist Bloc.

This is a difficult and exacting role at best. It is particularly difficult where so many nations are divided, not only by the power struggles and rivalries of the moment, but also by mutual fears and suspicions whose origins are buried deep in history. This unsettled situation has been further complicated by the intervention of the Soviet Union in the area. . . .

The principal threat in the Far East, as well as in South and Southeast Asia, is Communist China, for the Soviet Union is unlikely to initiate a war in the Pacific alone. Although the situation in the Far East has remained fairly stable during the last year, the threat of aggression from Communist China has not abated. It may well be that the logistic effort involved in the Chinese Communist attack on India will detract from their ability to undertake military adventures elsewhere. But we know from experience that the pressure can be quickly shifted from India to Southeast Asia, Korea or Formosa, or even Japan or the Philippines, and we must continue to help guard all of these areas. . . .

The most critical problem at issue between East and West in Europe continues to be the fate of Berlin. Our sharp confrontation of the Soviets in the Caribbean no doubt upset their agenda for Berlin. Their stationing of nuclear armed ballistic missiles in Cuba was directly related to that agenda. The psychological if not the military threat that these missiles would have posed to our own homeland was apparently the trump card which Mr. Khrushchev intended to play in the next round of negotiations on the status of Berlin.

The setback dealt Soviet plans in Cuba may have postponed an incipient crisis in Berlin, but did not remove the latent danger in that area. East Germany is still in dire straits, both economically and politically. The freedom and prosperity of West Berlin still stand in stark contrast to the oppression and misery behind the wall. . . . Although from our point of view, the obvious solution would be to improve the political, social, and economic conditions in East Berlin and, for that matter, in all of East Germany, the Communists instead still hope to solve the dilemma by obliterating freedom in West Berlin.

This we cannot permit. . . . We cannot abdicate that responsibility without casting grave doubts on our determination and ability to defend freedom in Europe, or, for that matter, anywhere else in the world.[34]

This view of the world scene was bound to affect McNamara's evaluation of the functions of the major forces in the American arsenal and the level of strength that he should attempt to achieve with respect to each. Inevitably, he gave first consideration to the capability for strategic nuclear war. The probability of such a war no doubt was low; but, if it did occur, the consequences would be frightful. Moreover, the probability was almost certainly low precisely because the United States had been keeping its guard up. McNamara had every intention of continuing that stance. He also advocated taking out insurance against the remote event that deterrence might fail. He was explicit on both counts to the Congress.

What we are proposing is a capability to strike back after absorbing the first blow. This means we have to build and maintain a second strike force. Such a force should have sufficient flexibility to permit a choice of strategies, particularly an ability to: (1) Strike back decisively at the entire Soviet target system simultaneously, or (2) Strike back first at the Soviet bomber bases, missile sites and other military installations associated with their long-range nuclear forces to reduce the power of any follow-on-attack—and then, if necessary, strike back at the Soviet urban and industrial complex in a controlled and deliberate way.

Now the foregoing is not to say that we can forecast the nature of a nuclear attack upon the United States. In talking about global nuclear war, the Soviet leaders always say that they would strike at the entire complex of our military power including government and production centers, meaning our cities. If they were to do so, we would, of course, have no alternative but to retaliate in kind. But we have no way of knowing whether they would actually do so. It would certainly be in their interest as well as ours to try to limit the terrible consequences of a nuclear exchange. By building into our forces a flexible capability, we at least eliminate the prospect that we could strike back in only one way, namely, against the entire Soviet target system including their cities. Such a prospect would give the Soviet Union no incentive to withhold attack against our cities in a first strike. We want to give them a better alternative. Whether they would accept it in the crisis of a global nuclear war, no one can say. Considering what is at stake, we believe it is worth the additional effort on our part to have this option.[35]

McNamara himself had always been, and remained, doubtful that the Soviets would accept the alternative of avoiding cities.

Today we know that the great majority of the Soviet strategic force, both their bombers and their missiles, are in soft configurations. Under these circumstances it seems almost inconceivable to me that were the Soviets to attack the United States they would attack other than our cities, because they have no possibility of holding in reserve forces for later use against our cities with any expectation that those forces would survive a U.S. attack.

And this leads me to the conclusion I have already stated, that under today's circumstances I personally believe any nuclear attack by the Soviet Union on the United States will include an attack on the major urban areas of the United States.[36]

This was a terribly grim conclusion. McNamara nevertheless persisted in wanting to maintain the option of the counterforce strike. Not only were the alternative types of nuclear exchange even grimmer; in time, the Soviets might change. McNamara was not exactly optimistic about the prospect, but he insisted on being ready for it.

There are in a sense three second strike capabilities that you could plan for. One is what I would call a city destruction force only. That is relatively small. [Deleted]

The second capability would be what I would call a second strike salvo capability. This would let everything off at once, that is fire everything at once, against military targets and urban targets. That would be a much larger force than the first force.

But the third force is the largest of all which would permit you to launch in waves a second strike and a second strike prime, one against their military targets and the other against their urban centers.

And that third force, that third type of second strike capability requires that you have greater numbers than either of the other two. It requires communications links and command headquarters that would survive, for a much longer time, than the communications links or command headquarters required by either of the other two forces.

Now this is the only reason that we consider that third contingency. As I say, I think it is a rather unlikely one. And, as a matter of fact, under today's conditions, I think it is so improbable it is not worth thinking about, because the Soviet force is soft, they wouldn't strike us with only a part of that force but would launch all of it. But in the future, as the character of their force changes, it is conceivable, although not likely, that they might strike our military installations with a first strike, withholding certain forces to later strike the cities.

Now I don't want to be misunderstood on this. I don't think that is probable. But I think it is sufficiently possible to warrant spending our resources to protect ourselves against it.[37]

There remained the difficulty that the resources invested in the approach became subject to the laws of diminishing returns. As McNamara explained it:

A very large increase in the number of fully hard Soviet ICBM's and nuclear powered ballistic missile-launching submarines would considerably detract from our ability to destroy completely the Soviet strategic nuclear forces.

It will become increasingly difficult, regardless of the form of the attack, to destroy a sufficiently large proportion of the Soviet's strategic nuclear forces to preclude major damage to the United States, regardless of how large or what kind of strategic forces we build.

Even if we were to double and triple our forces we would not be able to destroy quickly all or almost all of the hardened ICBM sites.

And even if we could do that, we know no way to destroy the enemy's missile-launching submarines at the same time.

We do not anticipate that either the United States or the Soviet Union will acquire that capability in the foreseeable future.

Moreover, to minimize damage to the United States, such a force would also have to be accompanied by an extensive missile defense system and a much more elaborate civil defense program than has thus far been contemplated.

Even then we could not preclude casualties counted in the tens of millions.[38]

To the anguish of the Air Force, this meant placing a limit on the size of the strategic offensive forces. McNamara explained the formula as follows:

In planning our second strike force, we have provided, throughout the period under consideration, a capability to destroy virtually all of the "soft" and "semi-hard" military targets in the Soviet Union and a large number of their fully hardened missile sites, with an additional capability in the form of a protected force to be employed or held in reserve for use against urban and industrial areas.[39]

The role to be played by these forces would be vital but specialized. As McNamara put it: "Our objective is the defeat of the Communists. I do not believe we can achieve that victory by engaging in strategic nuclear war." If the strategic forces of the two countries were unleashed,

there would be such severe damage done to this country that our way of life would change, and change in an undesirable direction. Therefore, I would say we had not won. In another sense of the word "win" we would win. We would win in the sense that their way of life would change more than ours because we would destroy a greater percentage of their industrial potential and probably destroy a greater percentage of their population than they destroyed of ours. By "ours" I am speaking of the United States. I suspect that in terms of facilities the amount of industrial destruction in the West would exceed that of the Soviet Union. This is so because you would have to add to the destruction in the United States the probable destruction of Western Europe. My personal opinion is . . . we cannot win a nuclear war, a strategic nuclear war, in the normal meaning of the word "win."[40]

In these circumstances, McNamara did not see the strategic forces as an all-purpose weapon.

There is no question in my mind but that our nuclear forces are there for the purpose of deterring the Soviets from doing something.

But the question is, what will they deter the Soviets from doing? Now I feel quite certain that if the Soviets are rational, our strategic forces program will deter the Soviets from launching a first strike against this country.

I say that for the very simple reason that, if they did, we would utterly destroy them, and I mean completely destroy them. I am not talking about the kind of destruction that the Air Force said it could or did accomplish in World War II. I am talking about completely destroying the Soviet Union as a civilized nation. . . .

It is not a deterrent force in the sense that it will deter all political and military aggression by the Soviets. It did not deter them from putting pressure on Berlin when we had a near nuclear monopoly in the early part of the decade of the 1950's. It did not deter the Communists from invading Korea. It did not deter them from building a wall in Berlin. It did not deter the Communist . . . attempt to subvert Southeast Asia. . . . It did not deter their attempt to move offensive weapons systems into Cuba. And I think that is an excellent illustration of the type of action that nuclear superiority, measured in terms of numbers, has not deterred up to the present time. . . . I should go one step further, to say that . . . the strategic nuclear power which we are proposing, large as it is and superior as it is, is not a universal deterrent to all forms of Soviet political and military aggression. We must have other deterrent forces.[41]

One of the other deterrent forces was the combined tactical nuclear capability of the Army and the Air Force. Just as Mc-Namara preserved the option to use the strategic nuclear forces, and maintained options within the option, so he insisted on the retention and even expansion of the tactical nuclear forces. As he pointed out early in 1963: "We have placed several thousand nuclear weapons in Europe. They are there at the present time. It would be our policy to use them when it is necessary to protect our vital interests."[42] There were various ways in which they could be used: in conjunction with the strategic forces; for the conduct of a local nuclear campaign of great intensity; in a selective and highly discriminating fashion; and in token fashion to demonstrate the American determination to proceed, if necessary, down the nuclear slope. McNamara wanted these options too. But he was not an enthusiast about any of them.

Nuclear weapons, even in the lower kiloton ranges, are extremely destructive devices and hardly the preferred weapons to defend such heavily populated areas as Europe. Furthermore, while it does not necessarily follow that the use of tactical nuclear weapons must inevitably escalate into global nuclear war, it does present a very definite threshold, beyond which we enter a vast unknown.[43]

McNamara was reminded that the recent exposition of *Soviet Military Strategy*, edited by Marshal V. D. Sokolovskii, seemed to take for granted the use of nuclear weapons in a major land campaign. He remained unimpressed. It was an attempt, he thought,

to explain what I consider to be an inconsistency between their nuclear strategy on the one hand, and their conventional forces on the other. . . . But nowhere in the book that I saw is there a sophisticated analysis of nuclear war, exactly how you carry out large-scale ground operations with the exchange of literally thousands and thousands of nuclear warheads between the two sides, and what the role of a 3,200,000 military force would be under the circumstances was not at all clear to me. . . . It is inconceivable to me how you send troops through an area in which there may have been literally hundreds of nuclear bursts. . . . It is as though the people who were writing the statements had never really had exposed to them the destructive power of nuclear weapons.[44]

Strong tactical nuclear capabilities were useful for the purpose of deterring the Soviets from initiating a nuclear campaign. But McNamara obviously did not regard them as the preferred means to the accomplishment of American political objectives. The interests of the United States were best served, in his view, by primary reliance on major conventional forces.

To this end, McNamara took still further steps in his budget for fiscal year 1964. He increased the Army's active duty strength from 960,000 to 975,000 men in order to test some new ideas about divisional organization and mobility. He continued to insist that the Army reserve components satisfy two specific requirements: the ability on short notice to augment significantly the Active Army during periods of grave international tension or during limited wars; and the ability to provide a base for a large-scale mobilization in the event of general war. To provide adequate support for the ground forces, he maintained the tactical air force at twenty-one fighter wings, continued their modernization, and increased their non-nuclear supplies. The Navy and the Marines also received additional funds for the improvement of their conventional capabilities. And Mc-Namara gave particular attention to the capability for quick reaction to any conventional aggression. He pushed three different methods simultaneously. As he described the scheme:

We have large forces deployed abroad—the equivalent of 6 divisions in Europe, 2 divisions in Korea, 1 division in Okinawa, etc. We have substantial amounts of equipment and supplies pre-positioned in Europe and the Far East and aboard . . . "floating depot" ships. We have a large central reserve of general purpose forces in the continental United States and we are building the airlift required to move these forces promptly to wherever they might be needed.[45]

McNamara took one other step of great significance with respect to all three Services. Describing its implications for the Army, he said:

Last year, as a first step toward insuring some internal balance within the total of Army stocks, I established equipment and supplies to support a 22-division force (16 Active and 6 Reserve component divisions) for a specified period of time, with an average of two-thirds of the force engaged at any one time.

Now we propose to take the next step toward a higher state of readiness and raise the procurement objective to provide the initial complement of combat equipment required for 16 Active and 6 priority Reserve component divisions, plus such replacement spares and combat consumables as are necessary to maintain 16 divisions and supporting forces in combat for the entire period between D-day and the time when our production lines would be able to catch up with the rate of combat consumption.[46]

In other words, existing forces would be able to fight, not for days, not for weeks, but for an indefinite period of time.

But were these forces large enough to handle the most probable range of threats without resort to nuclear weapons? With respect to the guerrilla threat, the problem was not primarily one of American manpower. McNamara had already more than tripled the Special Forces units intended for the counter-insurgency mission. He also had arranged for the training of 24,000 foreign nationals under the Military Assistance Program for fiscal year 1964 alone. For the rest, the chief responsibility would lie with the local forces on the spot. Where overt and organized aggression was concerned, McNamara pointed out that

our general purpose forces, to a large extent, are intended for the support of our allies around the world. Their required size and character, therefore, are greatly influenced by the size and character of the forces supported by our allies, as well as by the size and character of the forces which threaten the free world.[47]

In other words, one way of ensuring an effective conventional defense, and limiting the American requirement for general purpose forces, was by the maintenance and support of strong allied capabilities. That, as McNamara never tired of pointing out, was a key function of the Military Assistance Program.

Over sixty per cent of the total program will be allocated to *eight* key countries in South Asia, the Far East and the Near East, each of which is on the periphery of the Sino-Soviet Bloc, and confronts a direct threat of Communist aggression. These countries are: Viet-Nam, Thailand, the Republic of China, Korea, Greece, Turkey, Iran and Pakistan. Although the threat is external in most cases, the emphasis is on internal guerrilla warfare and subversion in Viet-Nam, where it is actually under way, and in Thailand where it is an imminent danger.[48]

McNamara underscored the importance of the program by saying further that "if I had to choose between a billion dollar reduction in economic aid, a billion dollar reduction in military assistance, or a billion dollar reduction in remaining defense requirements, I would choose the latter."[49]

There were other ways, also, to obtain a large number of conventional options from the planned level of forces. McNamara listed them in an important set of conclusions that he had reached about the capability of the United States and its allies to resist Communist aggression by non-nuclear means.

(1) Readiness and mobility can greatly reduce requirements for general purpose forces. This is simply the principle of getting there first with the most, before the situation deteriorates and greater forces are required to recover lost ground.

(2) Modern equipment, weapons, and munitions in sufficient quantity to support the existing forces in combat until production can catch up with consumption are far more important at this particular point in time than more military units.

(3) Proper support of indigenous forces on the scene would give a greater return to collective defense than additional U.S. forces.

(4) The presently programmed forces, in general, could by non-nuclear means alone, counter a wide spectrum of Sino-Soviet Bloc aggressions in regions other than Europe.

(5) With regard to Europe, the presently programmed U.S. forces, together with the present forces of other NATO countries, would not be able to contain an all-out conventional Soviet attack without invoking the use of nuclear weapons.[50]

The last point raised the nub of the problem. Despite McNamara's preference for conventional defenses, despite the revised estimates of Soviet air and ground strength, the defense of Europe still rested precariously on the nuclear deterrent. The most important conventional option, the one on which McNamara undoubtedly set the greatest store, continued to elude him. He could have attempted to command the option out of American resources alone. But that would have made nonsense out of NATO as an alliance; it was economically undesirable; and it was politically unacceptable. The United States was already fulfilling its commitments to the Alliance. With twenty-one tactical air wings, nineteen divisions in the Active Army

and Marines, a high-priority reserve of six Army and one
Marine divisions, and the most powerful Navy in the world, it
could already contribute to a much larger effort. The rest was
up to Europe. In order to complete the concept of multiple
options and primary dependence on non-nuclear means, Mc-
Namara had to win the acceptance of the European branch
of NATO. It proved to be his most complicated task.

CHAPTER 3

Dialogue with NATO

I T IS EASY for Americans to treat the North
Atlantic Treaty Organization as but one of many obligations and possible assets. Yet Europe, for many centuries, has
stood proudly at the center of international affairs. The countries which are members of NATO command great resources,
manpower, and traditions. They have largely recovered, at least
materially, from the effects of World War II. Not only is their
independence from communism a vital interest of the United
States; they also have the capacity to contribute significantly to
the defense of the West. With a population of over 300,000,000
people and a gross national product of more than $350 billion
a year, they are by themselves superior to the Soviet Union in
basic strength. McNamara, in fact, saw in that strength the way
to realize more fully the concept of multiple options. Strong
European conventional forces, joined with those of the United
States, would free the vital European sector of Western defenses from complete dependence on a nuclear strategy. And
that, McNamara wanted very badly indeed. Although accused
of downgrading NATO, he probably attached more importance
to it than any of his predecessors. His solicitude may even have
been too great.

At the same time that McNamara sought a conventional

build-up in Europe, he opposed the proliferation of nuclear weapons among the allies. In his opposition, of course, he followed the lead of the President. He thus found himself in the difficult position of proposing a somewhat novel course of action to NATO, opposing the advocates of independent European nuclear capabilities, and trying simultaneously to maintain the cohesion of the Alliance. It was a difficult balancing act to perform.

Part of the difficulty arose from the sheer diversity of views in Europe. It is easy and appealing to speak of Europe or NATO as though it were a unit with a single policy. Needless to say, it is not; and McNamara had to justify his views to fourteen other nations with distinctive and often irreconcilable ideas about strategy. He found, in doing so at the periodic ministerial meetings of NATO, that achievement of a consensus on strategy, forces, and budgets was a slow and laborious process. One reason for the slow pace of change lay in NATO's peculiar history. Once before, in 1952, the Alliance had set itself ambitious non-nuclear goals. But in 1954, under the influence of the Eisenhower New Look, it was decided to base strategy and requirements on two major assumptions: first, that the dominant military threat to Western Europe was a massive invasion by the overwhelming hordes of the Red Army; and second, that the only way to stop it was by the use of nuclear weapons. Perhaps even more than in the United States, nuclear weapons grew to be considered the quintessence of military power in NATO. General Norstad slightly modified the second assumption by introducing the idea of the pause. A Soviet invasion of Western Europe would be met initially by non-nuclear resistance; but this would only be of short duration—just long enough to test Soviet intentions and afford the Kremlin an opportunity to draw back before NATO ignited the nuclear fires.

So heavy a reliance on nuclear weapons inevitably caused the development of several politically influential attitudes. Key European leaders now took the position that deterrence rather than the conduct of war was the principal if not the only purpose of the armed forces. And they believed fervently that the effectiveness of the deterrent was intimately related to the expressed determination of the West to use nuclear weapons at the outset of any Soviet attack. Further, they held the view that a conventional build-up would weaken the effectiveness of the deterrent by encouraging the Soviets to believe that nuclear weapons would not in fact be used immediately to repel an invasion.

These beliefs created a host of problems for their holders. To begin with, the Europe of 1961 was a booming society with six of its members embarked on the experiment of economic and possibly political federation through the European Economic Community. The heavy dependence on the United States which had characterized the previous fifteen years no longer satisfied a group of nations who had recovered their prosperity and were accustomed to a central role in world affairs. Yet in the West, the United States held a virtual monopoly over nuclear weapons. Inevitably, this fact aroused a conflict of emotions: doubts about the willingness of the United States to use nuclear weapons; fear that the United States might withdraw from Europe; frustration over continued dependence on the United States for this vital element of power. Much of the controversy surrounding NATO between 1961 and 1963 sprang from this environment of doubt, fear, and ambition. Many influential Europeans wanted something different from the existing arrangements. But they could not agree among themselves about objectives, they trusted one another even less than they did the United States, and they had no particular inclination to incur the costs and risks of greater independence.

These currents of feeling made the prospects for a change in NATO strategy somewhat uncertain. It was doubtful that the non-nuclear build-up, on which the President and his advisers set great store, would receive enthusiastic support. And the Administration's known aversion to any further diffusion of nuclear weapons was unlikely to win popularity contests among government leaders in France, Germany, and Italy.

How, in the circumstances, to move toward a more respectable conventional capability in Europe, avoid the proliferation of national nuclear capabilities, and meet the tangled interests of the European members of the Alliance was a nice question of substance and strategy. Complexity was compounded by the lingering special relationship between the United States and Britain on nuclear matters, the determination of President de Gaulle to develop a French nuclear capability, German insistence on a forward defense of Europe which would prevent any territory of the Federal Republic from being overrun, and the persistent American balance of payments deficit—approaching $3 billion a year—which placed serious limits on American freedom of action. The program that would satisfy everyone, including the Americans, was not obvious.

President Eisenhower had complicated matters still further by attempting to mollify those Europeans who sought an increased measure of self-sufficiency in nuclear defense capabilities. He had recommended liberalizing the Atomic Energy Act so as to facilitate supplying nuclear weapons to allies. And Secretary of State Herter, at a ministerial session of the NATO Council in December, 1960, had proposed a multilateral force for the Alliance equipped with medium-range ballistic missiles. The idea here was that a force that was jointly owned and manned by NATO would answer some of the European concerns about the American nuclear monopoly and yet avoid the more dangerous alternative of national nuclear capabilities. At the same time, however, President Eisenhower coupled these suggestions with the hint that "some changes in U.S. force deployments may become advisable in light of continuing studies of overall U.S. programs." In other words, Eisenhower continued to support NATO's nuclear strategy and was apparently willing to furnish the European allies with additional nuclear capabilities in return for a reduction of the expensive American presence in Europe. Superficially, it looked like an appealing compromise.

The Kennedy Administration found it unacceptable, principally because of its stress on nuclear weapons. As Kennedy's advisers saw the problem, there were some obvious actions that the nuclear deterrent could be counted on actually to deter. But there remained a large set of aggressions which had not been deterred in the past and were unlikely to be in the future—unless someone set the record straight by using nuclear weapons in response to one of these acts. No one seemed eager to validate the nuclear deterrent in this particular way. Yet Europe was alive with possibilities for small-scale action: in Berlin, on the flanks of NATO, and against the friendly neutrals. Consequently conventional rather than nuclear forces seemed to be the real need of the day.

Former Secretary of State Dean Acheson undertook the initial responsibility for devising a formula that would provide for the conventional build-up yet meet some of the European concerns. His general conclusion was that conditions did not call for a change in existing NATO strategy, but rather the fulfillment by the European allies of their existing commitments of manpower and equipment. This would have meant giving General Norstad thirty active and thirty reserve divisions on the critical central front instead of the equivalent of sixteen active divisions and a scattering of reserves that were then at his disposal. Acheson theorized that a thirty-division force, backed by competent reserves, would provide Norstad with a real capability for enforcing a pause on the Soviets and enable the President to avoid the onus of using nuclear weapons immediately. The use of nuclear weapons was not precluded under this theory; Acheson was simply trying to buy a little time, and also enable statesmen to consider the employment of force without having always to step at the outset into the nuclear abyss.

President Kennedy reflected this line of thought when he addressed the Canadian Parliament on May 17, 1961. He also attempted to anticipate future European concerns about the validity of the nuclear deterrent. He explained:

Our NATO alliance is still, as it was when it was founded, the world's greatest bulwark of freedom. But the military balance of power has been changing. Enemy tactics and weaponry have been changing. We can stand still only at peril.

NATO force structures were originally devised to meet the threat of a massive conventional attack, in a period of western nuclear monopoly.

Now, if we are to meet the defense requirements of the 1960's, the NATO countries must push forward simultaneously along two major lines:

First, we must strengthen the conventional capability of our alliance as a matter of the highest priority.

To this end, we in the United States are taking steps to increase the strength and mobility of our forces and to modernize their equipment. To the same end, we will maintain our forces now on the European continent and will increase their conventional capabilities. We look to our NATO allies to assign an equally high priority to this same essential task.

Second, we must make certain that nuclear weapons will continue to be available for the defense of the entire treaty area, and that these weapons are at all times under close and flexible political control that meets the needs of all NATO countries. We are prepared to join our allies in working out suitable arrangements for this purpose.

To make clear our own intentions and commitment, the United States will commit to the NATO command area five—and subsequently still more—Polaris atomic-missile submarines, subject to any agreed NATO guidelines on their control and use, and responsive to the needs of all members but still credible in an emergency. Beyond this, we look to the possibility of eventually establishing a NATO sea-borne missile force, which would be truly multi-lateral in ownership and control, if this should be desired and found feasible by our allies once NATO's non-nuclear goals have been achieved.[1]

The President's words did not strike a particularly responsive chord in Europe. Aversion to a conventional build-up remained high on three counts. It might weaken the credibility of the nuclear deterrent; it was costly; and it would do no good in view of the supposedly overwhelming power of the Red Army. Furthermore, although the missile gap was disappearing as an issue in the United States, it still remained a matter of grave concern in Europe. The fear continued that, somehow or other, the United States would leave its allies in the lurch rather than use nuclear weapons. Deputy Secretary of Defense Gilpatric informed a news conference on June 6, 1961, that "the current doctrine is that if NATO forces were about to be overwhelmed by non-nuclear attacks from the bloc countries, that NATO would make use of nuclear arms."[2] Still the doubts persisted.

The advent of the Berlin crisis gave particular urgency to these issues. The United States advanced the view that the most effective deterrent to action by Khrushchev would be a build-up of conventional forces, and proceeded accordingly. The Europeans, on the other hand, continued to fret about what this would do to the nuclear deterrent. McNamara found it somewhat puzzling that whenever the Soviets increased their military expenditures, a stir of apprehension spread through the West, whereas an increase in American strength tended to be interpreted as a sign of weakness. He made the point to a House subcommittee more than a year later:

As evidence of my very strong belief that an increase in our conventional forces, taking place, as it is today, at a time when we are not only maintaining but increasing our nuclear forces, in no way detracts from the deterrent, I cite the Soviet Union. I do not place any less credence in their deterrent because they have maintained their conventional forces and, as a matter of fact, reversed a plan to reduce those forces.[3]

Paul Nitze, on a visit to London in December, 1961, tried his hand at allaying the concern about the credibility of the nuclear deterrent. He faced the issue of the missile gap head on, and said:

There was always a certain degree of misunderstanding concerning the so-called missile gap. The question was not so much one of relative numbers but one of the potential vulnerability of our strategic deterrent. Much has been and is being done to reduce that vulnerability. Furthermore, it appears to be the consensus of the intelligence community, both in the United States and in the United Kingdom, that the Soviet deployment of ICBM's has proceeded less rapidly than it was once feared it might. There has never been any doubt that the West possesses by far the greater nuclear force, including delivery capability, than does the U.S.S.R. Now that the problems of vulnerability, dispersal and command and control have become manageable, we believe that this force, including the U.K. nuclear forces and the NATO forces deployed on the Continent, give the West a definite nuclear superiority. We further believe this superiority can be maintained into the future, as improved weapon systems are developed and deployed by both sides. Furthermore, we believe this superiority, particularly when viewed from the Soviet side, to be strategically important in the equations of deterrence and strategy.

Nitze went on to attack the notion that a build-up of NATO's non-nuclear forces was defeatist, divisive, and deleterious to the credibility of the nuclear deterrent.

We can ask ourselves the question, what it is that is likely to affect Mr. Khrushchev's judgment on whether aggressive courses of action on his part will be likely to bring him unacceptably close to the danger of nuclear war. I should think the most important persuader is to be found in Western nuclear capabilities, their survivability against anything his forces can do, their penetration capabilities against his defenses, their responsiveness to responsible control, and their accuracy, numbers and power. On this score, as I have said earlier, the facts support a very credible deterrent indeed. I personally know of nothing significant which the Alliance could do but isn't doing within the probable time frame of the Berlin crisis, to improve the capabilities part of the nuclear deterrent.

Another part of the deterrent is the indications Mr. Khrushchev and his advisers receive from Western words and actions as to Western determination to protect its vital interests. Mr. Kennedy and Lord Home, among others, have expressed to Mr. Khrushchev and to Mr. Gromyko Western determination to see vital Western interests in Berlin defended in clear and unambiguous terms. I doubt whether much would be gained if we were to adapt to our purposes a much used Soviet tactic and dwell often and at length upon what would happen to Moscow or other Soviet areas if given numbers of thermonuclear weapons were to strike them. Mr. Khrushchev already knows the facts.

What we are left with then are actions which can leave no doubt in the Soviet mind that we mean to follow a course of action, if they persist in their aggression, which will bring about a new situation in which the danger to them of nuclear war is very great indeed. Let us assume two different hypothetical situations [with respect to Berlin]. In the first situation the central NATO front is very lightly covered. It is subject to the risk of deep penetration by Soviet non-nuclear forces starting from a standing start. The only option which the West has, to demonstrate its determination to have its vital interests respected, is to initiate the action with the use of nuclear weapons. In the second situation, the NATO front is firmly held on a continuous line. There are enough reserve forces to mount a really serious non-nuclear probe in the air corridors or along the autobahn. That probe can be thrown back by a full application of Soviet non-nuclear power, but only by involving Soviet and NATO in a major fight.

If you were sitting in the Kremlin, which situation would be considered most likely to bring you face to face with nuclear war if you persisted in a train of actions violating what the West considers to be its vital interests? To me, the answer is clear. If I were in the Kremlin I would be much more concerned in the second situation; I would consider it much more likely that the West would find it politically possible to initiate action in defense of the Berlin access routes from the second posture than from the first.[4]

Whether it was this kind of argument or the raw fact of Soviet pressure on Berlin that caused movement, the Allies did make some effort to improve their strength in 1961. McNamara, at a press conference in November, reported what they had accomplished.

I believe that General Norstad . . . had about 20 formal divisional organizations to start with, but that was the equivalent of only 16 full divisions because the 20 divisions were undermanned in part. His strength has built up in two respects: (a) undermanned divisions are being brought to strength, and (b) additional divisions are being provided. And as a result of both actions, he expects to

have approximately 25 effective divisions at the conclusion of the
buildup, approximately January 1st.[5]

A change of this magnitude was all to the good from Mc-
Namara's standpoint. But much still needed doing with respect
to NATO's reserve forces, its logistic position, and its active air
and ground components. And the nuclear ghosts haunting Europe still had not been laid to rest. American assurances about
the superiority of the West's nuclear capabilities were accepted
in Europe, especially after McNamara had briefed the NATO
Ministerial Council on the relative nuclear strengths of the
United States and the Soviet Union. Recognition even dawned
that the United States, with its 7th Army, 17th Air Force, and
6th Fleet all stationed in Europe, was not likely to vanish suddenly from the scene. Some European observers went a step
further and acknowledged that an American President would
feel obliged to use nuclear weapons against an invader rather
than allow these forces to be overrun. But now the nuclear argument proceeded on a different tack. The Americans could be
counted as reliable for the time being, but who could say what
would be the situation in another ten years. Meanwhile, if
Western nuclear superiority was as great as now seemed to be
the case, why should the Europeans strain themselves to provide more conventional power? The intent of the argument
was twofold: to justify the establishment of a nuclear capability
within Europe and to oppose any further demands on European
manpower. At the same time, any suggestion by the United
States that it might withdraw the reinforcements sent to Europe during the Berlin crisis met with outraged protests.

Again, a difficult set of choices confronted the United
States. It could simply sit quietly and not press for further
change in NATO's forces. It could accept this new set of arguments, subscribe in effect to the view that the United States
would soon become an unreliable ally, and help other nations
(but how many?) to acquire modest nuclear capabilities. Or it
could continue on the course set in 1961. Doing the latter meant
pushing simultaneously along four related lines: arguing for the

conventional build-up, offering to support a NATO nuclear capability, advising the allies in greater detail than had previously been the custom of American views on nuclear warfare, and bringing them more into the business of nuclear policy-making. It was this last alternative that the Administration chose to implement.

McNamara's discussions of NATO at the outset of 1962 were relatively low-keyed, and he tended to accentuate what was being accomplished rather than what needed to be done. He dwelt on the Berlin crisis at some length with the Committee on Armed Services of the House of Representatives and said:

The events of the last year have convinced us that the NATO forces in Europe must be greatly strengthened. While we will always be prepared to use our nuclear weapons when needed, we also want to have a choice other than doing nothing or deliberately initiating a general nuclear war; or as President Kennedy said, a choice between "inglorious retreat or unlimited retaliation." No one can put a precise figure on what the conventional strength ought to be, but we do know it must be more than what we had available last year.

Clearly this is not a problem solely for the United States but rather for all the NATO partners. But we, as the strongest of the NATO partners, have a duty to provide the leadership and set the example. Accordingly, through the measures recommended by President Kennedy and approved by the Congress last year, we significantly increased our general purpose forces. And I can report that our NATO partners are responding to our example. As a result NATO will soon have on the central front in Europe the equivalent of 26 divisions, including the 5 fully manned and ready U.S. divisions and their supporting forces. At home, we have on active duty an additional 10 combat-ready divisions—6 Regular Army, 2 Army National Guard, and 2 Marine Corps divisions.[6]

That was progress. But if NATO was to cover the four-hundred-mile central front in adequate strength, and still command the forces necessary to engage in the relief of Berlin, additional ready divisions would be required. Since the feasibility of coping with the Red Army on the ground had long been in

question, McNamara addressed the issue, this time in Chicago.
He pointed out that

we have augmented United States forces in Europe. Our European
Allies have increased the number of their ready divisions. We have
prepositioned more than 100,000 tons of equipment and several
thousand vehicles required by both armored and infantry divisions.
And we have deployed to Europe nearly 300 tactical fighters.

Then, he went on:

While we still depend on our nuclear superiority to support the
NATO alliance, it is important to realize that the Soviet bloc forces
are not unlimited, nor without their own problems. A simple comparison of numbers of Allied and bloc divisions takes no account of
the fact that many of the bloc divisions are a good deal smaller at
full strength than our own, many are under strength, and some of
them may be highly unreliable. The important point to bear in mind
is that NATO has a strong defensive capability. Its further growth
is only limited by the degree to which its members are willing to
devote resources to the task.[7]

The message was clear. Europe, in conjunction with the
United States, could do whatever needed to be done in order
to provide a major conventional defense on the central front
and at the same time protect the interests of the West Berliners.
McNamara, no doubt, found it difficult to believe that the opportunity would not be grasped. The nuclear deterrent was
such a specialized thing; its coverage had never been very large;
and its failure, followed by a nuclear exchange, would result
in millions of casualties. It seemed a weak and dangerous foundation on which to base an active foreign policy. Yet it soon
became clear that, in Europe, nuclear weapons remained a
panacea and that the French, as they worked toward an independent nuclear capability, were setting an example that others
might be tempted to follow. McNamara at last decided that
he must meet this challenge in the most explicit possible way.
The occasion chosen by the Secretary was the semiannual
meeting of NATO's foreign and defense ministers assembled

at Athens early in May. The task he had set himself was a
burdensome one, perhaps too heavy for a single speech to bear.
He wanted to expose his audience to the way in which the
United States planned its nuclear operations, explain the problems raised by the existence of other national nuclear capabilities, and underscore the vital but limited role in deterrence
played by strategic nuclear forces. By all accounts, he held his
audience enthralled for nearly an hour. Never before had the
NATO ministers heard so detailed an exposition of American
thought on major strategic problems. Little more than a month
later, on June 16, 1962, McNamara delivered the commencement address at the University of Michigan in Ann Arbor. It is
generally accepted that this address represented an abbrevi-
ated version of his Athens speech. Even so, he said a great deal
to what must have been a somewhat bemused group of gradu-
ating seniors. At that time, he told them:

. . . NATO is involved in a number of controversies, which must
be resolved by achieving a consensus within the organization in
order to preserve its strength and unity. . . .
It has been argued that the very success of Western European
economic development reduces Europe's need to rely on the U.S.
to share in its defenses.
It has been argued that the increasing vulnerability of the U.S.
to nuclear attack makes us less willing as a partner in the defense of
Europe, and hence less effective in deterring such an attack.
It has been argued that nuclear capabilities are alone relevant in
the face of the growing nuclear threat, and that independent national nuclear forces are sufficient to protect the nations of Europe.
I believe that all of these arguments are mistaken. I think it is
worthwhile to expose the U.S. views on these issues as we have
presented them to our allies. In our view, the effect of the new factors in the situation, both economic and military, has been to increase the interdependence of national security interests on both
sides of the Atlantic and to enhance the need for the closest co-
ordination of our efforts.
A central military issue facing NATO today is the role of nuclear
strategy. Four facts seem to us to dominate consideration of that

role. All of them point in the direction of increased integration to achieve our common defense. First, the Alliance has over-all nuclear strength adequate to any challenge confronting it. Second, this strength not only minimizes the likelihood of major nuclear war, but makes possible a strategy designed to preserve the fabric of our societies if war should occur. Third, damage to the civil societies of the Alliance resulting from nuclear war could be very grave. Fourth, improved non-nuclear forces, well within Alliance resources, could enhance deterrence of any aggressive moves short of direct, all-out attack on Western Europe.

Let us look at the situation today. First, given the current balance of nuclear power, which we confidently expect to maintain in the years ahead, a surprise nuclear attack is simply not a rational act for any enemy. Nor would it be rational for an enemy to take the initiative in the use of nuclear weapons as an outgrowth of a limited engagement in Europe or elsewhere. I think we are entitled to conclude that either of these actions has been made highly unlikely.

Second, and equally important, the mere fact that no nation could rationally take steps leading to a nuclear war does not guarantee that a nuclear war cannot take place. Not only do nations sometimes act in ways that are hard to explain on a rational basis, but even when acting in a "rational" way they sometimes, indeed disturbingly often, act on the basis of misunderstandings of the true facts of a situation. They misjudge the way others will react, and the way others will interpret what they are doing. We must hope, indeed I think we have good reason to hope, that all sides will understand this danger, and will refrain from steps that even raise the possibility of such a mutually disastrous misunderstanding. We have taken unilateral steps to reduce the likelihood of such an occurrence. We look forward to the prospect that through arms control, the actual use of these terrible weapons may be completely avoided. It is a problem not just for us in the West, but for all nations that are involved in this struggle we call the Cold War.[8]

McNamara went on to point out that, pending an agreement on arms control, the prudent strategist must design his forces and plans with the terrible contingency of nuclear war in mind. As he put it, "Simply ignoring the problem is not going to make it go away." But what did one do if these cataclysmic circum-

stances arose? McNamara now came to one of the main points
in his argument.

> The U.S. has come to the conclusion that to the extent feasible,
> basic military strategy in a possible general nuclear war should be
> approached in much the same way that more conventional military
> operations have been regarded in the past. That is to say, principal
> military objectives, in the event of a nuclear war stemming from a
> major attack on the Alliance, should be the destruction of the
> enemy's military forces, not of his civilian population.
>
> The very strength and nature of the Alliance forces make it pos-
> sible for us to retain, even in the face of a massive surprise attack,
> sufficient reserve striking power to destroy an enemy society if
> driven to it. In other words, we are giving a possible opponent the
> strongest imaginable incentive to refrain from striking our own
> cities.[9]

McNamara was attempting here to point out what, in the
American experience, was required both to maintain effective
deterrence and be prepared for the remote but awful event that
deterrence might fail. He then proceeded to outline some of
the implications of the requirement.

> The strength that makes these contributions to deterrence and to
> the hope of deterring attack upon civil societies even in wartime
> does not come cheap. . . . During the coming fiscal year, the
> United States plans to spend close to $15 billion on its nuclear
> weapons to assure their adequacy. For what this money buys, there
> is no substitute.
>
> In particular, relatively weak national nuclear forces with enemy
> cities as their targets are not likely to be sufficient to perform even
> the function of deterrence. If they are small, and perhaps vulnerable
> on the ground or in the air, or inaccurate, a major antagonist can
> take a variety of measures to counter them. Indeed, if a major antag-
> onist came to believe there was a substantial likelihood of it being
> used independently, this force would be inviting a pre-emptive first
> strike against it. In the event of war, the use of such a force against
> the cities of a major nuclear power would be tantamount to suicide,
> whereas its employment against significant military targets would
> have a negligible effect on the outcome of the conflict. Meanwhile,

the creation of a single additional national nuclear force encourages the proliferation of nuclear power with all of its attendant dangers.

In short, then, limited nuclear capabilities, operating independently, are dangerous, expensive, prone to obsolescence, and lacking in credibility as a deterrent. Clearly, the United States nuclear contribution to the Alliance is neither obsolete nor dispensable.[10]

That was by no means the end of the difficulty with small, independent nuclear capabilities. McNamara discussed, by implication, some of the other problems.

At the same time, the general strategy I have summarized magnifies the importance of unity of planning, concentration of executive authority, and central direction. There must not be competing and conflicting strategies to meet the contingency of nuclear war. We are convinced that a general nuclear war target system is indivisible, and if, despite all our efforts, nuclear war should occur, our best hope lies in conducting a centrally controlled campaign against all of the enemy's vital nuclear capabilities, while retaining reserve forces, all centrally controlled.

We know that the same forces which are targeted on ourselves are also targeted on our allies. Our own strategic retaliatory forces are prepared to respond against these forces, wherever they are and whatever their targets. This mission is assigned not only in fulfillment of our treaty commitments but also because the character of nuclear war compels it. More specifically, the U.S. is as much concerned with that portion of Soviet nuclear striking power that can reach Western Europe as with that portion that also can reach the United States. In short, we have undertaken the nuclear defense of NATO on a global basis. This will continue to be our objective. In the execution of this mission, the weapons in the European theater are only one resource among many.[11]

Put somewhat differently, McNamara found it hard to believe that a strategic nuclear exchange would not involve all the nuclear powers. Consequently, he was appalled at the prospect that such an exchange might start in an uncoordinated way and involve the wrong mixture of targets. Yet that seemed the most likely result of a proliferation of national nuclear capabilities. Rather than add strength, it might increase weakness, particularly if each of the nuclear powers—fearful of being drawn into a nuclear war not of its own choosing—tried to narrow the scope of its responsibilities to that of self-defense. An alternative to this kind of division and chaos had to be found. McNamara suggested one.

We want and need a greater degree of Alliance participation in formulating nuclear weapons policy to the greatest extent possible. We would all find it intolerable to contemplate having only a part of the strategic force launched in isolation from our main striking power.[12]

At the same time, McNamara pledged the United States "to maintain powerful nuclear forces for the Alliance as a whole." He also went on to stress what he regarded as NATO's real salvation. The maintenance of powerful strategic nuclear forces for purposes of deterrence was all well and good.

But let us be quite clear about what we are saying and what we would have to face if the deterrent should fail. This is the almost certain prospect that, despite our nuclear strength, all of us would suffer deeply in the event of major nuclear war.

We accept our share of this responsibility within the Alliance. And we believe that the combination of our nuclear strength and a strategy of controlled response gives us some hope of minimizing damage in the event that we have to fulfill our pledge. But I must point out that we do not regard this as a desirable prospect, nor do we believe that the Alliance should depend solely on our nuclear power to deter actions not involving a massive commitment of . . . hostile force. Surely an Alliance with the wealth, talent, and experience that we possess can find a better way than extreme reliance on nuclear weapons to meet our common threat. We do not believe that if the formula, $e = mc^2$, had not been discovered, we should all be Communist slaves. On this question, I can see no valid reason for a fundamental difference of view on the two sides of the Atlantic.[13]

McNamara, in other words, was pleading with Europe to consider its own self-interest as well as that of the United States. A strategy based solely on deterrence, and nuclear deterrence at that, seemed almost a frivolous way to treat the Soviet threat. It had already failed to deter a number of provocative acts and it was likely to remain of limited utility in the future. What, in fact, was most troublesome about European aspirations was not the search for nuclear independence; although that was troublesome enough. It was the belief that nuclear weapons would really prevent all evil from occurring. To McNamara, with his concern about uncertainty and his desire for options, such a gamble was incomprehensible. He virtually said as much as he approached the conclusion of the Ann Arbor speech.

With the Alliance possessing the strength and strategy I have described, it is most unlikely that any power will launch a nuclear attack on NATO. For the kinds of conflicts, both political and military, most likely to arise in the NATO area, our capabilities for response must not be limited to nuclear weapons alone. The Soviets have superiority in non-nuclear forces in Europe today. But that superiority is by no means overwhelming. Collectively, the Alliance has the potential for a successful defense against such forces. In manpower alone, NATO has more men under arms than the Soviet Union and its European satellites. We have already shown our willingness to contribute through our divisions now in place on European soil. In order to defend the populations of the NATO countries and to meet our treaty obligations, we have put in hand a series of measures to strengthen our non-nuclear power. We have added $10 billion for this purpose to the previously planned level of expenditures for fiscal years 1962 and 1963. To tide us over while new permanent strength was being created, we called up 158,000 reservists. We will be releasing them this summer, but only because in the meantime we have built up on an enduring basis more added strength than the call-up temporarily gave us. The number of U.S. combat-ready divisions has been increased from 11 to 16. Stockpiled in Europe now are full sets of equipment for two additional divisions; the men of these divisions can be rapidly moved to Europe by air.

We expect that our allies will also undertake to strengthen further their non-nuclear forces, and to improve the quality and staying power of these forces. These achievements will complement our deterrent strength. With improvements in Alliance ground force strength and staying power, improved non-nuclear air capabilities, and better equipped and trained reserve forces, we can be assured that no deficiency exists in the NATO defense of this vital region, and that no aggression, small or large, can succeed.[14]

The Ann Arbor speech produced a substantial reaction, not all of it favorable. Some European observers classified it as another piece of American arrogance; others as a confession of weakness. But while it set off a great deal of debate, it did virtually nothing to change either the force structure or the strategy in NATO. The defense budgets of most of the allies continued to decline as percentages of their gross national products. President de Gaulle, for his part, remained adamant in his determination to build a French nuclear capability. And whatever the force of McNamara's arguments, the desire for a European role in nuclear affairs, and conviction about the invincibility of the Red Army, persisted within NATO. The chances of acquiring the option to deal with a Soviet invasion of Western Europe on a non-nuclear basis still could not be counted too high.

After Ann Arbor, the question arose as to whether the time had not come to consolidate what gains had been made and await the views of the European allies about the future strategy and force structure of NATO. But two events occurred during the summer and autumn of 1962 that sent McNamara back into the campaign for additional non-nuclear capabilites. The first was the re-evaluation of Soviet air and ground strength, which provided increasing evidence that the now-traditional view of the Red Army, pouring across Germany in vast numbers, was a myth. The reality seemed to be a maximum effort of between 50 and 60 Soviet divisions plus whatever satellite forces could be supported on the central front, without allowing for the attrition and interdiction that superior allied air power could impose. Here, in other words, was a threat of sufficiently modest proportions to permit an extended Allied defense. In fact, the same force goals that NATO had carried on its books for so long—30 active and 30 reserve divisions assigned to the central front—looked quite adequate as the basis for such a defense.

The second event concerned the Skybolt missile. The Skybolt was an air-to-surface ballistic missile intended to be launched from a B-52 bomber at targets a thousand miles away. Its principal justifications were that it would complicate an enemy's defense problem and extend the life of the bomber by enabling it to fire the missile, if desired, outside the range of the air defenses. The British, with the cancellation of their Bluestreak ballistic missile program, decided in 1960 similarly to extend the life of their bombers by purchasing the Skybolt. The scrapping of this missile thus would affect significantly the future of the independent British nuclear deterrent. Yet scrap it McNamara and the President decided to do. The development of Skybolt had proved more lengthy and much more costly than anticipated; its launching platform, the bomber, would be vulnerable on the ground; the missile itself would not be very accurate; and other ballistic missiles—sea-based as well as land-based—could perform more effectively the same missions at approximately the same cost. These other missiles, moreover, were already available in the form of Polaris and Minuteman, while Skybolt was still going through development and test. Skybolt, in short, did not look like a particularly attractive investment. The time had come to cut the loss.

The reassessment of Soviet conventional strength offered McNamara the opportunity to press his case for the non-nuclear build-up in NATO. Cancellation of Skybolt raised most immediately the fate of the British independent deterrent, but it also brought in its train questions about the role of Europe in NATO nuclear affairs. The case for the non-nuclear build-up went before the December ministerial meeting of NATO in Paris. President Kennedy and Prime Minister Macmillan met at Nassau shortly thereafter and reached agreement on the steps to be taken in the wake of the Skybolt cancellation. The two events led McNamara to reflect at some length on American policy toward NATO as he reported to the Congress in

January, 1963, on the military posture of the United States.
He acknowledged at the outset the changing relationship between the United States and Europe.

European NATO, with a population of more than a third of a
billion and a gross national product of well over $350 billion a year,
is still a principal bastion against the spread of communism. The
six Common Market nations, plus the United Kingdom, by themselves have a total population, a military manpower pool and a
GNP well in excess of that of the Soviet Union. Moreover, the rate
of economic growth of the Common Market nations compares very
favorably with that of the Soviet Union and they have been able to
provide their people with a much higher standard of living.

With the continued growth and extension of the Common
Market, coupled with an increasing degree of political integration,
in time there will inevitably develop in Europe a new power center,
more nearly the equal of the Soviet Union and its European satellites. With the manpower, production capacity, and technical and
scientific skills available to them, the nations of Europe should not
only be able to provide larger contributions to their own defense
but should also be in a position to contribute more to the defense
of freedom in other parts of the world.

In view of this growing strength, some basic changes in our
present arrangements with our NATO partners would be very much
in order. We have no desire to dominate NATO. In fact, we would
be very happy to share more equitably the heavy burdens we now
carry in the collective defense of the free world.[15]

The difficulty was that no senior partners in this burden-
sharing had as yet made their appearance. The result was that
the United States still carried not only a great burden, but also
a proportionately large share of the responsibility for leadership
and direction within the Alliance. This, McNamara noted, was
particularly true in respect of the strategic nuclear forces, the
great bulk of which the United States was providing precisely
for the defense of NATO. He then elaborated on the nature of
that particular responsibility.

NATO is founded on the concept of collective defense. We have
all agreed that an attack upon one would be considered an attack

against all. Therefore, a decision to invoke the use of strategic nuclear weapons with their tremendous destructive potential and speed of delivery against another nuclear power would almost inevitably involve all the members of the alliance in a global nuclear war.

Moreover, the targets against which such weapons would be used must, as a practical matter, be viewed as a single system. Because of the speed at which such an exchange would take place—and as missiles become the predominant part of the strategic nuclear forces on both sides, the time would be reduced to minutes—decisions must be made and executed promptly. Targets must be allocated to weapons in advance (of course, with options) and in a very carefully planned manner, taking into account the character of the targets, their urgency, importance, and degree of hardness, as well as the character of the weapons, their range, yield, accuracy, and speed.

Clearly, under these conditions, a partial and uncoordinated response could be fatal to the interests of all the members of NATO. That is why we have consistently stressed the importance of a single chain of command, to be employed in a fully integrated manner against what is truly an indivisible target system.[16]

McNamara did not insist that the strategic nuclear force must be owned, controlled, and operated exclusively by the United States. That was not his point.

The essential point here is . . . that we must avoid the fragmentation and compartmentalization of NATO's nuclear power, which could be dangerous to us all. If our European NATO partners wish to create a European strategic nuclear force, we certainly should have no objections. But we should insist that that force be closely integrated with our own so that it could be jointly targeted, and directed in a coordinated fashion.

Furthermore, we are convinced that such a force could be successfully built only as a collective European undertaking and not on the basis of separate national efforts. We well know the heavy costs involved in creating and maintaining a strategic nuclear force. Our own nuclear forces cost us about $15 billion a year, almost as much as all of our European allies, together, spend on their total defense programs. Even assuming a continued high rate of economic growth, it would take the combined resources of all of them to create a truly significant nuclear capability with which to face the Soviet threat. That is why I said last year at Ann Arbor that weak "national" nuclear forces operating independently would be very costly and of questionable effectiveness.[17]

McNamara went on to point out that the United States had never opposed a nuclear capability for the European members of NATO.

In fact, we have for many years been providing them with tactical nuclear-capable weapon systems, although the nuclear warheads are retained, in accordance with our laws, under U.S. control. We have provided training in the use of these weapons to a large number of allied military personnel. We are making every possible effort to keep our NATO partners fully informed of the problems of nuclear war and the measures we are taking to deal with them. And last year we announced that we had earmarked a fully operational Polaris force to the NATO Command.[18]

McNamara might have added what he was to announce later, namely that the United States had increased the number of tactical nuclear weapons in Europe by more than 60 percent during the past two years. This was hardly the behavior of a power that intended, as some rumor had it, to withdraw from the Continent. Nor did it suggest that the United States was bent on keeping nuclear weapons out of its allies' hands in all circumstances. If anything, the implication was that NATO had already become a rather substantial nuclear power. Still, there was the question of symbols as well as substance. This led McNamara to a discussion of the agreements with Great Britain at Nassau.

The immediate issue between the two Governments . . . arose from our judgment that the Skybolt air-to-ground missile should not be developed and procured for our own strategic forces. . . . This judgment created a major problem for the United Kingdom, which had planned to buy 100 of these missiles to equip their Vulcan bombers in order to extend the useful life of these aircraft through the 1960's.

In 1960, the United States entered into an agreement with the United Kingdom to make available, under certain conditions, Skybolt missiles, if we proceeded with production. We undertook to bear the entire cost of the Skybolt development. The British undertook to bear the costs of adapting the missile to their bombers and their warheads. The entire agreement was contingent upon the successful development of the missile and its use by the United States. In the event that we found it undesirable to complete the program, the British would have the right to continue further development at their own expense.[19]

McNamara pointed out that the Skybolt program had been in trouble from its inception and that the British were kept informed of the difficulties. In December, 1960, and again in December, 1961, the British Minister of Defense learned that the United States had grave reservations about going ahead with production of the missile. When the United States decided that its interests would be best served by cancellation of the program, McNamara gave the Macmillan government more than a month's notice of what was in store. The decision, when it occurred on December 11, 1962, therefore did not come as any surprise to the British. The Kennedy Administration had acted with perfect propriety within the terms of the agreement. Nevertheless, as McNamara continued with his account:

The President, wishing to assist the United Kingdom in every possible way to adjust to our cancellation of Skybolt, explored with the British Prime Minister at Nassau a number of possible alternatives. As one alternative, the President offered to continue the development of Skybolt as a joint enterprise with the United Kingdom, with each country bearing equal shares of the future cost to complete development, after which the United Kingdom would be able to place a production order to meet its requirements. This offer went considerably beyond the original agreement, under which the United Kingdom would have had to stand the full cost of further development, but the British Prime Minister decided not to accept it in the light of the uncertainties involved in the project.
Another alternative suggested by the President was the use of the Hound Dog missile, but because of the technical difficulties

involved in adapting this missile to the British V-bombers, the Prime Minister declined this suggestion also.

A third alternative considered was the sale of Polaris missiles to the United Kingdom, with that country furnishing its own submarines and warheads. This was the alternative suggested and favored by the United Kingdom. Both the Prime Minister and the President recognized that such an arrangement could not only meet the needs of the United Kingdom but could also open up entirely new opportunities for enhancing the unity and cohesion of the NATO alliance by making possible the creation of a truly multilateral NATO nuclear force. The United States will not only sell to the United Kingdom the Polaris missiles and associated equipment but will also provide technical assistance and such other support as may be later agreed upon. The ballistic missile submarines constructed under the agreement will be assigned as part of a NATO nuclear force and targeted in accordance with NATO plans. The United States, on its part, will assign at least equal forces to the NATO Command. And, except where supreme national interests are at stake, these forces will be used solely for purposes of international defense of the Western alliance.

To make a start in the development of a multilateral NATO nuclear force, it was agreed that some part of the United States and United Kingdom nuclear forces already in existence would be assigned to NATO and targeted in accordance with NATO plans.

The President also decided that the United States should invite France, the only other NATO nuclear power, to participate in this multilateral force on terms similar to those offered the United Kingdom. It is also contemplated that other NATO nations will be invited to participate in such a force, although the specific method of participation has not been decided upon.[20]

McNamara thought that the Nassau Pact would be "a major milestone in the long march to a truly interdependent Atlantic alliance." Certainly it represented a major concession by the United States to European concerns about their nuclear future. However, its full effects still remained uncertain a year later. President de Gaulle summarily rejected the Polaris offer and at the same time blackballed Britain from the European Economic Community. In May, 1963, NATO created an interallied

nuclear force consisting of the existing national nuclear-capable
forces already committed to the Alliance, the British V-bomber
squadrons, and five Polaris submarines. By August it had acquired a Belgian commander, or nuclear deputy, under
SACEUR and representation at the headquarters of the Strategic Air Command. And in fulfillment of the third part of the
proposal, the United States undertook negotiations with various
members of the Alliance for the purpose of establishing a
NATO-wide, mix-manned, fleet of ships armed with Polaris
missiles—known as the multilateral nuclear force. France continued to stand aloof from all these initiatives; whether the
other members of the Alliance would find their nuclear ambitions satisfied or merely whetted thereby remained still to be
seen. The United States, perhaps naïvely, had tried to be constructive.

To McNamara, the proposals for NATO nuclear forces did
not lessen the need for the conventional option in Europe, and
he pointed out to the Congress what he saw as its justification.

The possibility that we may have to fight non-nuclear wars in
southeast Asia, the Middle East, and other areas of the world is
accepted, generally, without argument, but not so with regard to
Europe. Many people would believe that any military action in
Europe, short of a very minor probe, would require the immediate
use of nuclear weapons, and I stress the word "immediate." Certainly, a massive attack on Western Europe would have to be met
with whatever weapons are required to counter it. That has always
been the policy of the Western alliance. And, I have repeatedly
stated . . . that even in limited war situations we should not preclude the use of tactical nuclear weapons.

However, we may well be faced with situations in Europe where
it would not be to the advantage of ourselves or our allies to use
even tactical nuclear weapons initially—provided we had the capability to deal with them through non-nuclear means. Nuclear
weapons, even in the lower kiloton ranges, are extremely destructive
devices, and hardly the preferred weapons to defend such heavily
populated areas as Europe. Furthermore, while it does not necessarily follow that the use of tactical nuclear weapons must in-

evitably escalate into global nuclear war, it does present a very definite threshold, beyond which we enter a vast unknown.

This does not mean that the NATO forces can or should do without tactical nuclear weapons. On the contrary, we must continue to strengthen and modernize our tactical nuclear capabilities to deal with an attack where the opponent employs such weapons first, or any attack by conventional forces which puts Europe in danger of being overrun. We mean to defend Europe with every kind of weapon needed.

But we must also substantially increase our non-nuclear capabilities to foreclose to our opponent the freedom of action he would otherwise have, or believe he would have, in lesser military provocations. We must be in a position to confront him at any level of provocation with an appropriate military response. The decision to employ tactical nuclear weapons should not be forced upon us simply because we have no other way to cope with a particular situation.[21]

McNamara, in making these arguments, was engaged in a balancing act of the most delicate character. If he stressed too strongly the nuclear superiority of the United States over the Soviet Union, and underplayed the likely devastation of a thermonuclear war, he simply caused the Europeans to ask why they should increase their conventional forces above the existing levels. If he depicted the horrors of nuclear war, and suggested that Europe could and should be defended by conventional means, he invited the old cry that the United States was undermining the nuclear deterrent, that the United States itself could no longer be depended upon, and that the Europeans must have nuclear capabilities of their own in order to assure their safety. And if he pointed out that the Soviets were six feet rather than ten feet tall with respect to non-nuclear arms, he risked the reply that a further non-nuclear build-up by Europe therefore was unnecessary. No matter which way he turned, the mystique of nuclear deterrence stood in his way. It seemed virtually impossible to convince the Allies that nuclear capabilities long since had been found wanting as an all-purpose deterrent. European leaders simply attributed the failures of the past to a lack of will that could be remedied in the future. It seemed equally difficult to persuade them that the cost of a major conventional option was well worth incurring in a highly uncertain world. The temptation in Europe was to rely instead on the threat of escalation—a series of conventional and nuclear tripwires linked like firecrackers, which would explode with automatic and increasing fury if the Soviets tried to press through them.

A countervailing temptation in the United States was to point out that the Alliance had deluded itself all too long about the real worth of nuclear weapons; that their principal value lay in their ability to deter a nuclear attack by the Soviet Union. But McNamara and his principal advisers were not prepared to go to either extreme. They remained impressed by all the uncertainties; what they wanted still was not a complete reversal of NATO strategy, but a much greater degree of freedom within the existing concept. Paul Nitze, in March, 1963, described the goals, accomplishments, and reasoning of this approach.

He adverted first to the Nassau proposals, saying:

At first, the critical fact of NATO was that the collective defense of Western Europe rested almost solely upon the U.S. pledge of its nuclear monopoly. Thereafter, as Western Europe regained its economic and political strength, it has increased its contribution to the over-all defense task, and the voice of the European powers in collective NATO policy decisions has grown commensurately. This is eminently appropriate, and at Nassau last December President Kennedy and Prime Minister Macmillan proposed an even greater move in this direction. The proposals entailed allocations from national forces to a NATO nuclear force and creation of a multilateral NATO nuclear force through which all members of the Alliance desiring to do so might participate in the ownership, control, and operation of the nuclear element of the collective defense.[22]

These measures were intended to reassure Europe about the availability of nuclear power for its defense. But Nitze insisted that neither the American nor the European wing of the Alliance could make its proper contribution to the defense of the free world independently of the other. And this led him to a consideration of the threats to Europe and the forces most appropriate to their deterrence.

For the greater part of its history NATO has concentrated on the threat of a massive non-nuclear invasion of Western Europe to be met by a Western nuclear response. Strategic concepts, forces and defense expenditures have largely been designed for this contingency. However, the probability that the Communists would deliberately choose this form of attack seems small. Although the Soviets are moving steadily toward a strategic nuclear force protected by air defense, hardening, mobility and dispersal similar to ours, the NATO powers are, and can continue to remain, ahead in most relevant dimensions of nuclear power. Today, in a full nuclear exchange, whether or not the Soviets should strike first and without warning, they would not achieve a victory even in the technical military sense and they would be open to huge destruction. In the face of such a reality, a deliberate nuclear or an all-out conventional attack on Western Europe by Communist forces is simply not a rational politico-military act.[23]

What Nitze was saying, in effect, was that since a Soviet attempt to seize Europe would be met, if necessary, by the full power of American nuclear retaliation, massive invasion did not look like a very likely prospect. The implication, as he interpreted it, was that

we must concurrently prepare to meet a second, more likely set of contingencies—potentially more profitable and less dangerous to the Soviets and therefore more probable—namely, a series of Communist probes, exploitations of weak spots, military actions at the lower end of the spectrum, and efforts to divide the West. Communists demonstrate both a proclivity for bold political actions against a background of impressive military force and also careful calculation of risks and a staunch desire to keep events under their own control. Because they can be expected sensibly to avoid high risks of nuclear war or events leading to it, their military actions against the West at any one moment are likely to be controlled in size and aimed at limited objectives. In such circumstances, NATO will surely wish to have the choice of avoiding immediate use of nuclear weapons; it would be neither wise nor credible for us to build our doctrine and our forces on the premise that every pinprick must be met by nuclear war.

Of course, neither we nor they can discount the possibility that a conflict arising at lower levels of violence may lead to a major engagement using solely non-nuclear weapons or using nuclear weapons only tactically or escalating to a full nuclear exchange.[24]

If, in the face of this range of possibilities, NATO placed all its reliance on nuclear deterrence, some of the contingencies might be all the more likely to materialize. Thus, a revolt in East Germany, or a new blockade of Berlin, could easily occur despite the threat of nuclear retaliation. And if the threat were fulfilled:

A full nuclear exchange would in all probability—if not certainly— devastate the West so badly that the outcome might be "victory" in the technical sense only. Of course, we need strong nuclear forces. But even when the West had a virtual nuclear monopoly, this did not, by itself, deter all forms of Communist political and military aggression. Clearly, the military power supporting Alliance foreign policies must include non-nuclear forces able to apply a wide range of effective counterpressures against the background of a formidable nuclear deterrent. Without them, NATO might be reduced to inaction, or weak action, resulting in a serious setback, a missed opportunity, or even disaster.[25]

Nitze was trying to hammer home a lesson learned by all high American policy-makers, whatever their Administration or political affiliation. It was that the decision to use nuclear weapons is so awesome that most other alternatives look better at the time—if they exist; and they usually do. To talk in the abstract about the circumstances in which nuclear weapons might be used; that was one thing. To confront a crisis and have to make a choice; that was quite another matter. Nitze put the issue somewhat more circumspectly:

In such circumstances, a strong non-nuclear forward defense would help NATO develop advantageous courses of action—local and global, diplomatic and military—without going to nuclear war, at least initially, and without dangerously weakening our over-all position.

Furthermore, a strong non-nuclear posture would confer large political benefits on the Alliance, especially its European members. It would give a sense of freedom and initiative that primary reliance on nuclear power does not provide, increase bargaining power with the Soviet Union, and enhance the attractive power of Western Europe to Eastern Europe.[26]

By Nitze's calculations, achievement of this favorable non-nuclear posture was well within the realm of feasibility. He referred to the "myth of overwhelming Soviet non-nuclear superiority over the West." Then he suggested:

From the USSR, however, it may look as if it is NATO which has the hordes. Why? Because NATO has more men under arms and greater over-all strength than the Russians, both worldwide and in Europe. Worldwide, NATO has 5.8 million men under arms to a total for the Warsaw Pact countries of 4.3 million. NATO ground forces total 3.2 million of whom 2.2 million are in Europe. Active army units of the Soviet Union (not counting the satellites) total about 2 million men. . . .[27]

The main task ahead, in these circumstances, was to meet "presently prescribed NATO goals in both quality and quantity —including well-trained, ready reserves." The United States had already done its part.

In budgetary terms, we allocated $4 billion more for non-nuclear forces in FY 1962 than originally planned, and further increases are proposed in succeeding budgets. The number of combat ready Army divisions has been increased from 11 to 16 in the last two years, and we have greatly improved the air- and sealift capabilities of our forces, as well as their equipment and readiness. We have more than 400,000 men in Europe now and within 30 days can deploy very sizable additional forces there. We are fully meeting our commitments.

Our NATO Allies have also taken significant steps in the last few years . . . toward the attainment of NATO force goals. But they should shoulder an even greater portion of the financial and man-power burdens of the Alliance . . . a really worthwhile NATO non-nuclear defense posture requires full attainment of NATO goals with well-equipped units of high quality, backed up by ready reserves. This goal can be achieved with reasonable additional efforts, but neither Western Europe alone nor North America alone can or should provide all the resources for it.[28]

It remained quite uncertain, by the autumn of 1963, to what extent these arguments had taken effect or whether the United States had found the right formula for effecting a change in the forces and strategy of the Alliance. Interestingly enough, the country which had lived longest with the atom—the United States—seemed most skeptical about its ability to cover the en-tire spectrum of military conflict. Britain continued to pro-pound a strategy of tripwires, but without much conviction. Her main interest apparently lay in avoiding any substantial increase in defense expenditures. Germany professed to be-lieve that the key to her defense lay with low-yield nuclear weapons, even though, according to an authoritative American source, the Soviet tactical nuclear capability "is a blunt and imprecise instrument, better suited to operating in conjunction with a strategic exchange than in limited nuclear conflict."[29] France, as the newest member of the atomic club, mustered the greatest enthusiasm of all for the deterrent role of nuclear weapons and seemingly aspired to replace the United States as the chief guarantor of Europe. It would be difficult to say that this amounted to a consensus within the Alliance.

Nevertheless, NATO had changed in several ways since 1961. The interallied nuclear force was a fact. The multilateral nuclear force continued as a subject of active discussion and ne-gotiation. The American re-evaluation of Soviet conventional capabilities was gaining acceptance, even though disagreement remained about its implications for NATO policy. On the score of policy, sufficient open-mindedness now prevailed to permit the Secretary-General of NATO to take inventory of the capabilities and resources of the Alliance and analyze the alternative strategies that member states were pressing for adoption. And, above all, the conventional strength of NATO had increased. True, the goal of thirty active and thirty reserve divisions remained to be attained, and the European members of NATO were still spending their resources inefficiently. But the gap between aspiration and reality had narrowed. And the crises of Berlin and Cuba, if they had revealed nothing else, had shown that deterrence might indeed fail, and that major non-nuclear forces would then be welcome as a supplement to the nuclear capabilities of the Alliance. McNamara might not have won the battle for the major conventional option in Europe. It was too early to say, after thirty-four months, that he had lost it.

CHAPTER 4

The Long View

THE DEFENSE ESTABLISHMENT is invariably described as the servant of foreign policy. Whether used to deter acts of violence, support demands, or meet opposing force, military power is supposed to accomplish ends other than victory; indeed, victory, however defined, is simply a means to other ends of policy—not an end in itself. But force is a blunt instrument, not a scalpel, and difficult to make obedient to the objectives of policy. War itself may be a political process, but it leaves terrible marks on the societies that employ it. In doing so, it frequently distorts and enlarges the objectives it was intended to serve. Nuclear war could even obliterate all objectives.

McNamara quickly showed himself to be acutely conscious of the fractious nature of military power. His search for a substantial number of military options and his emphasis on the less destructive forms of violence were all intended to provide controlled and useful force in an environment of great uncertainty. As a result of his efforts, the President could apply military power with a delicacy of touch unmatched in postwar American history. Even so, McNamara was not entirely content with his handiwork. Large budgets, for example, held no intrinsic fascination for him. As a citizen, he was acutely aware of the heavy burdens placed upon his countrymen by the current costs of defense, and he was equally conscious that these resources could be put to more exciting alternative uses. He knew only too well that there were important competing claims on the national economy and he was intensely sympathetic to them. He was also concerned about the American balance of payments deficit and the role of the defense establishment in contributing to it. He suffered, too, from occasional discouragement about European attitudes. To provide the multiple options required for deterrence and action in an uncertain world, he needed greater European cooperation than he had obtained thus far. He still could not be entirely confident that the other members of NATO would make the necessary effort. He had therefore to ask himself from time to time whether the United States could continue indefinitely in its current contribution to Europe's defense. The balance of payments deficit and the prolonged differences over strategic concepts did not augur well in that respect.

But, above all, the nuclear dangers concerned him. No high policy-maker can go for long under modern conditions without recognizing that a nuclear war could actually occur. McNamara himself quickly became a veteran of two nuclear crises—over Berlin and Cuba—and he did not like what he saw. While he had actively promoted the continuing build-up and protection of American nuclear power and had committed himself to the doctrine of flexible and controlled response in the use of that power, he did not proceed along this course with any great enthusiasm. No other alternative seemed feasible at the time, but McNamara did not wish to foreclose any opportunity to reduce the nuclear hazard.

The traditional alternative to armaments as a means to security is, of course, disarmament. For some years now, the Department of Defense, in recognition of the importance of disarmament proposals and negotiations in American foreign policy, has had a Deputy Assistant Secretary of Defense for

Arms Control and a Special Assistant for Arms Control to the
Joint Chiefs of Staff. Under McNamara, these proved to be active and constructive offices. McNamara himself set the tone
even while presiding over the largest peacetime defense budgets in American history. As he noted to the Congress, in presenting the budget for fiscal year 1964:

> Although . . . we are proposing to increase our military strength
> and enhance our security, we should not lose sight of the fact that
> the central objective of our national policy is, in President Kennedy's
> words, "a peaceful world community of free and independent states,
> free to choose their own future and their own system as long as it
> does not threaten the freedom of others."

The Cuban missile crisis was still fresh in his mind at this
juncture, and he remarked:

> As the events of last October have so forcefully demonstrated, the
> expanding arsenals of nuclear weapons on both sides of the Iron
> Curtain have created an extremely dangerous situation not only for
> their possessors but also for the entire world. As the arms race
> continues and the weapons multiply and become more swift and
> deadly, the possibility of a global catastrophe, either by miscalcula-
> tion or design, becomes ever more real.
> More armaments, whether offensive or defensive, cannot solve
> this dilemma. We are approaching an era when it will become
> increasingly improbable that either side could destroy a sufficiently
> large portion of the other's strategic nuclear force, either by sur-
> prise or otherwise, to preclude a devastating retaliatory blow. This
> may result in mutual deterrence but it is still a grim prospect. It
> underscores the need for a renewed effort to find some way, if not
> to eliminate these deadly weapons completely, then at least to slow
> down or halt their further accumulation, and to create institutional
> arrangements which would reduce the need for either side to resort
> to their immediate use in moments of acute international tension.
> The United States and the Soviet Union, as the two great nuclear
> powers, are the nations most directly endangered by these weapons
> and therefore have a great mutual interest in seeing to it that they
> are never used.[1]

This was the most pessimistic possible view of a future strategic nuclear war. It assumed that the antagonists would start or finish by attacking one another's great urban concentrations. But whether or not a nuclear conflict would result in such an orgy of irrationality and destruction, it was difficult to quarrel with McNamara that a future of ever increasing nuclear armaments was hideous to contemplate. However, as he himself admitted, "until we can find a safe and sure road to disarmament, we must continue to build our own defenses."[2]

The adamant refusal of the Soviet Union to consider any realistic measures of inspected disarmament did not, however, mean to McNamara and his associates that the United States should construct its military power without regard to restraints. They took much to heart the idea that arms control was in many ways as important as disarmament. John T. McNaughton, an Assistant Secretary and formerly Deputy Assistant Secretary of Defense for Arms Control, on one occasion explained in some detail the Department's philosophy and policy in this respect. He challenged the assumption "that any U.S. gain in security necessarily implies a concomitant Soviet loss. This assumption," according to McNaughton, "is wrong."

Indeed, it may be that the one distinguishing characteristic of all "arms control" measures . . . is that of a design to achieve *mutual* improvement of security.

Another popular assumption is that all arms control measures—measures with the characteristic just described—must be negotiated. This too is wrong. The feature of enhancing simultaneously the security of both sides characterizes a multiplicity of measures running across the spectrum from negotiated disarmament agreements, through reciprocal initiatives and through unilateral acts which involve only rational adjustment by the other side, to purely unilateral measures involving no reciprocation or adjustment by any other country.

Until quite recently, relatively little attention was paid to the possibility of mutual improvement of security through use of non-negotiated techniques. Yet, not only are decisions in this area of crucial importance to our national security, but they are being made

today and every day, to a large extent by the Defense Department
in the fields of strategic doctrine, force structure, and research and
development.[3]

McNaughton argued that, while the United States and the
Soviet Union have great conflicts of interest, each no doubt de-
sires to avoid "the eruption, escalation or prolongation of nuclear war by accident or miscalculation." He described three
kinds of unilateral arms restraints designed to reduce these
dangers:

First, those designed to prevent war "by accident"—through an
unauthorized or unintended firing of a nuclear weapon.

Second, those designed to prevent war "by miscalculation"—
through lack of time or absence of doctrine to permit deliberate,
controlled response, especially in crises.

And third, those designed to reduce the damage should a war
occur—for example, by building firebreaks against escalation of
conflict, by pursuing a strategy which is anti-military rather than
anti-population, and by ensuring that the power to stop a war is
preserved.[4]

The explosion of a nuclear device by accident, McNaughton
pointed out, could conceivably trigger a nuclear exchange.
He described what had been done to reduce the probability of
such a dangerous event.

On the administrative side, only the President may authorize the
use of atomic or hydrogen weapons. And the devolution of this authority is carefully controlled.

There is also the so-called "two-man rule" which requires at least
two responsible individuals to be present at every level of operation or handling of nuclear weapons. When a weapon is in storage,
at least two men stand guard. If a message is given to use the
weapon, at least two men verify its authenticity. In order to arm or
fuse a bomb so that it will go off, independent but necessary actions
are assigned to at least two different men. No one man, even a
commanding officer, is authorized to depart from this rule. And
the men who handle these weapons are very carefully screened in
the first instance and rescreened periodically thereafter. In this connection, Deputy Secretary Gilpatric [has] signed two directives

tightening rules regarding storing and transporting nuclear weapons and regarding traits of personnel who may not have access to them.

Another administrative measure, one which has recently been publicized—quite inaccurately, I might note—by a best-selling novel, is the so-called "fail-safe" procedure which in essence precludes SAC planes from proceeding beyond a predetermined point without an explicit "go" order, an order which must come from the highest authority and which cannot be triggered by some mechanical failure. It is designed to permit an enhanced retaliatory capability without any corresponding increase in the danger of accidental war.[5]

In addition to these administrative restraints, physical safeguards had been devised to prevent accidents.

On the physical side, there are various devices built into the weapons themselves which prevent improper use. For example, there may be an arming switch which can be tampered with only by disassembling (and therefore by disarming) the weapon and which can be activated only by remote control or by the insertion of a "key" held in careful custody. Also, there is the simple device of making the required arming actions too much for one man to handle. It would take an octopus, and one with a 20-foot reach, to ready a one-man fighter-bomber for armed take-off. Barricades on the field provide additional safeguards against unauthorized use. As for missiles, the critical power supply for the "button" may be provided—in this age of automation—by a man in a distant corner turning a hand crank not unlike the one used on an ice cream freezer. There are many other similar devices.

Devices functionally similar to those just mentioned prevent the accidental explosion of a nuclear weapon. It is difficult to set off a nuclear weapon; several things have to happen in the proper sequence, and finally a set of electrical signals—not one but a certain pattern—has to reach the explosive part of the warhead with split-second timing. Everything has to be done just the way the designers planned, or there will be no nuclear explosion. A bomb accidentally dropped from an airplane, burned in a fire, or even hit by lightning would not go off. It is designed so that, at most, the high explosive part might go off, producing the effect of a World War II bomb.

There are, then, a wide array of administrative and physical restraints on a nuclear firing by accident or violation of authority.[6]

Another type of unilateral arms control discussed by Mc-Naughton involved the adoption of methods for preventing a mistake in the decision-making process. As McNaughton defined the problem:

The classic means for preventing grave errors of judgment is to go cautiously, to take adequate time for decision. But inherent in the age of rocket warfare is the fact that one cannot count on having time. Strategic weapons today can travel as far in a minute as they could in World War II in an hour. And as important as their speed is their power. Unlike any pre-atomic strategic weapons, they have the capability of determining a war's conclusion at its outset unless the opposing nuclear force is to some extent invulnerable.

What if our radar shows unidentified objects approaching over the Pole? Or what if our detectors indicate one or two nuclear explosions in the Midwest? The fear of a surprise attack, the knowledge that avoiding it might spell national survival, could dominate decisions on how to respond to ambiguous information.

If time is permitted to be of the essence, this kind of fear can be reflected back and forth like images in a room of mirrors. If one side knows that the other side may have reason to react hastily and has forces capable of inflicting severe damage on his strategic capability, the first side will itself become super-alert and prone to just the same kind of over-fast reaction it anticipates from the other side. This in turn will cause the other side to tighten its grip on the trigger. And so on.

The only way to break this cycle of "reciprocal fear of surprise attack" is to move to a situation where *at least one side has time*— that is, a situation where, for one side at least, an enemy first strike will not be decisive. This means assuring that retaliatory forces, even if caught with little or no warning, will survive the attack.[7]

McNaughton advised that the key word here was "survivability." If survivability could be obtained, then there would be time. And that, of course, was what the United States was purchasing for its strategic forces.

Its reliance is shifting away from bombers on the ground protected only by substantial warning, and from missiles in known,
exposed locations. It is shifting partly to bombers on ground or air
alert under positive control, but mainly to missiles that are widely
dispersed and hardened underground or effectively concealed by
means of continuous mobility. The coming generation of land-based
missiles, the Minuteman, will be emplaced individually in underground silos widely separated from each other. . . . An attacker
would have to use at least one of his missiles to destroy one Minuteman and it is calculated that he would have to allot more than one
of his missiles to each Minuteman to have any confidence that he
had achieved his mission. Submarine-based missiles also serve to
reduce or eliminate the advantage of an enemy strike. There now
are nine Polaris-bearing submarines in service [at the end of 1962],
each carrying sixteen missiles. Five additional submarines have been
launched but are not yet commissioned. Construction will continue
at the approximate rate of one per month until a total of 41 are
deployed with the fleet. An attacker would have a most difficult
time tracking down and destroying more than a few such submarines before the missiles from the other submarines could strike
back.

The net result . . . is that at present and in the foreseeable
future the United States can be confident that its forces will ride
out any attack. The attacker could be sure that the response of the
United States would be swift, but not so swift that the President
would lack time to evaluate the attack and match the United States
response to the factual situation. A potential enemy need not fear
the fears of the United States, and the United States need not fear
that he fears its fears; so one side need not be under compulsion
to attack the other whenever the situation becomes confused.[8]

Time, however, would have no value unless a directing brain
could use it appropriately. This meant, in McNaughton's words,

preservation of the chain of command, from the President down to
the forces in the field. The demands on the command system have
multiplied with the dangers of the nuclear age.

In view of the speed with which situations may develop, a 24-
hour-a-day capability to respond is required. There must be continuous provision for virtually instantaneous communication be-

tween the President, as Commander-in-Chief, and the military commands, and from commanders to forces.

The ambiguous evidence of attack with which the United States might be confronted poses an additional challenge, which can be met only by a command and control system possessing great flexibility, and the ability to assemble, evaluate and utilize accurate and complex information.

In addition, the command and control system must be capable of coping with the kind of accidents described earlier, and also with potential enemy attack, coordinated or uncoordinated. In military jargon, it must have great "redundancy." What this means is that the system requires multiple "brains" and multiple "nervous systems" in case one or another set of facilities is lost.

The Defense Department and the rest of the Government have been giving top priority to meeting these requirements. The steps being taken have two purposes. One, which is familiar, is to assure that United States forces can react instantly and properly when called upon—that is, to assure that they can be used if and when they are supposed to be used. The other purpose of the new command and control measures, and this is the point especially relevant here, is to guarantee that those forces will *not* be used when they are *not* supposed to be used. One small example of the kinds of things that are and can be done is the Strategic Air Command's airborne command and control system. In operation since 1961, the "Airborne Command Post" uses specially modified aircraft which maintain continuous contact with the National Military Command Center and Air Force Command Post in Washington and the Strategic Air Command's underground and alternate command and control network.[9]

McNaughton had already suggested that arms control did not necessarily end when war began. Now he emphasized that many of the techniques used to prevent war could also be important in the termination of a war and possibly in keeping a nuclear conflict from becoming completely apocalyptic.

Steps which the United States is taking in the command and control field to assure that war does not *start* by miscalculation have already been described. These same measures are designed to assure that a war does not *continue* by miscalculation. They are designed to assure that United States forces can be used or not used, as the case may be, in a controlled and deliberate way, subject at all times to the direction of the highest civilian authority.

Such flexibility means that the United States will not be faced with "all or nothing" decisions. Though it will be capable of an all-out attack, the nation will have a much wider choice, so that it can pick the strategy which is best for the United States and not just worst for the enemy. And, perhaps most important, command and control flexibility means that there will be a way to stop a war before all the destruction of which both sides are capable has been wrought.[10]

At the time McNaughton was reporting, the "hot line" for emergency communications between the White House and the Kremlin had not been agreed to or installed. Furthermore, it did not fall into the class of unilateral measures of arms control he was discussing. Another measure, somewhat more surprisingly but quite logically, did. If arms control extended into war itself and included the objective of limiting damage, then, said McNaughton, that raised the question of targets in a thermonuclear conflict. Targets, in turn, led him to a discussion of the controlled response strategy from the standpoint of arms control.

The first interest of the United States Government is the protection of people. It can and must ensure that they will not be the incidental victims of a strike intended not for them but rather for Western strategic forces. Two major efforts are being made to prevent such incidental destruction of population. A third effort is directed toward protecting people from being the intentional victims of a nuclear strike.

The first effort is to separate geographically our military forces from our cities. This is being done. Of the most effective United States deterrent systems, one—Minuteman—will be dispersed through less densely settled areas, and another—Polaris—will be at sea.

The second effort is civil defense. The President has proposed a civil defense program capable of saving tens of millions of people from death caused by fallout if there should be a war.

Of course, these two efforts do not prevent an unfriendly power from deliberately targeting cities, but they are consistent with the third United States effort—to provide itself with a "city-avoidance" targeting option and with a reserve of protected firepower and the targeting flexibility required to give an enemy a strong incentive to avoid striking the cities of the Free World.[11]

McNaughton recognized that this rather novel connection of arms control with the strategy of controlled response would stir up controversy. In fact, he acknowledged that the strategy had already been attacked by some of the most dedicated supporters of arms control and disarmament. This, he thought, was primarily because of the prevalence of two beliefs,

one fallacious, the other questionable. First, there is the assertion that "city-avoidance" must equal "disarming first strike." This is wrong. The United States does not think in terms of hitting first. The "city-avoidance" strategy is no more nor less than an affirmation that, whatever other targets may be available and whoever initiates the use of nuclear weapons, the United States will be in a position to refrain from attacking cities. But it will have in reserve sufficient weapons and it will have the targeting flexibility to destroy enemy cities if the enemy strikes cities first.

The second principal criticism which has been raised is that this targeting strategy makes nuclear war more likely by reducing the expected damage, and so is contrary to the objectives of both arms control and deterrence. But is this so? Who really knows? Uncertainties probably dominate the calculations. The resulting damage under any strategy would be so great that nuclear war would be elected only in the case of the most extreme provocation.[12]

The refutation of the second criticism could have been put even more strongly. But McNaughton went on to argue the value of the strategy from the standpoint of arms control.

The open declaration of a "city-avoidance" option (as compared with mere secret preparations for "city-avoidance") is, in a sense, notice served. It is a notice in accordance with which an enemy may well expect the United States to behave in case war is forced upon us. The purpose of making the declaration is not to solicit an "agreement" to rules of nuclear war. It is rather to be sure that a potential enemy is aware of the new choice it has. If it values the lives of its citizens, it should take steps to create for itself a targeting option to spare the cities of its enemies.

One should not attribute too much to this strategy, however. Nor should one spin out its implications too far. Nothing can be certain or even highly probable in this dark area. The Soviets may not reason as we think they do. And reason may not prevail in times of high crisis. The main point is that the United States must have a strategy of one kind or another with respect to targeting cities, and the "city-avoidance" strategy appears to be a move in the right direction—a move which could reduce the damage should war occur. It is an arms restraint the success of which does not depend upon negotiation in the normal sense and one which incidentally stands to benefit both sides.[13]

There were a number of other areas which McNaughton chose not to discuss in any detail. For example, he did not try to explain the rationale underlying the American drive for more non-nuclear power. But he did point out that the policy was designed to fill an important gap in the spectrum of deterrence, and that it might well reduce both the risk of war and the risk of escalation if war should somehow start—which, after all, reflected the objectives of arms control even though it involved an increase rather than a reduction of arms. His main point was that military decisions could be and were being made with arms restraint very much in mind. As he put the problem, "It no longer suffices, if it ever did, simply to 'get there fustest with the mostest.'" In fact, there were some ways "in which 'getting there' too early or with too much" might run directly counter to the national interest.

We must, in every decision we make, concern ourselves with the factors of stability and of the dynamic effect on the arms race. This is so whether the decision lies in the area of strategic doctrine, force structure or research and development. That is, when faced with the need to make decisions in any of those three key areas, we should have two questions in mind:

How will the action affect stability—stability against technological surprise, against accidents and unexpected or misleading events, against a tendency for every confrontation to spiral upward in violence?

And, how will the decision contribute to either quickening or dampening the arms race over time—will it lead to added destructive capability in the world, to our material impoverishment, to the distortion of our way of life? And in this connection, the remark made by the President . . . is pertinent: "There is just a limit to how much we need as well as how much we can afford to have a successful deterrent. . . ."

In answering these questions, one should have no illusions about the future. Certainly the Free World faces a continuing "elbowing" process perpetuated chiefly by the countries that are dedicated to revising the world to their own image. Even if disarmament is achieved, the "elbowing" will continue at the non- and sub-military level among nations fully capable of rearming on short but varying lead times.

The question is how to "elbow" through the "elbowing" crowd with sufficient protection of the interests of the Free World.

Until general and complete disarmament is achieved, there will be no foolproof way of preventing nuclear war if vital interests are to be protected. But there are many things that can be done to reduce the various risks. Many of these things are in the field of restraints, or wise management of one's own armed forces.

The United States is adopting measures which assure that its military might will be intelligently composed and controlled. We can hope that the Soviet Union is prepared to adopt similar measures for its own security and the security of the world.[14]

No doubt McNamara shared this philosophy. And on several occasions he showed a comparable interest in the kind of controls that McNaughton had discussed. On the subject of nuclear proliferation, for example, he held very strong views indeed. As he told a press conference shortly after his much-publicized Ann Arbor speech:

The points I emphasized in Ann Arbor included the point that weak nuclear forces operating individually under the control of a single nation were dangerous, obsolete, and costly. It has been the policy of this government, and will continue to be the policy, to deter the proliferation of national nuclear forces. That was the major point I emphasized at Ann Arbor.[15]

He could see nothing but trouble growing out of an expansion of the nuclear club. One way or another he wanted to exercise that kind of arms control. Like McNaughton, he also looked upon powerful and protected nuclear capabilities as conducive to restraint. As he informed Stewart Alsop:

Because we have a sure second-strike capability, there is no pressure on us whatsoever to preempt. I assure you that we really never think in those terms. Under any circumstances, even if we had the military advantage of striking first, the price of any nuclear war would be terribly high. One point I was making in the Ann Arbor speech is that our second-strike capability is so sure that there would be no rational basis on which to launch a preemptive strike.[16]

In fact, McNamara went even one step further and seemed to indicate a preference for a somewhat comparable capability in the Soviet Union. His reasoning on this point was intriguing. Again, he told Alsop:

I believe myself that a counterforce strategy is most likely to apply in circumstances in which *both* sides have the capability of surviving a first strike and retaliating selectively. This is a highly unpredictable business, of course. But today, following a surprise attack on us, we would still have the power to respond with over-whelming force, and they would not then have the capability of a further strike. In this situation, given the highly irrational act of an attempted first strike against us, such a strike seems most likely to take the form of an all-out attack on both military targets and population centers. This is why a nuclear exchange confined to military targets seems more possible, not less, when *both* sides have a sure second-strike capability. Then you might have a more stable "balance of terror." This may seem a rather subtle point, but from where I'm sitting it seems a point worth thinking about.[17]

By this reasoning, the cause of arms control, broadly defined, would be more advanced if the Soviets acquired a stronger and better protected strategic nuclear capability than McNamara apparently thought they had in 1962. Still, even this kind of possibility was not exactly heart-warming, and McNamara remained an eager seeker for ways of bringing the nuclear competition under a greater degree of more formal control. When the Soviets broke the nuclear test ban moratorium in the autumn of 1961, he was in the forefront of those urging the President to resume American nuclear tests. His responsibilities as Secretary of Defense could not permit him to do otherwise. But he remained steadfast in his belief that a properly inspected test ban would work to the advantage of the United States as well as the Soviet Union and he consistently advised Congressional committees to that effect. His reasons became apparent in the statement supporting the limited test ban treaty which he presented to the Senate Foreign Relations Committee on August 13, 1963.

McNamara began his comprehensive defense of what he called "the three-environment nuclear test ban" (in the atmosphere, underwater, and in outer space) by describing the military context in which the treaty would take effect.

In reporting to the Armed Services Committee in January, 1962, I said that "there is no question but that today our strategic retaliatory forces are fully capable of destroying the Soviet target system, even after absorbing an initial surprise attack." Earlier this year I was able to report to that committee that "allowing for losses from an initial enemy attack and attrition en route to target, we calculate that our forces today could still destroy the Soviet Union without any help from the deployed tactical air units or carrier task forces or Thor or Jupiter IRBM's."

The sum of these statements is that the United States has nuclear superiority. We are determined to maintain that superiority. In order to achieve it, we maintain a total number of nuclear warheads, tactical as well as strategic, in the tens of thousands. There have been very substantial increases in our nuclear forces over the last five years, and further substantial increases are programmed. In the past 24 months alone, there has been:

A 100 per cent increase in the number of nuclear warheads in the strategic alert forces;

A 60 per cent increase in the tactical nuclear forces deployed in Western Europe.

During that period the megatonnage of our strategic alert forces has been more than doubled and during the next 24 months it will be further increased. At the same time, during the past 24 months there has been:

A 45 per cent increase in the number of combat-ready Army divisions;

A 30 per cent increase in the number of tactical air squadrons;

A 30 per cent increase in airlift capability;

A 100 per cent increase in ship construction and conversion to modernize the fleet;

A 200 per cent increase in the special forces trained to deal with counterinsurgency threats.

I regard as essential to our national security the maintenance of a military posture such that we can absorb any initial surprise attack and strike back with sufficient power to destroy the aggressor. My assessment of the proposed treaty is made from that point of view—from the point of view of what is best for the security of the United States.[18]

Since Secretary of State Rusk had already testified to the political implications of the treaty, McNamara focused on its military benefits and risks. His first concern was with the effects of the treaty on the military balance between the United States and the Soviet Union. How, in particular, would it change the problem of maintaining American nuclear superiority?

Any examination of the direct effects of the treaty on the military balance must contain an appraisal of the existing technological and military capabilities of the United States and the U.S.S.R. And the examination must assess the direction in which the military balance is likely to move on the two alternative roads open to us. That is, the examination must compare the situation of unrestricted testing in all environments with the situation under the test ban—with testing restricted to the underground environment.

I shall start with a comparison of the capabilities of the United States and U.S.S.R. in the field of nuclear technology to put the question of the military balance in proper perspective.

The most commonly used standard for comparing technological

capabilities is yield-to-weight ratios. This is not the only relevant criterion, but it is the one concerning which we possess the most information. By this standard, the Soviet Union appears to be technologically more advanced than we are in the high-yield range, in the tens of megatons; below that yield, the relative capability shifts progressively in favor of the United States. Below a few megatons, the United States appears to be clearly superior in yield-to-weight ratios.

With respect to the very light weights, suitable primarily for tactical purposes, Soviet yield-to-weight ratios are a less accurate measure of relative capability. In this area the United States has performed many more tests; and such analysis as has been made indicates that the United States has superior quality weapons.

The apparent Soviet technological advantage at the upper end of the yield spectrum has resulted from a considered decision by the United States not to concentrate effort in this field, as I shall discuss in detail a little later.

The United States advantage in the low and intermediate part of the yield spectrum is in my judgment a very important advantage. Our high yield-to-weight ratio in the relevant range has facilitated the development of more powerful warheads for Minuteman and Polaris without concomitant increase in vehicle size or decrease in range. It is because of this that the United States has had the advantage over the Soviets of being able to deploy large numbers of hardened and dispersed Minuteman missiles and a large number of long-range sub-launched Polaris missiles. And United States superiority in the lower ranges facilitates further development of relatively small warheads which would be used to assure penetration by saturation of sophisticated and very elaborate ballistic missile defenses.[19]

The picture presented by McNamara thus was one of greater versatility in the American than in the Soviet nuclear arsenal. It was also a picture of a much larger American arsenal. But the size and composition of the nuclear stockpile does not by itself determine the balance of military power in this sinister realm. McNamara pointed out as much.

The purely military aspects of the strategic balance of course include many factors in addition to the exact state of nuclear technology. . . . These other factors include the numbers of weapons and their accuracy; the variety of systems; their dispersal, mobility and hardening; decoy and salvo techniques; and the possible deployment, in the future, of an antiballistic missile system.

The net of the relevant factors is that the United States nuclear force is manifestly superior to the Soviet Union's.

The United States force now contains more than 500 missiles— Atlas, Titan, Minuteman, Polaris—and is planned to increase to over 1,700 by 1966.

In addition, the United States has S.A.C. bombers on air-alert and over 500 S.A.C. bombers on quick-reaction alert. By comparison, the consensus is that today the Soviets could place less than half as many bombers over North America on a first strike; the Soviets are estimated to have today only a fraction of as many ICBM missiles; and their sub-launched ballistic missiles are short-range, require surface launch and generally are not comparable to our Polaris force. Between now and 1966, it is estimated that our ballistic missile numerical superiority will increase both absolutely and relatively.

Further, the United States at present has in stockpile or planned for stockpile a large number of nuclear explosives for tactical purposes. These weapons are planned for employment on the battlefield, in anti-submarine warfare, and against aircraft; they consist of warheads for artillery, battlefield missiles, demolition munitions, bombs, depth charges, air-to-air missiles and surface-to-air missiles. The yield spectrum associated with these weapons extends from the subkiloton range to hundreds of kilotons. The consensus is that the United States is presently superior in design, diversity and numbers in this class of weapons.

That is the very general picture. It is the picture of existing and continuing United States nuclear superiority.[20]

The question to which McNamara now addressed himself was how this relatively favorable situation would be affected by the limited test ban. His immediate reply was concise.

I can say that most of the factors will not be affected at all— not accuracy of missiles, not variety of systems, not their dispersal or mobility, and not numbers. There are four areas, however, which deserve special attention. I want now to narrow my focus and discuss in detail the four aspects of the strategic balance which have been of particular concern. They are:

> very large yield weapons;
> missile-site survivability;
> anti-ballistic missile defense;
> missile penetrability.[21]

The controversy about the desirability of the test ban centered on these four areas, and McNamara felt obliged to express a judgment as to whether a cessation of tests in the atmosphere would, first, put the United States at a disadvantage in these areas relative to the Soviet Union; and second, affect adversely the over-all balance of nuclear power. His analysis went into considerable detail.

In the area of very large yield weapons the Soviets appear now to have some advantage in the area of nuclear technology. They have demonstrated a device of 60 megatons which we believe could be weaponized at about 100 megatons. As an aircraft-carried bomb, the Soviets' scaled-up 100-megaton weapon would be suitable only for vulnerable high-altitude or suicide low-level delivery. The Soviets probably have no missile at this time which will deliver a 100-megaton warhead to ICBM ranges, although even under a test ban, the Soviets could elect to develop such a missile.

The United States, without any further testing, can develop a warhead with a yield of 50 to 60 megatons for B-52 delivery.

With testing in the atmosphere the United States could improve considerably our yield-to-weight ratios for very large yield weapons. Some experts believe that almost no significant improvements in the technology of these weapons can be made by testing underground. Others have concluded that by testing at yields of about one megaton underground, some improvement in high-yield weapons design could be achieved and that new warheads—for example, a 35-megaton warhead for our Titan II—could be developed and stockpiled with confidence that they would work.

But the question is, and has been for some time: Is there a military advantage to the United States in deployment of very high-yield weapons? For some years we have examined this question.

One possible use of the very high-yield weapons would be to

deliver them by missile and detonate them at altitudes of 100,000 feet and above, presumably over cities. Detonation at such altitudes could cause significant thermal damage—fire—over hundreds of square miles. But a better way to achieve even greater destruction, and a way which is within the present United States capabilities, is to divide the attack among several smaller weapons so as to saturate any defenses.

Another potential mission for the very high-yield weapons might be to use them to strike very hard underground targets. As for this mission, the judgment is that, except for command posts placed thousands of feet deep in rock, the objective can be achieved at least as well by the expenditure of larger numbers of smaller weapons. In any case, it seems agreed that command posts can be constructed at sufficiently great depths to preclude their destruction even by surface detonation of 100-megaton bombs. Vulnerability of command and control locations can also be reduced by the use of alternate mobile, airborne command posts. The United States already has such posts in operation.

As a result of our consideration of these very high-yield weapons, we have concluded that there are two military disadvantages to deploying them as contrasted with deploying a larger number of smaller weapons. First, our studies indicate that for most missions directed at military targets, we can achieve a higher confidence of kill by using two or three smaller weapons instead of one very large one; for a given resource input we achieve higher target destruction with our smaller systems. Second, very high-yield warheads are relatively inferior as second-strike, retaliation weapons; it is much more difficult and costly to make them survivable—to harden, camouflage or make mobile the huge missiles required to deliver these weapons.

I point out, therefore, that no consensus has even been formed with regard to the wisdom of a 100-megaton versus a 50-megaton bomb. I could not predict with any confidence whether we would make a significant investment in the larger bomb even in the absence of the proposed treaty.

But I can state with full confidence that the absence from our arsenal of a bomb greater than the one we can build under the treaty will not impair the effectiveness of our strategic forces.[22]

Since the Soviets had already tested a nuclear device yielding approximately sixty megatons, scientists and military leaders were concerned that the Soviets might have discovered certain weapons effects that would increase the vulnerability of American retaliatory forces. McNamara addressed these concerns under the heading of missile-site survivability. He explained that the American strategic missile force was designed to survive, and, he asserted, "it will survive."

Our missile force is deployed so as to assure that under any conceivable Soviet first strike, a substantial portion of it would remain in firing condition. Most of the land-based portion of the force has been hardened, as well as dispersed. Minuteman silos are designed to withstand thermal and pressure effects and ground-motion effects of typical Soviet weapons detonated at relatively close distances. The Minuteman control posts are protected by extreme hardening. In addition, we have duplicative facilities which will in the future include the capability of launching each individual Minuteman by a signal from airborne control posts.

Large yield nuclear tests in the atmosphere, on or near the ground, would help us to determine with greater precision the degree of hardness of Minuteman sites. However, we believe the Soviets have conducted no such tests. We can achieve, by underground tests of substantial yields, a significant reduction in certain existing uncertainties. And, it must be remembered that the United States has already had considerable experience with low-yield surface and near-surface detonations which have been used to study the effects of surface bursts on hardened structures such as missile sites.

So the United States now has a substantial amount of information in this area of hardened missile-site vulnerability. Our knowledge of the Soviet testing program leads us to believe that their uncertainties are at least as great as ours. Uncertainties of this kind, and others—into which we must count uncertainties about the accuracy of Soviet missiles—will continue to be compensated for by conservative designs, wide dispersal and large quantities of missiles.

Furthermore, the most pessimistic view of these uncertainties suggests a vulnerability ratio for our hardened, dispersed Minuteman sites of less than two sites killed on the average by a single very large-yield Soviet missile. It is clear that the Soviets do not have anything like the number of missiles necessary to knock out the Minuteman force, nor do they appear to have any present plans to acquire such a capacity. If they were to undertake the construction and deployment of a large number of very high-yield missiles, we would probably have knowledge of this and would have ample time to expand our Minuteman force or to disperse it more widely.

We know, and the Soviets know, that in the event of a surprise Soviet first strike, at least a substantial proportion of our Minuteman missiles will survive. Also, we and they know that the Polaris submarines at sea and many strategic aircraft will survive. We can say with assurance that even after such a Soviet strike, the total surviving United States strategic nuclear force will be large enough to destroy the enemy.[23]

A strategic nuclear force must not only have a diversified arsenal of weapons and be able to survive an enemy surprise attack; it must also be able to counterattack, penetrate enemy defenses, and destroy its designated target system. Otherwise it is not an effective deterrent. McNamara had argued that the test ban treaty would not limit the ability of the United States to satisfy the first two requirements. But what about the problem of penetration? McNamara now had to deal with the role of the antiballistic missile (or ABM) in preventing penetration. As he put it, "Interception and penetration are opposite sides of the same coin." If an effective ABM were feasible, and if its effectiveness depended critically on nuclear information available to the Soviet Union, but not the United States, then the case against the test ban would be strong. McNamara faced this issue, first, by explaining the nature of the antiballistic missile system.

An ABM system consists of several types of radars, the interceptor missile and the very complex computing equipment at a ground station to control the radars and to direct the interceptor missile. The various radars serve to detect incoming objects in space, to distinguish the incoming warhead from other objects in nearby space, to track the incoming warhead, and to track and control the interceptor missile, which is targeted on the incoming warhead by the computing equipment.

In designing an antiballistic missile system, the major factors are reaction speed, missile performance, traffic handling capacity, capacity for decoy discrimination, resistance to blackout effects, and warhead technology.

The last two of these depend on nuclear testing.[24]

In other words, only a small part of the solution to the ABM problem turned on information about nuclear weapons and their myriad effects. How, in McNamara's view, did the United States stand in regard to this kind of information?

With respect to warhead technology, the United States now has the capability, without further testing, to weaponize a variety of possible ABM warheads, including those within the yield range desired by the designers of the Nike-X system [an advance over the Army's Nike-Zeus]. These or larger warheads can be improved even further by underground testing under the treaty. The ABM system which we are now designing will provide us with a high confidence of achieving low-miss distances. The ABM warhead designs which we now have or can develop through underground testing will provide a high probability of killing Soviet warheads even if they incorporate advanced technology far beyond what now exists.

As for the blackout problem—and these observations, incidentally, apply to communications blackouts as well as to ABM radar blackouts—Soviet and United States experience appears to be comparable though not identical. By theoretical analysis of presently available data, we believe we can adequately predict effects over the range of yields and altitudes in which we are most interested. We will be able to design around the remaining uncertainties.

The best present judgment is that our design efforts are comparable in magnitude and success with those of the Soviets. Any deployed system which the Soviets are likely to have in the near future will probably not be as effective, almost certainly not more effective, than the Nike-Zeus. It should be noted that the United States decided not to deploy the Nike-Zeus because its effectiveness was inadequate.

One important point stands out in connection with the antiballistic missile: The ABM problem is dominated by factors un-related to the treaty—by reaction speed, missile performance, traffic handling capacity, and capacity for decoy discrimination. A fuller understanding of the blackout phenomenon—which would result from tests prohibited by the treaty—might at most permit some reduction in the number of ABM radars required at an ABM site.

Thus, with or without a test ban, we could proceed with the development of an ABM system.[25]

In short, if what McNamara argued about the development of the ABM was true, then the United States and the USSR stood on equal terms and the real issue concerned the proba-bility with which a modern ICBM could penetrate this kind of defense. McNamara explained the nature of the measures and countermeasures involved in the battle between the ICBM and the ABM.

Penetration of an enemy antiballistic missile system depends on the capability to destroy, disrupt or saturate the system. Current penetration philosophy concentrates on saturation, and is dominated by problems of decoy design and salvo techniques as well as of nuclear technology.

The problems of nuclear technology here relate to the vulner-ability of the ballistic missile warhead to kill by blast or by radia-tion. The latter vulnerability can but the former cannot, be fully tested underground. We have not, and we believe that the Soviet Union has not, explored by full-scale high-altitude tests the vulner-ability of re-entry vehicles to blast.

Atmospheric testing would enable us to confirm the enhanced resistance of new, hard warhead designs to blast. Without the con-firmation which dynamic tests of re-entry would provide, we will have to rely on extensive extrapolations, and therefore there will be greater uncertainties than would otherwise exist.

But regardless of the design of any Soviet ABM system, in view of the warhead improvements we can make under the treaty, of the massive United States force available to saturate their defenses, and of the array of penetration aids which are being developed and can continue to be developed and improved by underground testing where necessary, the United States will continue to have the capability—and the Soviets know that we continue to have the capability—to penetrate and to devastate the Soviet Union if a retaliatory blow is required.[26]

McNamara's judgment, in short, was that, even with the treaty, the United States could maintain the diversified capability necessary to survive an enemy's attack and penetrate his defenses. Which also meant being able to destroy his targets. Moreover, the treaty was a two-way street. As McNamara explained it:

In putting a net judgment on the direct military implications of the treaty on the military balance, we must bear in mind that the issue is not whether the United States alone should make, or give up, the progress in nuclear technology which is involved. We must remember, as we consider the progress open or closed to the United States in the various testing environments, that the Soviets will have the same opportunities open or closed to them. If testing continued indefinitely without limit as to test environment or size of yield, the most likely ultimate result would be technical parity between the United States and the U.S.S.R.

Except for the very high-yield weapons area (where, as I have pointed out, we have had no great interest) unlimited underground testing by both sides would also tend to produce technological parity. But, by limiting Soviet testing to the underground environment, where testing is more difficult and more expensive, and where the United States has substantially more experience, we can at least retard Soviet progress and prolong the duration of our technological superiority. A properly inspected comprehensive test ban would of course serve this purpose still better.

This prolongation of our technological superiority will be a principal direct military effect of the treaty on the future military balance. I believe it to be a significant one.[27]

The gradually wasting asset of superiority in nuclear technology would, by this analysis, decline more slowly with rather than without the treaty—assuming that the Soviets did not cheat. But opponents of the treaty had also raised this possibility, and so McNamara had to deal with the risk of illegal, clandestine tests.

Assessment of that risk required an examination of any advantages to be gained by the Soviet Union in clandestine testing in any of the three prohibited environments, and of the means available to the United States to detect and identify such tests. Our examination concluded that the Soviet Union could obtain no major results by testing in the atmosphere and deep space or underwater without incurring high risk of detection and identification.

Let me point out that the only advantages of illegal testing in the three prohibited environments would be either to develop weapons with yields in the multimegaton range (since designs for weapons with yields up to 10 megatons or more can be checked by lower yield tests underground) or to determine the weapons effects of explosions which cannot be carried out at all, or not so well underground. There will probably be no cost advantage to illegal testing in the prohibited environments because keeping the tests secret will add to the expense and difficulty of the experiments.

Multimegaton weapons developments tests would have to be conducted more than 20,000,000 miles from earth—80 times as far away as the moon—if they were to have a good chance of escaping detection by a ground-based system such as could be installed rapidly with the cooperation of Western and possibly some neutral nations. The United States on its own can deploy earth and solar satellite systems for detection of deep-space nuclear explosions; for the former, an earth satellite system, we have a first launch scheduled for September or October, this year [1963]. Such detection systems would offset attempts by a violator to "shield" his space tests from our detection devices or, if no attempt were made to shield the test, would force clandestine tests even of a megaton to distances in the hundreds of millions of miles. In addition to scientific detection and identification means, other intelligence resources can make significant contributions to the exposure of deep space tests.

While tests at extreme ranges are a technological possibility, they would involve years of preparation plus several months to a year of actual execution, and they could cost hundreds of millions of dollars per successful experiment.

Weapons-effects tests that require the presence of atmosphere to be ionized (to produce blackout) or which depend on the earth's magnetic field cannot be carried out in deep space. Effects of earth shock on hardened missile sites of course could not be measured in space. Other effects tests in connection with antiballistic missile defense could be measured in deep space; but they can also be measured underground.

I conclude that, as a practical matter, illegal clandestine testing in deep space is not a reasonable proposition for the Soviet Union, and, in any event, is one against which we can protect ourselves.

In the lower atmosphere, small tests above the surface of the Soviet Union will be detected even if their yields are in the low kiloton range.

In the upper atmosphere—say above six miles high—the principal purpose of clandestine tests would be for determining weapons effects. Effects tests in the upper atmosphere have been performed in the past with a very large amount of elaborate equipment and telemetry of the results. Such an operation, in addition to running a substantial risk of detection by geophysical means, is quite vulnerable to detection by conventional intelligence means and could probably not be chanced under a test ban.

Over the U.S.S.R. or Communist China only very low-yield tests, with quite limited objectives, could have a good chance of escaping discovery. These tests could not produce significant advantages.

In certain remote parts of the world such as the South Pacific, the threshold of evasion of geophysical detectors in the upper atmosphere will be somewhat higher and the chance of recovering a debris sample might be rather small. However, it is most unlikely that the Soviets will try to take advantage of this situation. An upper atmosphere test would be difficult to perform from shipboard and might require several vessels properly deployed around the test point. Preparations for such a test would be relatively easy to discover.

Measurements of effects of underwater nuclear explosions have not been as important as the measurements of the atmospheric effects because many of these measurements can be performed with high explosive charges. A violator might like to perform a nuclear test to determine over-all vulnerability of submarines and surface vessels with their associated electronic gear. Such a test would almost certainly be detected.

In summary, then, conduct of any potentially important clandestine test would clearly not be a simple, easily concealed, high-confidence operation. Therefore, looking at the problem from the Soviet side, there will always be the imponderable risk of detection through conventional intelligence in addition to the risk from the operations of the United States scientific detection and identification system. My scientific advisers believe that such tests might permit some reduction in A.B.M. system costs. But they would not make the difference between an effective and an ineffective system.[28]

Although the risk of successful clandestine testing might not seem high, there remained the problem of a surprise abrogation of the treaty. It was not easy to forget, after all, the way in which the Soviets had broken the test moratorium in 1961 with a large series of experiments, and the length of time it had taken the United States to ready its own program of atmospheric tests thereafter. Was it possible that the Soviets might suddenly denounce the treaty, ignore the three months' waiting period, and start testing in such a way as to obtain an important military advantage? McNamara acknowledged the risk of a surprise abrogation, but he did not foresee that any major military advantage would result from it.

The consensus is that the Soviets could not in a single series of tests, however carefully planned, achieve a significant or permanent lead in the strategic field, much less a "super-weapon" capable of neutralizing our deterrent force. Moreover, as long as (1) we maintain the vitality of our weapons laboratories and (2) we retain the administrative and logistic capabilities required to conduct a test series in any environment, the Soviets even with surprise will not be able to achieve a significant time advantage. Therefore, surprise abrogation does not pose a serious threat to our national security.

We will maintain the vitality of our weapons laboratories. We will continue to conduct a program of underground tests as necessary to meet our military requirements. As I stated earlier, practically the complete range of weapons development tests (with the exception of experiments with very high yields) and some weapons effects experiments can be carried out underground. This ongoing test program will also include tests designed to lay the foundation for a major atmospheric series to be conducted in case of Soviet abrogation.

The second requirement—to retain the administrative talent and other resources required for quick expansion of our test program into additional environments—can clearly be met if we have the necessary will. We have that will. We have the determination to retain a readiness to test in every relevant environment. This is a firm national policy. Its existence will not only render the risk of abrogation minimal, but will also constitute a strong deterrent to abrogation.[29]

In the light of these assurances, and McNamara's earlier judgment that the test ban would not affect the nuclear balance of power, an observer might well wonder why McNamara would regard the treaty as any measure of arms control at all. It would, presumably, halt the addition of further radioactive fallout to the atmosphere. It might slow somewhat the pace of nuclear technology. But the United States and the Soviet Union would still be free to test underground, to add to their nuclear stockpiles, and to work on the improvement of their nuclear capabilities virtually without restraint. That, indeed, was the burden of much of what McNamara had been saying. What, then, would change from the standpoint of arms control? McNamara came to this question as he related the treaty to the proliferation of nuclear weapons capabilities among other nations. As far as he was concerned, "the possibility of the further diffusion of nuclear weapons poses a severe threat to our national security."

Proliferation of nuclear weapons capability would:

1. Increase the likelihood of accidental detonation of a nuclear weapon;
2. Increase the risk of "small" nuclear wars which could catalyze a big one between the two great powers;
3. Cause important and destabilizing shifts in regional power balances.

At least eight countries, in addition to the four present nuclear powers, will be able to acquire at least a few nuclear weapons and a crude delivery capability—possibly including medium-range rockets during the next 10 years.

With testing limited to the underground environment, the potential cost of a nuclear weapons development program would increase sharply for all signatory states. And, since testing underground is not only more costly but also more difficult and time consuming, the proposed treaty would retard progress in weapons development in cases where the added cost and other factors were not sufficient to preclude it altogether. One of the great advantages of this treaty is that it will have this effect of retarding the spread of nuclear weapons.[30]

McNamara may yet prove to have been too optimistic in his expectation that the treaty would place great obstacles in the way of nations seeking nuclear weapons. France and Communist China have not adhered to it; other countries may proceed with nuclear programs even without testing; and it may yet become possible to acquire nuclear weapons without the trouble and expense of a great research effort. Nevertheless, the treaty represented a measure of nuclear restraint, however limited, and for that reason McNamara enthusiastically supported it. He explained his basic reasons to the Senate Committee on Foreign Relations.

In his inaugural address, the President made this plea to the peoples and leaders of the Soviet bloc and the Western alliance. He said, "Let us begin anew—remembering on both sides that civility is not a sign of weakness and sincerity is always subject to proof. Let us never negotiate out of fear. But let us never fear to negotiate."

For a long time, this proposal went unheeded behind the Iron Curtain. Negotiations were treated as exercises in propaganda. And by crude threat and subtle machination, the Soviets continued to explore for weakness in the capabilities and the will of the Western alliance. Meanwhile, we took the steps which I have described to assure that our arms were sufficient beyond doubt. We have created an enormous military force, powerful and flexible enough to guarantee our ability to deal with aggression under all contingencies.

And in Cuba, in Vietnam, in Berlin and elsewhere around the globe, we have demonstrated that our will matches our might.

Yet—and this is a key point—I cannot allege that the vast increase in our nuclear forces, accompanied as it was by large increases in Soviet nuclear stockpiles, has produced a comparable enhancement in our security. In terms of absolute numbers, we have gained more. But, as the President stated, "A full-scale nuclear exchange lasting less than 60 minutes, with the weapons now in existence, could wipe out more than 300,000,000 Americans, Europeans and Russians. . . ." It is clear that the absolute growth of Soviet capability to inflict damage on the United States has narrowed the range of contingencies in which our nuclear deterrent is credible.

The Soviet Union's acceptance of the United States proposal for a three-environment test ban offers some evidence that its leadership has at last grasped an essential fact—that the sheer multiplication of a nation's destructive nuclear capability does not necessarily produce a net increase in its security. The limited ban is, of course, only a beginning. It will not end the threat of nuclear war. It will not reduce the existing stockpiles of nuclear weapons. It will not halt the production of nuclear weapons. It will not prevent qualitative weapons improvement of many kinds. But it will retard the proliferation of nuclear weapons, a proliferation which would increase the risk of nuclear wars. And, probably more important than purely military implications, the treaty should provide us with an opportunity to test the sincerity of Soviet protestations about their desire to explore more sweeping arrangements for preserving the peace. It provides us with this opportunity at a minimum risk. For even if the Soviets fail to abide by this agreement and even under the doubtful contingency of Soviet testing in the prohibited environments without being detected, the United States will maintain its ability to survive a surprise attack with sufficient power to destroy the Soviet Union.

I do not pretend that this or any other agreement between great, contending powers can be risk-free. This one is not. I cannot guarantee that we will detect any single clandestine test the Soviets might attempt; but Soviet technical and military advisers cannot guarantee that we will not. I am convinced that even undetected clandestine tests will not alter the basic military balance.

Perhaps the most serious risk of this treaty is the risk of euphoria. We must guard against a condition of mind which allows us to become lax in our defenses. This agreement is a product of Western strength. Further progress in arms-control arrangements with the Soviet Union—progress which we all want to make—depends critically on the maintenance of that strength.

Thus, the risks under the treaty are either small or under our control, and the values of the treaty are substantial even if we consider only the military area. The scales are clearly tipped in favor of the treaty. . . . It has my unequivocal support.[31]

Although McNamara opposed uninspected agreements, he was reluctantly willing to accept a ban on the orbiting of nuclear weapons in space. In fact, Deputy Secretary Gilpatric had already announced in September, 1962, that "the United States has no program to place any weapons of mass destruction into orbit . . . such an action is just not a rational military strategy for either side for the foreseeable future."[32] The agreement in principle between the United States, the Soviet Union, and Great Britain in October, 1963, pledging to abstain from orbiting nuclear weapons in space, thus could be construed as yet another joint effort to remove a costly and dangerous area of competition from the East-West struggle. But the limited test ban and the understanding on orbiting nuclear weapons were indeed only a beginning. And, as McNamara had testified, they were a product of Western strength and determination. Sir Winston Churchill had advised the West that it must arm to parley; McNamara found the advice relevant to the prospects for arms control.

Whether further agreements to reduce and control the hazards of modern conflict would be forthcoming remained another one of the great uncertainties that had to dominate McNamara's calculations about strategic concepts, force structure, and budgets. Certainly he had no desire to close the door on arrangements that would enhance world security. But he remained committed to the view that additional progress in this direction would flow from American strength. While he had no

desire to aggravate the competition between East and West by
abrupt changes in the character and magnitude of American
military power, he recognized that arms control—broadly defined—might still require further increases in certain aspects
of Western capabilities. The approach of multiple options, with
continued emphasis on the non-nuclear end of the weapons
spectrum, left the country with the kind of flexibility that it
needed in the face of all the uncertainties. Not only did it offer
the President usable power—and therefore deterrent power
—in the event of future crises; it also permitted him greater
initiatives in the field of arms control. The more the power of
the United States rested on diversified capabilities, the easier
it would be to reach agreements on measures of arms control
without running the risk of immobilizing needed American
strength. And the larger the number of options, the smaller the
chance that, in the event of conflict, the catastrophe of general
nuclear war would ensue.

Short-run considerations as well as the long view thus continued to impel McNamara in the direction of multiple options
and controlled response. They also sent him on an unending
search for efficiency of choice and expenditure within the military establishment. The cost of multiple options ran high. To
achieve the appropriate balance of forces and the necessary
levels of combat effectiveness at minimum cost to the nation
required more than the establishment of clear-cut strategic
objectives. They obliged McNamara to find new ways of coming to grips with the policy-making process in the Pentagon.

CHAPTER 5

Cost and Effectiveness

THE PENTAGON symbolizes the American defense establishment in several important ways. It is enormous, with 7,000 offices, 150 staircases, 17½ miles of corridors, a shopping center, and more than 25,000 daily inhabitants. It is the product of a long and stormy evolution; within its walls four Services with a heritage of proud and independent traditions go about the uneasy business of coexistence, collaboration, and competition. It is also the center of that bewildering network of activities necessary to the functioning of a great military machine under the exigent conditions of the cold war. The responsibilities of the Pentagon are staggering by any measure. Its annual payroll alone amounts to $20 billion for 2.7 million active duty military personnel, supported by about a million civilians in the United States and approximately a quarter of a million overseas. It spends something like $35 billion a year on a wide variety of goods and services—aircraft, missiles, tanks, spare parts, food, clothing, construction, and utilities. It draws upon virtually every segment of the American economy and uses well over half of the nation's research and development capacity. Its world-wide operations involve it in the annual expenditure of almost $3 billion in other countries—to the understandable pain of those who must struggle with the deficit in the American balance of payments. Yet all this expenditure and activity has but one outstanding purpose: the production of usable and effective combat power sufficient to the maintenance of the nation's vital interests.

Two of the Pentagon's activities are central to this purpose. The first is the budget cycle, a year-round process which culminates each December in a statement of the defense establishment's requirements in money and forces. The budget, in effect, states the defense policy of the United States. Or, as McNamara has put it: "I equate planning and budgeting and consider the terms almost synonymous, the budget being simply a quantitative expression of the operating plans."[1] The other central activity, at least in peacetime, is the expenditure of the appropriated funds for the procurement and maintenance of the needed combat power.

The performance of these functions looks deceptively simple. The actuality, as the Eisenhower Administration discovered, is quite different. The problem lies not so much in drawing up a budget or in disbursing resources. Rather it rests in the process of relating basic strategic concepts to forces and budgets, and in seeing that funds are spent in the most economical way commensurate with the objectives. Despite those who believe in determining the budget first, or the requirements first, what we can actually do in the field of deterrence and defense depends very much on how much we are willing to spend. Similarly, how much we are willing to spend may well depend, among other things, on the type and level of military effectiveness that we can achieve with additional increments of resources. And exactly how we spend the available resources will determine the amount of combat power that we actually acquire. The ability to reduce the costs of procuring a needed item of equipment can mean either an increase in the amount of equipment purchased or a reallocation of resources to the achievement of other important objectives. Cost and effectiveness thus are intimately related.

The determination of budgetary needs and the achievement

of efficiency in the expenditure of resources for the requisite
types of military capabilities is an intrinsically difficult task. It
has been complicated in the Pentagon by several important
conditions. Although the sheer magnitude of the defense organization cries out for decentralized decision-making and
management, Service traditions and rivalries make a large
measure of decentralization in budgetary and disbursement
practices very difficult indeed. The problem is complicated still
further by the fact that neither the Services nor the unified
and specified commands embody distinct and noncompetitive
combat functions. Each has claims which are related in important ways to those of the others. These competing claims
have become greatly magnified with the impact of a rapidly
changing technology on the weapon systems of the Services.
Thus, to take a familiar example, the Polaris submarine with its
sixteen ballistic missiles, a Navy system, can perform the same
function as the Air Force's Minuteman missile in its protected
silo. How much to purchase of each is in itself a hard decision;
its difficulty is not reduced by rivalries between the Air Force
and the Navy. Nor can the problem be satisfactorily resolved
by letting each Service decide independently the procurement
policies for its preferred systems. That road is bound to lead
to great redundancies in some types of capabilities and serious
shortages in other categories. An over-all view and centralized
responsibility is required for this kind of decision.

The Eisenhower system of budgeting did not embody these
essential characteristics. According to Alain Enthoven, Deputy
Assistant Secretary of Defense for Systems Analysis:

It had several important defects, perhaps the most important of
which was the almost complete separation between planning and
decision-making on weapon systems and forces, on the one hand,
and budgeting on the other. . . . In other words, the long-range
plans for weapon systems, forces, and all of their supporting elements were made by the Services on the basis of their estimates
of the forces required to assure our national security. Generally
speaking, costs were not introduced systematically, either to test

the feasibility of the whole program or for purposes of evaluating the efficiency of the allocation.

Budgeting, on the other hand, had as its point of departure the guideline dollar totals laid down by the Administration and based on estimates of the burden the economy could or should bear. The result was a gap. The "required forces" always cost much more than the Administration and the Congress were willing to pay. The process by which the conflicting interests were resolved was unsystematic and wasteful because it led to unbalanced programs.

Furthermore, the Secretary of Defense did not receive adequate cost data. The budgetary system identified cost by object classes —Procurement, Military Personnel, Installations, etc.—the *inputs* to the Defense Department, rather than by weapon systems and forces, such as B-52 wings and Army divisions, which are the tangible *outputs* of the Department. . . . Moreover, cost data were presented and financial management was conducted at the Defense Department level on a year-at-a-time basis. The full time-phased costs of the proposed forces were not presented to the Secretary of Defense. Because the costs of most programs are small in their first years, this led to the starting of many programs that could not be completed at anything like existing budget levels. Although a certain amount of this is a desirable hedge against uncertainty, it is clear that there were a great many wasteful stretch-outs and cancellations of programs that would not have been started if the costs of all of the approved programs had been anticipated.[2]

This kind of procedure was unacceptable to McNamara. Not long after his arrival in the Pentagon, he described generally the role he visualized for himself. "I see my position here," he said, "as being that of a leader, not a judge. I'm here to originate and stimulate new ideas and programs, not just to referee arguments and harmonize interests. Using deliberate analysis to force alternative programs to the surface, and then making explicit choices among them is fundamental."[3] Nearly two years later he characterized his basic management philosophy in the following terms:

It is a philosophy based on a decision pyramid and a system of administration in which all possible decisions are pushed to the bottom of that pyramid. But for intelligent decisions to be made at the bottom of the pyramid there must be a framework within which those decisions can be made. Basic policies must be established against which a decision-maker at the lower levels can compare his decision and gain some confidence that he is acting in accordance with a pattern of decisions elsewhere in the organization. This will lead to unity and strength rather than an imbalance, which can only lead to weakness.

And it is the establishment of these policies that can only be done at the top.

The basic policy that we have established is a policy that shifts from a reliance on massive retaliation to the option response or capability. . . . Now, this is a shift required, we believe, because of a change in the character of Soviet military forces in the world environment in which we find ourselves as a nation operating. It is a shift, however, that requires a complete rebalancing of the military forces of this Nation, and it is not something, therefore, that could be simply turned over to the Services for them to decide unilaterally how they should proceed.

We must insure that the Army is balanced to the Air Force, that the Navy is balanced to the requirements of the Army, that the financial budget is balanced to the military force structure required as a foundation for our foreign policy.

It is this type of decision that comes up to my level and, until we translate this basic policy into a balanced force structure, I really know of no other way to follow. This isn't because I like to make decisions, and I don't happen to like to work six or seven days a week, twelve hours a day, but I don't know any other way to do it when passing through this transitional period.[4]

The method which McNamara chose to assist him in making these decisions was the planning-programming-budgeting system—largely the work of Charles J. Hitch, his Comptroller. McNamara described the system's function briefly as he expanded on his management philosophy.

It is through this system that we look at the defense effort as a whole. Major program priorities can be meaningfully determined only in terms of the total program, and a proper balancing of all the elements of the defense effort can only be achieved at the Department of Defense level. For example, the size of the Polaris force cannot be determined in terms of the Navy shipbuilding program or even the entire Navy program, but can be validly judged only in relation to all of the other elements of the strategic retaliatory forces—the B-52's, the Atlas, the Titan, and the Minuteman ICBM's. Similarly, the requirement for Air Force tactical fighters cannot be determined independently of the requirement for Army ground forces. All such interdependent decisions must be made at one place in the defense organization, and in this process the Joint Chiefs and the Secretary must play a major role. Alone among the elements of the Department, they have the overall vantage point from which to reach sound recommendations on balanced military forces.

While I believe that unified planning, programming, and decision-making are indispensable to the effective management of the defense effort, I am equally convinced that the actual operation of the program should be managed, to the maximum extent possible, on a decentralized basis. The defense effort is entirely too big, too complex, and too geographically dispersed for its operations to be managed from a single, central point.

Thus, the organization and management of the Defense Department must be based on the principle of centralized planning and decentralized operation.[5]

The planning-programming-budgeting system has become the device by which to do the centralized planning; through it, national security objectives are related to strategy, strategy to forces, forces to resources, and resources to costs. As described by Enthoven, the program "consists of a five-year projection of all forces, weapon systems, and other activities described in physical (or non-financial) terms, together with their costs, all as approved by the Secretary of Defense, plus a set of regular procedures for modifying the plan."[6] Hitch has gone into some detail about the process by which this five-year projection is maintained and modified.

The first phase of the decision-making process—military planning and requirements determination—involves the participation of all appropriate elements of the Defense Department in their respective areas of responsibility. This is the phase in which the Joint Chiefs

of Staff organization and the planners in the military departments
play a particularly important role. Although the system provides for
specific changes in plans and requirements at any time during the
year, there is a need for a comprehensive review and analysis, at
least once a year, of the entire longer-range military plan and the
forces required to support it. The product of this effort is the Joint
Strategic Objectives Plan (JSOP) which is prepared by the Joint
Chiefs of Staff with the assistance of the planners in the military
departments. The military plans and force requirements are developed on the basis of broadly stated national security policies and
objectives, and intelligence assessments of our opponents' likely
future capabilities. This is a dynamic process. Plans are continually
being modified as old assumptions are tested, new data are integrated, new intelligence information becomes available, and
alternative ways of accomplishing specific military tasks are examined and new choices made.[7]

Hitch now came to a critical part of the system: program
packaging. The force requirements are directly related to the
major military missions of the Defense Department; thus, whatever the Service origin of the forces—whether Army, Navy, or
Air Force—where they perform the same functions they are put
in the same package (of which there are nine), and displayed
for purposes of comparison as to cost and effectiveness. As one
example, all these forces which would perform the retaliatory
mission in a strategic nuclear war appear in the first program
package. According to Hitch, the Secretary then makes his
decisions about forces in terms of the program packages. As
Hitch describes the process:

During this programming phase we try:

First, to develop our programs on the basis of broad military
missions which cut across traditional organizational lines, rather
than on the basis of unilateral plans and priorities of the Military
Services;

Second, to relate resource "inputs"—manpower, matériel and installations—together with their costs, to military "outputs"—strategic
retaliatory forces, general purpose forces, and others;

Third, to coordinate our long-range military planning with short-range detailed budgeting by projecting our detailed programs at least five years into the future;

Fourth, to appraise our programs on a continuous basis;

Fifth, to control approved programs through a system of progress reporting;

And sixth, to provide both physical and financial data in forms suitable for making cost-effectiveness studies of alternative force structures.[8]

McNamara, testifying in 1962, explained further the reasoning behind the program packaging approach and the five-year projections.

Because of the great technical complexity of modern-day weapons, their lengthy period of development, their tremendous combat power and their enormous cost, we believe that sound choices of major weapon systems in relation to military tasks and missions have become the key decisions around which much else of the defense program revolves. But the full cost implications of these decisions, present and future, cannot be ascertained unless both the programs and their cost are projected over a period of years, ideally over the entire life cycle of the weapon system. Since such long-term projections are very difficult to make with any degree of accuracy, we have fixed on a 5-year period, which is short enough to assure reasonably accurate estimates and long enough to provide a good approximation of the full cost.[9]

Hitch points out the magnitude of the decisions and describes how they are approached:

We break down the cost of each program element into three categories—Research and Development, Initial Investment, and Annual Operating—each of which has its own particular significance in the decision-making process.

The first category, Research and Development, . . . represents the cost of bringing a new weapon or capability to the point where it is ready for operational use. Since the cost of development alone may run into very large sums, making a commitment to development is in itself a major management decision. For example, over $1.3 billion has already been committed to the Nike-Zeus anti-ballistic missile program, and another few hundreds of millions of dollars will be required just to complete the research and development phase. The decision to go ahead with only the development of the more advanced Nike-X represents an additional outlay of well over a billion dollars.

The Investment category represents the costs beyond the development phase required to introduce a new capability into operational use. These decisions many times involve outlays of 4, 5, and even more billions of dollars. Our investment in the B-52 force over the years is estimated at well over $7 billion, excluding the cost of tankers, air-to-surface missiles, etc.

The Operating costs are the annual recurring costs required to man, operate, and maintain the capability. Quite often the cost of operating a system over its expected life is more important than investment costs. For example, it costs us as much to operate and maintain an infantry division for one year as it does to equip it in the first place. Thus, operating costs can be crucial to the initial management decision to produce and deploy one weapon system as compared with another.

Therefore, wherever possible we try to estimate the total cost, including R&D, investment and operating costs through what we call the "first line life" of the weapon system before any decision is made to proceed with a major development.[10]

The third phase of the system, after planning and program packaging, is the preparation of the annual budget estimates. The military departments submit their budget estimates early in October. They are reviewed by the Office of the Secretary and then passed on to the President for recommended inclusion in his annual budgetary submission to the Congress. As Hitch points out, the actual submission takes the traditional form.

The Five-Year Force Structure and Financial Plan is an internal Defense Department tool and does not represent an approved program of the U.S. Government. The Congress . . . reserves unto itself the right to authorize and appropriate funds, year by year, against this proposed program, and even the President . . . is not unalterably committed to the five-year program in detail. It is essentially a planning tool—a road map, if you please—of where we hope to move over the next five years.[11]

The first five-year program was developed in connection with preparations for the fiscal year 1963 budget. Thereafter, with the original program as the starting point, the Department concentrated each year on projecting the plan by a year and on introducing changes and refinements into the program. According to Hitch, changes in the program were made as necessary, at any time during the year.

However, the majority of the important changes are concentrated in the three-month period, June, July, and August, following the completion of the annual JSOP by the Joint Chiefs of Staff. We hope that by the middle of August the Secretary will have substantially completed his program review so that the military departments can be furnished an approved program for the next five fiscal years 1965–69, upon which to base their budget estimates for fiscal year 1965.

The specific administrative procedure for making these changes is known as the "Program Change Control System." The basic elements of this procedure involve the submission of program change proposals by any major component of the Department of Defense, their review by all interested components, the Secretary's decision and finally, the assignment of responsibility for carrying out this decision to the appropriate military agency.[12]

Hitch argues that this formal change procedure helps to ensure:

1. that there is only one channel for major decision-making;
2. that proposed changes receive a rapid, but complete, review by all parties concerned;
3. that program decisions are made on the basis of the best information available, including a validation of their long-range cost implications;
4. that all major changes are made only after approval by the Secretary of Defense; and
5. that there is always available an up-to-date, approved five-year program for U.S. defense activities.[13]

It should be noted that the program change control system does not operate at quite the stately pace that one might expect on the basis of its formal description. McNamara, who has now been exposed thrice to the workings of the system, described, early in 1963, what happened on the first occasion.

This year, in contrast to last year when we had to develop a 5-year program from the ground up, we started the budgeting cycle with an approved program projected through fiscal year 1967. This was essentially the same program I presented . . . last year. We realized, of course, that changes in this program would be needed as time went on; first, to reflect the action of the Congress on our fiscal year 1963 budget, and then to take account of all the numerous changes which are bound to occur in the international situation, in our requirements for military forces, in technology, and in costs. Accordingly, we established last summer a program change procedure designed to provide an orderly method for proposing, reviewing, and approving program changes. The procedure affords all elements in the Defense Department concerned with a particular proposal a full opportunity to present their views. For example, an Air Force proposal to modify its airlift fleet would be referred to the Army for comment as a user; to the Navy because of its impact on the sealift requirement; to the Joint Chiefs of Staff as representatives of the using commands, as well as to appropriate parts of my office. When all of these views have been assembled, Mr. Gilpatric or I review each proposal and render a decision or, in some cases, ask for further study. Where major issues are involved we discuss the matter in greater detail with our principal military and civilian advisers. Indeed, such major issues as the RS-70, Nike-Zeus, strategic forces, and so forth, were given individual and extensive study by the Chiefs, and their views were considered before the decisions were made.

The program change procedure went into effect last July and, up until the time the budget estimates were submitted in early October, several hundred program change proposals were received. These program changes would have added about $40 billion to the previously approved 1964–67 program base. The sizable sums requested were by no means unexpected, inasmuch as we had eliminated the arbitrary budget ceilings which had been used prior to 1961.

The program change procedure has unquestionably increased the workload on the Office of the Secretary of Defense, but I was particularly anxious that nothing should be done to discourage the military departments from submitting any program change they felt was necessary for the defense of the Nation. This was consistent with President Kennedy's instructions to me to (1) develop the force structure necessary to meet our military requirements without regard to arbitrary budget ceilings; and (2) procure and operate this force at the lowest possible cost.

The total of the fiscal year 1964 programs and budgets submitted by the Services and defense agencies amounted to $67 billion. All of the budgets were carefully reviewed jointly by the budget examiners of my office and the Bureau of the Budget, as has been the custom in the past. The analyses resulting from this review were forwarded to me for decision. In consultation with our principal advisers, Mr. Gilpatric and I then thoroughly reviewed all of the outstanding issues. Our decisions were transmitted to the respective Services and, in the final step of our review, outstanding differences were resolved. As a result of this review, we were able to reduce the approximately $67 billion requested by the Services to the total of $53.7 billion in new obligational authority recommended in the President's budget.[14]

Although the five-year force projection and the program change procedure placed an extraordinarily heavy responsibility on McNamara, they also provided him with a more precise and integrated picture of American combat power than any previous Secretary of Defense had received. They also displayed for him in an orderly way the kinds of choices—expressed in terms of capabilities and costs—that he had available and must make in order to determine the shape of the military establishment. But neither five-year projection nor program change proposals could tell McNamara what automatically were the preferred choices. For that kind of advice he turned to another set of devices.

Perhaps the most important technique is that of operational research or systems analysis. Here, the war game or the exercise, with its vital military inputs, is wedded to considerations of cost so that the policy-maker can obtain some knowledge about the degree of military effectiveness that can be achieved with a particular capability for a given expenditure. As Hitch has pointed out,

> there is a need for . . . detailed and intensive analyses of special problem areas such as conventional vs. nuclear-powered aircraft carriers, the need for a new long-range interceptor aircraft, the use of aircraft to enhance Army mobility, etc.

Many of these special requirements studies are initiated by the Secretary of Defense to help solve particular problems which arise during his program and budget review or to fill gaps in the data available to him. Others are initiated by the military departments, the Joint Chiefs of Staff, or other elements of the Office of the Secretary of Defense.

In each case we are interested not only in the military worth of the proposed requirement but also its cost. In our view, military effectiveness and cost are simply two sides of the same coin and must be considered jointly in the decision-making process. For example, the value to our national security of a five percent increase in our capability to destroy a given target system can be decided only in relation to the cost of acquiring it—so long as we live in a world in which resources are limited.

We do not use systems analysis or cost/effectiveness studies as a substitute for sound and experienced military judgment but rather as a method to get before the decision-maker the relevant data, organized in a way most useful to him. There are and there should be many other inputs to the decision-maker, particularly in those areas which are not susceptible in whole or in part to quantitative analysis. While no important military problem is ever likely to be wholly susceptible to quantitative analysis, properly applied analytical techniques help to minimize the areas in which unsupported judgment must govern in the decision-making process.[15]

McNamara has described a typical case in which he found this type of analysis relevant.

> Now, one of the pertinent factors in the presentation of a Navy program is the Air Force program that is proposed to accomplish the same objective. And the only way I found to make an intelligent decision on the proposals of one service is to consider the actions of other services that relate thereto.

I can give the illustration of the Polaris. Whether we should have a 45-boat Polaris program, as the Navy has suggested, or a 29-boat program, as the Air Force thinks, is in part affected by the decision we make on the Air Force Minuteman missile program.[16]

Exactly how this particular problem of choice should be resolved, McNamara did not go on to say. But he did describe in surprising and lucid detail the analysis which would precede the decision.

A major mission of these forces is to deter war by their capability to destroy the enemy's warmaking capabilities [deleted]. With the kinds of weapons available to us, this task presents a problem of reasonably finite dimensions, which are measurable in terms of the number and type of targets or aiming points which must be destroyed and the number and types of weapon delivery systems required to do the job under various sets of conditions.

The first step in such a calculation is to determine the number, types, and locations of the aiming points in the target system.

The second step is to determine the numbers and explosive yields of weapons which must be delivered on the aiming points to insure the destruction or substantial destruction of the target system.

The third step involves a determination of the size and character of the forces best suited to deliver these weapons, taking into account such factors as—

1. The number and weight of warheads that each type of vehicle can deliver.

2. The ability of each type of vehicle to penetrate enemy defenses.

3. The degree of accuracy that can be expected of each system, i.e., the CEP, which we know as circular error probability.

4. The degree of reliability of each system, i.e., the proportion of the ready operational inventory that we can count on getting off successfully within the prescribed time.

5. The cost/effectiveness of each system, i.e., the combat effectiveness per dollar of outlay.

Since we must be prepared for a fast strike by the enemy, allowances must also be made in our calculations for the losses which our own forces would suffer from the initial enemy attack. This, in turn, introduces a number of additional factors into our calculations, including:

1. The size, weight, and effectiveness of a possible enemy attack—based on estimates of the size and character of the enemy's long-range strategic offensive forces and the warhead yields, reliability, and accuracy of their weapon systems.

2. The degree of vulnerability of our own strategic weapon systems to such an attack.

Clearly, each of these crucial factors involves various degrees of uncertainty. But these uncertainties are not completely unmanageable. By postulating various sets of assumptions, ranging from optimistic to pessimistic, it is possible to introduce into our calculations reasonable allowances for these uncertainties. For example, we can use in our analysis both the higher and lower limits of the range of estimates of enemy ICBM's and long-range bombers. We can assign to these forces a range of capabilities as to warhead yield, accuracy, and reliability.

With respect to our own forces, we can establish, within reasonable limits, the degree of reliability, accuracy, and vulnerability of each type of offensive weapon system and we can establish its ability to penetrate the enemy defenses under various modes of operation. Obviously, the last factor also involves an estimate of the size and character of the enemy's defenses.

This is, admittedly, a rather oversimplified version of the actual studies and calculations we made to help us determine the size and character of the Strategic Retaliatory Forces required, now, and over the next 5 or 6 years—to assure that we have at all times the capability to destroy any nation which might attack us, even after we have absorbed a first blow from that nation.[17]

Despite the fortunate absence of data about a strategic nuclear war, the problem and the requirements lent themselves, as McNamara pointed out, to relatively straightforward analysis. Making choices with respect to systems like Polaris and Minuteman, or the B-52, Skybolt, and the RS-70, could proceed with some confidence. Where limited war and the forces required for it were concerned, however, the difficulties proved substantially less tractable. McNamara gave a number of reasons for this comparative lack of precision:

1. The great diversity of units and capabilities included in these forces;
2. The relationship between our general purpose forces and those of our allies around the world;
3. The wide variety of possible contingencies that they must be prepared to meet;
4. The important role that the Reserve components play in these forces, the Reserve and National Guard components; and
5. The sheer number and diversity of weapons, equipment, and supplies involved.[18]

McNamara nevertheless persisted in his search for useful analyses. As he informed the Congress in 1963:

Last spring I asked the Chairman of the Joint Chiefs of Staff to establish a working group to study the requirements of U.S. general purpose forces to meet a number of possible non-nuclear combat situations in various oversea potential trouble spots. This group was headed by Vice Adm. H. D. Riley, the Director of the Joint Staff, with Lt. Gen. T. W. Parker, now Army Deputy Chief of Staff for Military Operations, serving as Vice Director, and included about 110 officers from all the services. Parallel studies were conducted in the military departments. The group was given considerable freedom to develop study situations which took the form of several different sets of assumptions and objectives. Then the group was provided with the latest intelligence data and was asked to examine the general purpose forces requirements to meet various kinds of enemy attacks in four broad geographic regions—Europe, the Middle East, southeast Asia, and northeast Asia. Including those examined by the military departments, some 16 different situations were studied.

In each of these situations, the specific requirements for ground forces and tactical air forces were examined in considerable detail. Requirements for naval forces, because of their special character, were examined primarily on a worldwide basis. This latter study proved to be particularly complex and difficult to define, and we will be giving it much more intensive study in future months.[19]

McNamara found the resulting analyses highly useful; but, he cautioned,

in an effort to keep them manageable, a certain degree of over-simplification was inevitable. We are under no illusion that any of these situations would actually develop exactly as postulated for purposes of the studies. They never do and we know it. Furthermore, each situation, of necessity, had to be examined solely within its own context and no attempt was made to evaluate its effect on the world situation as a whole. Conversely, the interaction of other likely world events on the particular situation under study was also omitted from consideration.

Nevertheless, with all of these limitations, the general purpose forces studies constitute a very useful approach to the problem of determining the force requirements for limited war.

They have been of great assistance in assessing the capabilities of our land and tactical air forces to cope with situations short of general war occurring in various parts of the world, in some cases in more than one place at the same time.

They have also given us a much better idea of what we could do with our non-nuclear forces in these kinds of situations, and a much better grasp of the size and composition of the forces—both our own and the enemy's—that would most likely be involved.[20]

Although this kind of analysis did not allow the comparison of alternative weapon systems and strategies to nearly the degree that characterized the war gaming of strategic nuclear conflict, it could take advantage of the experience that the Services had accumulated in conventional war. Consequently McNamara found it valuable—provided always that his advisers could support their judgments with data from that experience. If he became somewhat intransigent it was usually where he thought that advice and evidence had failed to coincide.

Such a failure had occurred, in his view, with respect to the Navy's requirements. As he told Congress:

We do not yet have acceptable situation-by-situation analyses of naval requirements comparable to those now available for ground and tactical air forces. Until such analyses become available we are accepting the Navy's general purpose forces as being generally the right order of magnitude and composition.[21]

This made it appear as though the Navy had gained its objectives without having undergone any trial by analysis. But appearances were deceptive. The major issue of policy was not so much the over-all size and composition of the Navy as it was the rate of its modernization. McNamara recognized the problem.

I am well aware that the Navy faces a difficult problem of "block obsolescence" and that well over half of today's fleet was built during or just shortly after World War II. While it is true that these ships are now approaching the 20-year mark, the useful lives of many combatant types still can be extended by rehabilitation and modernization. Support and auxiliary types, in most cases, can be maintained in a serviceable condition much longer than 20 years.[22]

In other words, even though he might not yet understand the basis for the Navy's requirements, McNamara refused to accept on faith the asserted danger of "block obsolescence." On the contrary, he set out to analyze the validity of the concept itself.

Tentatively, one new attack carrier, conventionally powered, will be started every second year. The last carrier was included in the fiscal year 1963 shipbuilding program and, tentatively, the next carrier will be started in fiscal year 1965, and another in fiscal year 1967. If we were to carry through the Navy's long-standing program of one attack carrier every other year, the Midway-class carriers would be 30 to 32 years old by the time they were phased out of the force, clearly demonstrating that the 20-year rule-of-thumb is an artificial standard for measuring the useful life of naval vessels.[23]

This kind of critical analysis no doubt was an inadequate substitute for a clear definition of functions and the establishment of a reasonably precise relationship between the budgets, force levels requested, and the tasks that could be performed. But lacking such a device did not mean that McNamara would abandon his efforts to test, by all logical means, proposals coming up to him.

The area of research and development, with a budget for fiscal year 1964 of about $5.5 billion, called for still another style of analysis and decision-making. McNamara was not happy with the way the program had been going.

Of the 10 or 15 major systems I examined at one particular time, systems we have procured over the last three to five years, no one of them had an actual cost less than 300 percent of the original estimate, and several of them had final costs that were approximately 1000 percent of the original estimate. This represented a serious penalty to the Government, a penalty, I believe, that at least in part we can avoid.[24]

That was not the only problem.

Research and development expenditures, whether measured in budget terms or in program terms, have been mounting steadily over the years, but too much of this effort is not producing useful results. What we want are weapons and equipment that the fighting man can use. We are not interested in supporting the intellectually challenging, but militarily useless, engineering "tour de force." If we are to make optimum use of our available scientific and engineering manpower resources, we must plan our program carefully and concentrate these resources where they will make the greatest contribution to our military posture.[25]

As part of the effort to allocate resources more efficiently in the highly uncertain field of research and development, McNamara inaugurated what he called a "program definition phase."

This is the phase in which we, together with our contractors, do our thinking and planning—before we start "bending metal."

Very briefly, the program definition phase begins with the solicitation of proposals from industry and involves a number of early study contracts whose purpose is simply to define the program, prior to authorizing full-scale development. In the early stages of the program definition phase we do not attempt to establish rigorous specifications, preferring to encourage initiative and innovation on the part of our contractors or contractor teams. Indeed, where competing approaches present an unusually difficult choice, we may support more than one approach throughout the whole program definition period.

Working together, a contractor team can explore in depth the many unknowns which are present in any new effort. They can accomplish the overall system design, define the subsystems and major components and begin the early stages of laboratory experimentation and design. Most important, they can identify the critical problems and make good estimates of how long and how much money it will take to solve them.

With this information at hand, we are in a much better position to decide whether or not to proceed with full-scale development. And if we decide on full-scale development, the basic scientific and management team will have already been established, with a visible history of successful collaboration during the program definition phase. Finally, it will be possible to make the decision for full-scale effort with far greater assurance that the cost estimates are sound, that the performance of the system will meet the promise, and that the military requirement will be filled at the time needed.

Prior planning, and even feasibility testing of "pacing" components, are a lot cheaper than having to reorient, stretch out, or terminate expensive projects after they have been started. There are, of course, exceptions to this general rule. Where a development can add a new and unique dimension to our military capability like the A and H bombs and the ICBM, great costs and risks are justified. But such cases are rare. The typical development promises, if successful, to achieve a capability that can also be achieved in other ways or represents an improvement of but modest proportions in our total military capability. In these cases the urgency is not as great and the employment of a more measured and orderly approach to development and production is fully justified. In fact, I have observed that in most cases careful and comprehensive prior planning actually saves time as well as money and results in more effective and more dependable weapons.[26]

McNamara gave the Congress two illustrations of weapon systems going through the program definition phase.

The mobile medium-range ballistic [missile] program . . . for which we are requesting large appropriations in fiscal 1964, has not yet progressed through the program definition phase. Until it does, we won't know for sure what we can accomplish with that weapon. After it passes through that phase, we may believe it is unwise to proceed further with it. Of course, next year we would come back and tell you that, why we arrived at that conclusion; and certain funds that might have been appropriated would remain unspent and, of course, you would wish to withdraw the appropriation.

Another project in the same status is Titan III. This is the large solid-propellant booster . . . which will have a capability of placing about 27,000 pounds in a low earth orbit. Its primary purpose is to give us a flexibility of solid propellants at a cost lower than the presently estimated costs for the liquid-fueled alternative, which is the Saturn booster.

. . . We have placed contracts with contractors to undertake the initial studies. . . . They run in the low millions. The total program is estimated to cost something on the order of $800 million. We are going to spend a few million dollars to find out what can be accomplished. As one of the committee members implied the other day, to complete it successfully will require technological developments which have not yet occurred.[27]

McNamara summed up the role of different techniques of analysis and decision-making in his management of the Pentagon when he explained:

In adding to a defense budget as large as the one we now have, we begin to encounter the law of diminishing returns, where each additional increment of resources applied produces a smaller increment of overall defense capability. While the benefits to be gained from each additional increment cannot be measured with precision, careful cost/effectiveness analysis can greatly assist in eliminating those program proposals which clearly contribute little military worth in relation to the resource expenditures involved. We have applied this principle throughout our program and budget reviews.[28]

McNamara derived several important benefits from the whole planning-programming-budgeting process with its emphasis on analysis done in terms of cost and effectiveness. Perhaps outstanding among them was that the system obliged both his military and civilian advisers to present and discuss major defense issues in terms that were readily comprehensible to him. It was now possible for the Secretary to discharge his legal responsibilities and choose knowledgeably among the many alternatives that confronted him. Moreover, the system—although by no means perfect in this respect—gave him a way of looking at functionally related aspects of the defense establishment, wherever these activities might be located organizationally. The ability to cut across organizational lines, and particularly to integrate both the complementary and competitive functions of the Services within the major program packages also permitted comparisons and a degree of efficiency which had been impossible with previous management techniques. This ability offered still another benefit; it reduced the need for the vast reorganizations that had shaken the Pentagon periodically since 1947. Responsibility for the management of the Department of Defense was clearly vested in the Secretary and he now had the means, through the planning-programming-budgeting process, to exercise his authority in a systematic and orderly way. In effect, he had found a substitute for unification of the Services and establishment of a single Chief of Staff.

The acquisition of these benefits did not mean that McNamara regarded further changes in the organization of the Department as irrelevant or unnecessary. Where reorganization would promote efficiency, where it would isolate and identify responsibility, he favored it strongly. A fundamental principle of management, in his view, was "never do anything at a higher echelon that can be done at a lower echelon."[29] He described his approach to organization early in 1962. Defense, to him, was a dynamic not a static endeavor.

The size and character of the defense effort is subject to constant change with shifts in the international situation and progress in military technology. And the way in which the Defense Establishment is organized to carry out its missions must be constantly adjusted to cope with these changes. To assist me in this task, I have established a small organizational and management planning group in the General Counsel's office to devote full time to the study of such matters.

In dealing with this problem of organization and management I have tried to avoid a doctrinaire approach. I am sure that there are several good ways in which to organize the efforts of the Defense Establishment, each with its own peculiar strengths and weaknesses. What I have tried to do during the last year is to deal with this problem on a case-by-case basis, correcting organizational arrangements and management methods and procedures wherever I was convinced that there was a better way of getting the job done. Each change was considered on its own merits and each was adopted only after the most careful analysis and review clearly demonstrated that an improvement should and could be made.[30]

McNamara's first major move was in the field of intelligence. Here, a large number of organizations had been doing "similar or parallel work, and unified direction of the Department's total intelligence activities was lacking. It was clear that the situation had to be improved."[31] McNamara attempted to improve it by establishing the Defense Intelligence Agency, or DIA.

Our principal objectives in establishing this Agency are to obtain unity of effort among all components of the Department of Defense in developing military intelligence and to achieve a strengthened overall capacity in the Department for the collection, production, and dissemination of defense intelligence information.

The organization will also achieve a more efficient allocation of intelligence resources, more effective management of all Department of Defense intelligence activities, and elimination of duplicating intelligence facilities, organizations, and tasks.[32]

DIA reports to the Secretary of Defense through the Joint Chiefs of Staff and is under their immediate supervision. It began by integrating the current intelligence activities of the Joint Staff and the three military departments. It also made possible the elimination of the Office of Special Operations from McNamara's own staff. Ultimately, if McNamara's expectations are fulfilled,

DIA will furnish all DOD current operations intelligence, assemble, integrate, and validate all DOD intelligence requirements, and produce all DOD intelligence estimates. It will also supervise Defense noncryptologic intelligence collection activities and will submit a consolidated DOD budget request for all intelligence activities [deleted]. In this way, we hope to strengthen and unify the Department's activities in this field and at the same time make the most efficient use of the intelligence resources at our disposal.[33]

A second major change was the creation of Strike Command (STRICOM). Commanded by an Army general, with an Air Force lieutenant-general as his deputy, STRICOM consolidates the eight divisions of the strategic Army reserve, the operational squadrons of the Tactical Air Command, and supporting airlift squadrons into one unit which trains together and "is instantly available for use as an augmentation to existing theater forces under the unified commanders, or as the primary force for use in remote areas."[34] Not only was STRICOM the embodiment of the Kennedy Administration's drive for a greater number of conventional options; it was also the means of bringing the Air Force and the Army back into the formidable air-ground combination which dominated the battles of World War II and Korea.

McNamara also pushed to get the three military departments "to bring their internal structure into line with present-day needs."[35] He was most notably successful with the Air Force and the Army.

In the Air Force the arbitrary distinction and divided responsibilities in the life cycle of a weapon system between development and production have been abolished. Weapon systems, from their inception through delivery to the using combat organization, are now managed by the new Systems Command. This combines the functions of the old Air Research and Development Command, the procurement elements of the Air Material Command, and the Air Force proving grounds. On the other hand, logistical support of the combat forces has now been concentrated in the new Air Force Logistics Command. This incorporates principally the supply and maintenance functions of the old Air Material Command.[36]

A similar reorganization of the Army's technical services was instituted. Even though Robert Lovett, a former Secretary of Defense, had compared such an undertaking with backing into a buzz saw, McNamara insisted on its necessity.

> While the organization of the Army General Staff in recent years has been improved, the technical services have largely retained their traditional independence. Each has its own R&D, production, training, personnel, supply, and other functions, thus compounding the possibilities for duplication. Whatever reasons may once have existed for the division of responsibilities among them and for their quasi-autonomous status, they no longer correspond with the organizational requirements of a modern Army.
>
> Under the . . . reorganization, the Department of the Army, other than the Army forces assigned to unified commands, would consist of three major commands and the departmental headquarters. The three major commands are the Matériel Development and Logistic Command, the Continental Army Command, and the Combat Developments Command.[37]

Perhaps the biggest change, and the one closest to McNamara's heart, concerned those supply functions common to all of the Services. As he explained to a White House Conference:

> For many years, Congressional Committees, private commissions, consultants and study groups have recommended that these support activities be organized on a Defense Department–wide basis. One large area which appeared to us to lend itself to centralized management was that of common supplies and services. A closer study convinced us that considerable economy and efficiency could be gained if all the common supply management activities were consolidated in a single agency directly under the Secretary of Defense. This we have done by establishing the new Defense Supply Agency.[38]

McNamara assigned five major responsibilities to the new Agency:

1. All the commodity single manager operating agencies previously under the Secretary of the Army and the Navy. (These, in

effect, are large buying and inventory management offices, located in various cities around the country.)

2. The Military Traffic Management Agency, previously under the Secretary of the Army.

3. The consolidated surplus sales offices, previously operated by the three military departments.

4. The National Surplus Property Bidders Control Center, previously operated by the Air Force.

5. The Armed Forces Supply Center (including the Federal Catalog and defense standardization activities) which previously reported to the Secretary of Defense through a council of general and flag rank officers of all the military services.

DSA will also administer the surplus property disposal program and the coordinated procurement program, and is now activating a new subordinate agency to take over management at the wholesale level of common electronic supplies now managed separately by each of the military departments.[39]

The Defense Supply Agency would operate primarily as a wholesale supply management organization,

buying from suppliers and selling to the military consuming organizations. The military departments will distribute the supplies acquired from DSA to their own using organizations in the United States and to the component forces of unified commands and specified commands, both overseas and in the United States.[40]

By early 1963, McNamara felt that DSA had begun to achieve economies in the expenditure of defense dollars.

Already, the new Agency has made possible a personnel reduction of 3,700 in the fiscal year 1964 budget with an operations and maintenance saving of $33 million. Inventory is expected to be reduced by $232 million during the current fiscal year with a further reduction of $112 million in fiscal year 1964. DSA now handles about one million supply items but the number of different storage points is being reduced from 77 to 11.[41]

The fascination which DSA held for McNamara was not simply a function of his determination to acquire a belt buckle common to the four Services or to standardize the undergarments of the young ladies in the military establishment. It also reflected his consuming interest in what he calls cost reduction. The planning-programming-budgeting system with its supporting analytical techniques gave him a basis for making rational choices with respect to the force structure and strategy of the United States. And cost considerations figured very largely in those choices. But it was one thing to determine requirements at minimum cost in an organization as large as the defense establishment; it was quite another to assure that the requirements were fulfilled with the maximum efficiency. McNamara had good grounds for believing that he had made progress on the first part of the task; the second part remained a constant challenge. As he pointed out to the President, "Seventy percent of every Defense dollar is spent on purchasing, construction, operating depots and bases, maintenance, transportation and communication services."[42] He was by no means convinced that this enormous sum—roughly $35 billion a year—was being spent with perfect wisdom.

The Defense Department had total inventories of real estate, equipment, and parts exceeding $138 billion. Of this total $42 billion were invested in munitions and spare parts. And of that $42 billion, approximately $13 billion had turned out to be surplus which would have to be disposed of at a fraction of their original cost.[43] Then there were the cost-plus-fixed-fee contracts which guaranteed the contractor his profit regardless of the efficiency with which he performed. McNamara looked into these and found, with respect to a number of major weapon systems, "that the final costs exceeded the original estimates by between 300 percent and a thousand percent. Now that wasn't solely because they were cost-plus-fixed-fee contracts, but it was importantly because they were cost-plus-fixed-fee contracts."[44]

Another major source of waste that McNamara noted was the parallel development of projects and systems designed for the same general mission.

The cost of developing new aircraft today is reckoned in the hundreds of millions of dollars. In the case of the B-70 the development of three prototype aircraft will probably cost us about $1.5 billion and they will still not be assigned as operational vehicles. The cost of developing a new major missile system is even higher. We have invested well over $1 billion in the Nike-Zeus already and the Atlas and Titan developments ran well over $2 billion each. Even the cost of developing a new aircraft engine to the point of production is about $150 million.

But this is only the beginning of the increased cost. If two models are produced where one could do the job, the cost of production is also increased. Two production lines instead of one must be set up and tooled and the economies of large-scale, repetitive production are lost, thus significantly increasing the cost per unit. Two separate pipelines of spares and unique support equipment instead of one must be established in the logistics system, with all the additional costs involved. And, finally, two sets of obsolete spares and support equipment instead of one will eventually have to be disposed of when the end item is finally phased out of the inventory.[45]

It was to minimize this kind of waste that McNamara established the cost reduction program. Describing it one day, he said, "This program is detailed. It has been laid out Military Department by Military Department, item by item. Each of the Secretaries has accepted his share of it. I carry around in my pocket the details of it which I discuss with them periodically. I check to make damn sure we are on the targets."[46] He did not claim that this was a new program. "It existed in the Defense Department, but it has never received the push, pressure and the action it has in the last year and a half."[47]

The push, pressure, and action took place in a number of different directions.

By redefining our logistics objectives to accord with approved Defense Department–wide contingency plans we were able to reduce our total stated matériel requirements by some $24 billion. By setting out realistic goals that could be achieved within a reasonable period of time, we have been able to assure that the readiness levels of all related elements of the military forces are raised together and maintained in balance, one with another.[48]

In this connection, McNamara took a look at pipeline requirements—that additional amount of supplies needed to fill the "pipeline" between the warehouse and the user. He was unhappy with what he saw.

We are . . . taking steps to get away from the use of often arbitrary and wasteful rule-of-thumb measures for determining pipeline requirements. Instead of simply adopting a standard factor for pipeline computations, we must, at least in the case of high cost, major end items and components, determine quantitative requirements on an item-by-item basis. . . . Let me give you a specific example: in the case of the M-88 tank recovery vehicle, we found that the substitution of a fully adequate transit pipeline factor of 55 days for the previously used arbitrary factor of 120 days enabled us to realize savings of $12.5 million on just this one item.[49]

These were only samples. McNamara concentrated his drive for cost reduction in three major areas. He referred to them as "buying only what we need," "buying at the lowest sound price," and "reducing operating costs." Each year he reported to the President on the progress made. In his 1963 report he noted the estimate of the previous year that "we could cut the Department's logistic costs by at least $3 billion per year within five years, and that we would realize about 25% of this goal in Fiscal Year 1963."

I have now completed a review of the results to date and the opportunities that lie ahead, and I find that they are greater than estimated last year:

1. *Savings in excess of $1 billion* were actually realized during FY 1963, compared with our estimate of $750 million last July.
2. The actions now planned for FY 1964 and 1965 will bring the *estimated annual savings, to be realized by FY 1967, to almost $4 billion,* compared with the $3 billion estimated last July.[50]

McNamara took pains to point out that these savings had not been and would not be achieved at the expense of national security, and he described for the President the increases in American nuclear and conventional power that had occurred during the past two years. He also expressed the conviction that the costs of these increases would begin to be balanced by the savings from the cost reduction program. He might have added, but did not, that an alternative would be to hold the budget constant and invest the savings in further combat power. Instead, he explained what he meant by "buying only what we need." One part of it was the refinement of requirements calculations.

The best way to ensure that we buy only what we need is to start at the very beginning of the procurement process—the setting of requirements. Through a systematic and intensive review of requirements calculations, we have been able to cancel $700 million of purchases which otherwise would have been made had our procurement programs still been based on planning factors and inventory levels considered necessary in past years. The largest part of this reduction occurred in spare parts for aircraft and missiles. We expect to increase these savings in fiscal years 1964 and 1965.[51]

Another way to save was by an increased use of excess inventories.

During FY 1963 almost $1.2 billion in excess inventories held by the Department and its contractors has been redistributed to other military users for current consumption or mobilization reserves. This is an increase of better than $200 million in the rate of reutilization, compared with FY 1961. Our goal for the next two years is to increase this rate to more than $400 million over the 1961 level.[52]

Since excess stocks represented about $12 billion, this was a critical area. One of McNamara's favorite examples of what could be done here was the case of the 2.75-inch rockets, of which the Air Force had a million in excess supply. The Army, which needed rockets for use on helicopters, took over the supply, instead of buying new rockets, and thereby saved $41 million in a single transaction.

Still another technique was to eliminate what McNamara

called "gold-plating" in specifications for equipment. This meant

a major effort to eliminate from our procurement specifications costly materials and fabrication processes not essential to the proper functioning of the item being bought. As a result, we are now averaging savings well over $1 million per week in reduced costs, and we expect these savings to triple during the next two years.[53]

As an example of what could be done in this area, McNamara displayed on television two turbine wheels from a generator in a nuclear weapon system. One was machined out of stainless steel and cost $175. The other was made of molded plastic at a cost of $2. The plastic wheel could do the two-minute job required of it just as well as the stainless steel wheel.[54] The latter was "gold-plated."

The second area of buying at the lowest sound price involved, first and foremost, shifting from noncompetitive to competitive procurement. According to McNamara:

Maximizing competition in Defense procurement is sound public policy. It is one of the most effective means of broadening the industrial base and ensuring that we obtain the lowest sound price on what we buy. The purchase of specialized military items, however, involves unique problems which tend to limit our opportunities to buy competitively. We are attempting, nevertheless, to expand continually the opportunities for competitive bidding even on these specialized items, and in the process of doing so we have achieved savings in the first ten months of FY 1963 of $195 million. We have found that when we are able to shift from a single source to a competitive procurement, we normally achieve a reduction in price of at least 25%. On 58 major procurements made competitively during the third quarter of FY 1963, the average reduction was 30% of the price formerly paid to the sole source producer.[55]

McNamara estimated that the Department had already shifted about $800 million worth of contracts from noncompetitive to competitive procurement. By fiscal year 1965 he hoped to let 40 percent of all contracts awarded on a competitive basis, as against roughly 36 percent in fiscal year 1962, and expected to save something on the order of $400 million.

Where competition was not feasible, it was still possible, in McNamara's view, to shift from cost-plus-fixed-fee to fixed price and incentive contracts.

The increasingly complex weapon systems resulting from the technological revolution of the 1950's led to a great expansion in the use of the cost-plus-fixed-fee (CPFF) contract. However, both Department and industry officials agree that CPFF contracts not only fail to provide incentives for economy, but actually deaden management efficiency by removing the need for either the Department or the contractor to estimate costs accurately, and to plan and control programs tightly.

Accordingly, last year we established specific goals for a reduction in the use of CPFF contracts by each Military Department in each of the three fiscal years 1963–1965. The goal for FY 1963 was to reduce such contracts to 25.8% of total contract awards (compared with 38% in the first nine months of FY 1961) with an ultimate goal of not more than 12.3% by FY 1965. This is a very ambitious goal but we are exerting every effort to meet it.[56]

By virtue of these efforts, the value of annual awards under cost-plus-fixed-fee contracts had declined by $3.2 billion from the high of fiscal year 1961, and the saving had amounted to about $320 million. McNamara's goal was to shift a total of about $6.8 billion into firm fixed-price and incentive contracts by fiscal year 1965 and to achieve a saving of about $680 million in the process.

The third major area, that of reducing operating costs, involved among other actions the termination of unnecessary operations. McNamara regarded the retention of unneeded real estate and facilities as one of the largest hidden costs in Defense Department operations. He reminded the President that, in 1961,

you instructed me to review thoroughly our utilization of real properties, and, wherever possible, to consolidate activities in order to eliminate unnecessary overhead costs, free personnel for higher priority duties, and release property which could be put to more productive use by the civilian economy. Accordingly, we have instituted a permanent program of inspection and review to achieve these objectives. During the past two years, actions have been initiated at over 400 locations in the U.S. and overseas which, when completed, will produce the following results:

Real estate returned to civilian use	265,905 acres
Industrial plants with commercial potential made available for sale	54 plants
Personnel being released or reassigned	53,310 men
Annual operating savings	316,000,000 dollars

During the next two years we expect to take additional actions which will increase the annual savings to almost $450 million, with further savings anticipated in later fiscal years.

The adverse impact of these actions on the local economies is being completely or substantially offset in many cases. The Administrator of GSA [General Services Administration] recently advised me that in calendar year 1962, 26 industrial plants released by Defense were sold at fair market value of $49 million, and that these plants are now employing 27,000 workers. In addition, we have an active program to assist employees and communities adversely affected by reduction or termination of Defense activities. This program has been successful in minimizing loss of employment as well as in turning the excess properties to productive non-Defense uses.[57]

The standardization and simplification of procedures represented yet another way of reducing operating costs.

During FY 1963, 16 different requisitioning systems were successfully consolidated into one standard system, eliminating extensive rewriting of information and wasted clerical effort. As a result, manpower reductions are beginning to occur, and over the next two years the value of clerical time saved should reach $20 million per year.

On October 1 [1963], we plan to introduce a new single multipurpose shipping document which is designed to replace the 81 different bills of lading and shipping forms now in use. The value of the man-hours which the new improved system is expected to save when fully operational is estimated at more than $30 million per year.[58]

Finally, consolidating and increasing the efficiency of operations seemed likely to have produced savings of $220 million during fiscal year 1963. The Defense Supply Agency alone had assured overhead savings of $31 million in fiscal year 1963, and had managed to reduce inventories by 10 percent, or $240 million. The Defense Communications Agency, established by McNamara's predecessor to run the long-lines communications of the military departments, had produced savings of $82 million as a result of consolidated procurement of leased line services and more effective utilization of existing Defense and commercial communications facilities. Such practices as increased use of economy class air travel, decreased cost of household goods shipments, and more economical use of airlift for cargo movements had resulted in savings of $13 million. And reforms designed to provide more economical maintenance of equipment, family housing, and other property had permitted savings in excess of $90 million. By such measures, McNamara hoped to increase the amount saved in this area to $400 million by fiscal year 1965.[59]

Like the planning-programming-budgeting system, the cost reduction program was intended, as McNamara advised the President, "to meet the heavy burden of national defense with the least possible demand on the nation's resources."[60] McNamara took great pride in both efforts. *The New York Times,* rather surprisingly, proved to be somewhat less enthusiastic. In a long editorial on July 13, 1963, it commented:

The recent memorandum to President Kennedy from Secretary McNamara asserted that through "improvements in operating efficiency" the Defense Department's logistic costs were reduced during the 1963 fiscal year by more than $1 billion without impairing combat strength.

Mr. McNamara's explanation of a budget rise, while cost reduction programs are in effect, is that combat forces are being greatly strengthened and modernized.

It is probably impossible, even for a skilled bookkeeper, to evaluate "savings" achieved. Probably no two experts would agree. There would certainly be disagreement from some sources, for instance, with the claim that combat effectiveness has been in no way reduced by the economies. The Navy, for example, has found it exceedingly difficult to keep all its planes flying, due in large measure to Mr. McNamara's insistence upon reduction in numbers of spare parts carried in inventory and the opening of spare parts bids to new contractors. Nevertheless, with his end objective—the installation of a modern, business machine system of keeping track of all naval aircraft spare parts—there can be no quarrel.

About still another point—the elimination of what Mr. McNamara calls "gold-plating" in specifications—there is also bound to be disagreement. A speed differential of a few miles an hour in an aircraft may appear in the Pentagon to be "gold-plating"; up yonder it can be life or death.

One of Mr. McNamara's most important points is the establishment of a "Logistics Service Center" in Battle Creek, Mich., where a central inventory of all excess stocks of each service is maintained, so one service may compensate its deficiencies from another's surpluses. Of even greater potential significance has been the shift (which Mr. McNamara did not initiate, but which he has greatly speeded) from non-competitive to competitive procurement, and from cost plus to fixed price and incentive contracts. More than any other single accomplishment this trend should at least reduce skyrocketing increases in unit costs of weapons systems.

These things are good. But, as in any economy drive, Pentagon officials must be careful not to cut bone and sinew, or reduce in effectiveness, by too much "standardization," the intangibles of service esprit and the sense of pride of elite units.[61]

Whether or not the criticisms and cautions of the *Times* had merit, they symbolized the uneasiness that McNamara's defense policies had begun to arouse. That there should be this concern was hardly surprising. McNamara had accomplished some rather remarkable changes. He had developed the approach of multiple options and had reoriented the American military establishment to accord with it. He had sponsored the planning-programming-budgeting process in such a way that the Secretary could now exercise an unprecedented degree of real control over the formulation and execution of defense policy. And, with his dedication to efficiency, he had instituted a serious campaign of cost reduction on a very large scale. Moreover, these revolutions had proceeded at a rapid pace. They were bound to be opposed. More and more, in fact, McNamara found himself at the center of controversy. Increasingly, it became evident that action followed by explanation was not enough. Despite the force of his logic, elements of discontent from all parts of the political spectrum were beginning to develop. Like so many of his predecessors, McNamara discovered that strategy had become a subject of lively public debate.

CHAPTER 6

Capitol Controversies

THE SECRETARY OF DEFENSE, like most high American public servants, stands in an almost blinding glare of publicity. He is also the target for a drumfire of criticism and the object of occasional words of praise. Whatever Mc-Namara may have expected in this regard, he and his policies proved no exception to the rule. The files in the Pentagon quickly filled with adverse comment on what he was doing to the Armed Forces and the organization of the Department of Defense. McNamara accepted the bulk of this criticism with remarkable equanimity. As he told an interviewer, "It is important to recognize that progress is a function of controversy—or conversely, controversy is a condition necessarily associated with progress."[1]

In addition, some of the comment proved less than trenchant. It was difficult to take seriously the critic who claimed that the United States was asking for too large a conventional build-up in NATO, and damaging the Alliance in the process, when he would not say what, in his opinion, would constitute the proper level of forces. It was equally difficult to become aroused by the commentator who inveighed against the multilateral nuclear force but suggested some vague form of Anglo-French nuclear collaboration as a substitute. More irritating, though no

more serious, was the journalist who compared a nonexistent
Eisenhower strategic nuclear program for the middle 1960's
with the tentative Kennedy program for the late 1960's, and
claimed that the results showed the United States engaged in
the process of unilateral disarmament. Perhaps only puzzling
was the critic who cited gleanings from the Soviet press about
future weapon systems, however costly and outlandish, as evidence that the United States was falling desperately behind in
the space, lunar, or stellar race. What the engineers call background noise inevitably accompanies a major shift in policy.
It is unlikely to have more than a transient effect on major
plans and programs unless it comprises better information than
was the case in these instances and more constructive alternatives than, for example, the suggestion that McNamara should
do what the Eisenhower Administration clearly did not intend
to do, namely, keep the aging B-47 force in service beyond the
mid-1960's.

This is not to say that McNamara was impervious to serious
criticism or that he did not have to account in detail for his
stewardship of the national defense. Each year he presented
to the committees of Congress responsible for defense matters
an extraordinarily detailed statement of what he had done,
what he proposed to do, and why he had selected a particular
course of action. Each year, in addition, he testified before
these committees for perhaps a total of a month in support of
his programs. And each year he faced a searching and frequently skeptical examination of his actions and proposals. The
arena of the Congressional committees, in short, was where the
most serious and meaningful controversies arose and where
McNamara, of necessity, made his defense. How, during the
months of the Kennedy Administration, did he fare?

On the surface, the record was a glittering one. Carl Vinson,
Chairman of the House Armed Services Committee, and a great
connoisseur of such matters, said on one occasion:

I want to say this. I say it from the very bottom of my heart. I
have been here dealing with these problems since 1919. I want to

state that this is the most comprehensive, most factual statement that has ever been my privilege to have an opportunity to receive from any of the departments of Government.

There is more information in here than any committee in Congress has ever received along the line that it is dealing with.

It is so full of information all one has to do is just study it.

You dealt with both sides of the problem. When you reach a decision, you set out the reasons why you reached that decision. You point out why—it probably could have been done the other way, but the other facts were superior and therefore you followed the method you did.

It is a magnificent statement.[2]

On the same occasion, Vinson exclaimed:

You made a superb witness. You know every phase of the Department of National Defense in the most remote detail. It is indeed refreshing to have a witness like you that can answer all the questions that run through the minds of 37 members of the committee.[3]

Congressman Bray, however, held a somewhat different view. He was reminded, after listening to McNamara, of a Civil War story.

There was a very avid southern fan who was telling everybody that they could whip the Yankees with cornstalks.

And his line of thinking finally prevailed, and they tried it—not with cornstalks, but they tried it.

Later, the same gentleman was running for Congress, in Georgia, and proclaiming, as Congressman Bray put it, "the greatest confidence in himself and his line of procedure." A prospective constituent reminded him:

"You told us before the war started you could whip those Yankees with cornstalks." He said, "We could have easily, but they did not use cornstalks."

I just wonder whether we will use cornstalks, the next time or not.

I don't mean that in a sarcastic manner, either.

I just hope that 10 years from now you will have equal confidence in your plan as you have today.[4]

Congressman Bray may not have represented the majority of McNamara's Congressional interlocutors, but he reflected a concern and an uneasiness which gradually mounted in the Congress as the defense program unfolded. Part of the uneasiness no doubt stemmed from the past nature of the relationship between Congress and the Department of Defense. Owing to the divisions and rivalries within the Department, Congress had formerly played the Services off against one another, influenced policies, and affected the magnitude and direction of defense expenditures in a variety of ways. Now, with McNamara exercising central control over the Department, commanding an enormous fund of knowledge, and presenting a carefully integrated defense program, these activities had become substantially more difficult. Even though relations with the Services remained close, and a number of senators and representatives retained reserve commissions and dedicated themselves to the pursuit of the interests of the Services with which they were associated, the room for maneuver and bargaining had declined.

It would be a mistake, however, to trace Congressional uneasiness solely to this apparent decline of influence. Much more important was a genuine concern about certain aspects of McNamara's policies. The reasons were not far to seek. Many members of the Congressional committees were veterans of the postwar hearings and conflicts over defense programs. They were highly knowledgeable. And they had played an important role in assuring the adoption of some of the key weapon systems in the American arsenal. Congressional pressure had had much to do with the decision to develop thermonuclear weapons, to push ahead with the Polaris program under forced draft, and to remedy deficiencies in the strategic nuclear posture in the wake of the first Soviet sputnik. The record testified that senators and representatives had every right to expect a respectful hearing for their views.

Congressional concerns manifested themselves primarily with respect to specific issues, but fell into three major categories.

The first had to do with the role of nuclear weapons in the American defense strategy. Secondly, there was the question of the kinds of weapon systems that the United States should be developing for its nuclear forces. And thirdly, Congressional concern focused on the relationships between the civilians and the military and the relative influence of the two groups in the resolution of major defense issues. Generally speaking, members of Congress did not oppose the conventional build-up; and they sympathized with McNamara's efforts to encourage a larger non-nuclear defense program in NATO. What bothered them most, aside from civil-military relations, was the question of nuclear policy.

One part of the nuclear question concerned the general adequacy of American strategic retaliatory forces. Here, two schools of thought were represented and they were diametrically opposed to one another. They might be labeled the "overkill" and the "underkill" approaches. The principal version of the overkill approach was that the United States and, to a lesser extent, the Soviet Union already had sufficient nuclear power to obliterate each other several times over—exactly how many times depends on who is doing the calculations. The inference drawn from these calculations usually was that the United States and, hopefully, the Soviet Union should stop expanding their nuclear forces and that the United States, at any rate, should consider actually reducing its nuclear capabilities to much more modest proportions. McNamara had not yet specifically dealt with this version of the overkill thesis, but his answer would probably have run somewhat as follows. Measures of adequacy are indeed important, especially in the nuclear field. However, careful calculations of sufficiency must take into account far more than presumed stockpiles of weapons and numbers of delivery vehicles. They must, at a minimum, consider where the weapons actually are, whether they are married to alert vehicles, who strikes first and at what kinds of targets, how well the targets are protected, what missions are assigned to the retaliatory forces, and how many weapons are required to execute these missions. What actually determines the appropriate level of forces is even more complicated than that. But whether or not the United States has an overkill capability depends critically on the factors taken into account by the calculations. In this connection, at least one rule of thumb seems applicable. A nuclear weapon in a stockpile is not a lethal weapon; it must be delivered and detonated to do its terrible damage. It is one thing to calculate in the abstract the number of megatons required to destroy the Soviet Union, and to deduce therefrom that the American nuclear stockpile far exceeds the necessary amount. It is something else again to assure the delivery of the requisite number of nuclear weapons against the Soviet target system—whether military or civilian or some combination of these—in the face of a possibly malevolent enemy who might have started the war by attacking American delivery vehicles and stockpiles. Presumably, it is this second and much larger number which the Secretary of Defense has the responsibility to provide.

A more complex version of the overkill thesis has it that the correct target for nuclear weapons is enemy cities, that even allowing for a malevolent opponent, a measure of sufficiency can be established, and that efforts to go beyond that number simply drive a prospective enemy into increasing his capabilities with the further consequence of an arms race and an increased danger of war. Adherents to this view argue that the United States has already exceeded the number of protected weapons required to do an unacceptable amount of damage to the Soviet Union. McNamara regarded the argument as an important one, as he showed in his testimony. He, too, was worried about the nuclear arms race and wanted to see it terminated. His advocacy of the limited nuclear test ban stemmed in part from that concern. But in the absence of other assured arrangements of arms control he continued to feel that there were worse alternatives for the country than a continuation of the gradual nuclear build-up. One such alternative might be a more rapid development of further national nuclear capabilities if other countries were to lose faith in the efficacy of the American nuclear umbrella. Another might be a confrontation such as had occurred over the Soviet missiles in Cuba, but with the Soviets having the advantage in nuclear arms. It is often said that nuclear superiority is cold comfort in a crisis; the lack of it, Khrushchev might argue, is the chilliest feeling of all. At any rate, McNamara remained of the opinion that the future— technologically, strategically, and politically—remained too uncertain for the country to hand the initiative in this field to the Soviet Union. Nonetheless, it was not an easy choice.

Perhaps because McNamara revealed what a hard choice it was, the opposite concern in the Congress developed a flourishing career. No one exactly suggested to him that he favored underkilling Soviet citizens. But it was not uncommon for senators and representatives to ask if his policies were not leading to nuclear stalemate or parity, which amounted to approximately the same thing. McNamara attempted to deal with this concern in a variety of ways. One way was to give his own interpretation of such terms as "stalemate" and "parity." For example:

"Stalemate" suggests that we are satisfied with an impasse that will not change. But change occurs continually. Technical factors which may change this offsetting capacity which now exists pretty much on both sides are constantly revealing themselves. We must watch pretty carefully and pursue all the research and development programs you are concerned with. We do not have a balance. We have a dynamic offsetting situation which may change, not overnight, but in the course of a few years.[5]

Exactly what constituted a "dynamic offsetting situation" McNamara did not say. He confessed, for his part, to be as uncertain about the meaning of "parity" as he was about "stalemate."

I do not mean overly to emphasize semantics, but I do not know how you define nuclear parity. I say if you do define it in one way, as it might well be defined, that is to say, numbers of weapons, we in no sense of the word are in a state of nuclear parity today. Our number of nuclear weapons in any category I am familiar with far exceeds the number of weapons in a similar category in the hands of the Soviet Union, in my opinion.[6]

By McNamara's standards, in fact, the situation was not one of parity but of American superiority. As he put it:

. . . I am trying to be very precise in stating the situation as I visualize it developing, particularly I wish to be precise in making clear that the military program we are presenting to the Congress for fiscal year 1964 will in any mind maintain a superior strategic nuclear force in the United States compared to the strategic nuclear force of the Soviet Union in a period covered by the program we presented to you.[7]

Thus, the real issue in McNamara's mind was not superiority versus parity but exactly what American superiority would mean in the awful event of nuclear war. On that score he was quite candid.

I do not believe we are either unimaginative, or lacking in skill, but I do believe that a careful assessment of the probable increases in the Soviet nuclear power as estimated by the experienced intelligence evaluators in our Government indicate that power will increase in such ways, particularly in such types, that there will not be a possibility for us to build a force that can destroy that power to such a degree that there will not remain elements so large as to cause severe damage to our Nation in retaliation for our destructive effort directed against that power.[8]

Some members of Congress immediately concluded from this kind of statement that a condition of strategic nuclear stalemate did in fact exist. McNamara, however, argued differently.

The extent of damage which the United States would be willing to accept must, in my judgment, always be related to the degree to which her security interests are involved in any given issue. For example, we have made it quite clear that the defense of Western Europe is as vital to us as the defense of our own continent and that we are prepared to back up our commitments there with our strategic nuclear power no matter what degree of damage might result should the deterrent aspect of this policy fail. . . . Being realistic, we must admit the Soviets are achieving a growing capability to inflict damage upon the U.S. mainland. The fact that the United States is maintaining a superior strategic nuclear power should not blind us to the growing destructive power of Soviet nuclear forces. This fact makes it increasingly important for us to make clear to the Soviet Union, in advance, those vital U.S. interests which we must support with our total power. The increasing capability of Soviet nuclear forces must not be permitted to lull our Allies, our own citizens, or our enemies into the belief that we would be less willing to defend these vital interests.[9]

As evidence of his conviction on this score, McNamara told Senator Symington: "I foresee no period in the future, let's say in the remaining years of this century, when we can, under today's conditions, operate without a strategic nuclear force of the type we are proposing for this 5-year period, no matter how large a conventional force we and our allies build."[10] What was more, this force had to have certain important characteristics:

I believe the initiation of thermonuclear war would not be a rational act, but I also believe under the press of circumstances it is entirely possible that such a war would be initiated, and I believe we must be prepared, therefore, to participate in such a war and to apply our nuclear forces. I further believe that any force that has such characteristics that it cannot be thought of as an operating force cannot serve as a deterrent, and therefore unless one has a force that has capabilities for actual operations and a force for which one has an operational plan, one, in my opinion, does not have a creditable deterrent.[11]

Despite these rather firm assurances, members of Congress wondered whether McNamara was not perhaps willing to accept stalemate and parity through measures of arms control and disarmament. He assured them that such was not the case.

My position is a very simple one on disarmament or arms control: I think we should engage in such agreements if and when, and only if and when, we can do so without reducing our power advantage.

It is perhaps oversimplified to say that the Soviets seek to dominate the present world but I believe that, and I think the only reason they don't dominate it today is, basically, because of the military and economic strength of the United States and, in my opinion, the only deterrent to their domination of the free world in the future will be the maintenance of that strength.

Now, I think that strength can be maintained under certain forms of arms control or disarmament. Other forms of arms control and disarmament in my opinion would reduce our net advantage over the Soviets, and I would be very much opposed to the latter and in favor of the former. This is the approach with which we view armament and disarmament proposals and arms control proposals and I . . . take a personal interest in these matters, as does Mr. Gilpatric, the Deputy Secretary.[12]

If that, indeed, was the attitude of the Department, why had McNamara concurred in the removal of the Jupiter missiles from Italy and Turkey? Could this act not be construed as unilateral disarmament and part of some secret deal with Khrushchev which included the removal of the Soviet missiles from Cuba? McNamara vigorously rejected this interpretation. The actuality, as he saw it, was one of modernization rather than disarmament.

We are planning to replace the Jupiter missiles in both Italy and Turkey . . . with Polaris missile submarines.

In 1957 when the decision was made to install the Jupiters, they, along with the Thors, were the only strategic missiles NATO had ready for deployment.

These missiles helped greatly to build up our early ballistic missile strength.

But with the rapid advances in technology and with the accelerating growth of our missile forces, they no longer form a major part of NATO's missile strength.

And this year alone [1963], for example, the number of operational strategic ballistic missiles in the Alliance will increase from approximately 450 to over 800.

And more importantly, as the Joint Committee on Atomic Energy noted in their report in February 1961, when they recommended the replacement of the Jupiter missiles with a mobile solid-fueled missile system, the Jupiter missiles are liquid fueled, easily located by the enemy, and vulnerable not only to conventional and nuclear attack but also to sabotage.

It seems to us desirable, therefore, for these reasons to replace . . . the Jupiters with the more modern weapon system.

The best available alternative is the Polaris system.

These submarine-borne Polaris missiles would have a very much higher probability of survival in the face of a sudden nuclear attack.

Aside from the present advantages of the Polaris system, it, unlike the Jupiter, has a growth potential extending for a period of years into the future.

And we therefore propose that the Polaris submarines begin operation in the Mediterranean the first half of this year [1963].[13]

In addition to these considerations, McNamara pointed out that "it costs us roughly $1 million a year per missile simply to maintain the missile in Turkey, and we pay that, and we see no need to continue that expenditure for such an ineffective weapon."[14] He could see no connection, in short, between the removal of the Jupiters and disarmament. The budgetary trend, after all, was all the other way. Defense expenditures for fiscal year 1961 had been $44.7 billion. For fiscal year 1964 they would run to about $52.4 billion.[15] That seemed rather a far cry from unilateral disarmament.

Despite the evidence, and these assurances, members of Congress wondered whether the Administration would actually be willing to use nuclear weapons if the occasion so required. The concern seemed to be, first, that the Soviets could overwhelm NATO with conventional forces; and secondly, that fear of nuclear escalation played too large a role in the calculations of the Administration. McNamara dealt with the first point in much the same terms as Nitze and Vance had done. The Russians, he said, "are not 10 feet tall in Europe."

When we credit the Russians with 140-odd divisions, with a total army strength of about 2 million, and when we recognize that in addition to the divisions, they must have in the army an overhead base to take care of patients, trainees, and others, that, perhaps, is a half to a third of the combat troops, you can see it is absolutely impossible for them to have divisions anything approaching ours in the number of 145 out of 2 million men.

Our Army considers that a division plus its support personnel should total roughly 40,000 men, and if you were to multiply 145 Russian divisions by 40,000, you have something on the order of 5,600,000, to which must be added at least a third, say, another 2 million men, for the necessary training base and overhead personnel. So you have a military force of 7½ million, which would be equivalent in strength per division to our divisions.

Now, the Russians do not require, perhaps, as much support personnel as we do for a variety of purposes. Perhaps their lines of communications are shorter, perhaps their traditions in relation to support are such as to get by with less than ours, but it is perfectly clear, I think, that one Soviet division is quite a different form of army force than one U.S. division.[16]

As for the problem of nuclear escalation, McNamara insisted that it had to be taken seriously. "At the moment," he maintained, "I am inclined to think there is very little chance of limiting a conflict that has already seen the rather widespread use of tactical nuclear weapons."[17] The cause of escalation, he thought,

will be the fear of one side or the other that the use of nuclear weapons by the other side is leading to their near-defeat, and a catastrophic defeat, which they would hope to minimize by initiating the use of strategic weapons. This is the circumstance, I believe, one side would be in, in the event that several hundred nuclear weapons had been used against it by the other side.[18]

To indicate how this fear might operate, McNamara cited the following case:

I would simply suggest if we were sitting here today and we received cables from Europe saying that in the case of our airfields—let's assume they were being attacked with [deleted] bombs by the Soviets, there are, let's say, 120 airfields—and we received cables from Europe that 120 [deleted] bombs had gone off, I think there would be a strong temptation on our part, and perhaps a requirement on our part, to assume that this was but the first step of a drive to subjugate the West, and that in our own interests to minimize our losses, we should respond with an overwhelming force. This is the problem, it seems to me, that both of us face under those circumstances. I am speculating now. I can't speak with certainty.[19]

In the circumstances, it seemed unwise to gamble the nation on the possibility that the use of nuclear weapons on a small scale would not cause escalation. McNamara did not rule out limited nuclear war even in Europe. But he continued to insist on the desirability of a major conventional option. That, he insisted, was not cowardice; it was a prudent regard for the national interest.

Congressional anxieties about the role of nuclear weapons in American strategy were accompanied by uneasiness over McNamara's policies with respect to the procurement of major weapon systems. This uneasiness expressed itself in opposite directions. On the one hand, members of Congress resisted the transition from bombers to missiles; on the other hand, they questioned whether enough was being done to develop new and radical capabilities.

The anxiety about the transition from bombers to missiles first took shape in Congressional demands that McNamara purchase a fifteenth wing of B-52's. McNamara would not bow to the demand and gave his reasons for refusing.

Procurement of another wing of B-52's would increase the operational inventory of that aircraft by only 7 percent [deleted] when they would be coming into the operational force. Furthermore, manned bombers present soft and concentrated targets and they depend upon warning and quick response for their survival under nuclear attack. This is a less reliable means of protection than hardening, dispersal, and mobility. Moreover, reliance on warning and quick response means that the bombers must be committed to the attack very early in the war and cannot be held in reserve to be used in a controlled and deliberate way. Finally, bombers are expensive. It costs about [deleted] billion to procure a wing of B-52's, together with its tankers and Skybolt missiles, and to operate it for 5 years. For the same cost, we can buy and operate for the same period of time about 250 hardened and dispersed Minuteman missiles or [deleted] about 6 Polaris submarines.[20]

The decision "did not mean that we did not want manned bombers. We already had many bombers but very few ballistic missiles. What we needed to do was to build a more balanced force of bombers and missiles, and to do that, we had to buy more missiles."[21]

In 1963, McNamara assured the Congress that he planned to continue a mixed force of missiles and manned bombers for at least the next five years.

Although most of the aiming points in the Soviet target system can be best attacked by missiles, the long-range bombers will still be useful in followup attack, particularly on certain hardened targets. Accordingly, all 14 of the B-52 wings will be maintained in the force. Advance attrition aircraft have been procured with prior year funds to support this force.

The B-47 subsonic medium bombers will be gradually phased out of the forces over the next several years. Some of these aircraft could be continued in operation for a longer period of time than now planned if the need should arise over the next year or two. Two wings of the B-58 supersonic medium bombers will be continued in the force throughout the program period.[22]

McNamara warned, however, that this very large force—more than seven hundred bombers—might grow increasingly vulnerable.

Since July, 1961, we have maintained approximately 50 percent of the manned bomber force on a 15-minute alert. Because this measure is essential to the survival of the force in a ballistic missile attack, we plan to continue it throughout the program period. But I should caution that a 15-minute ground alert may not be sufficient to safeguard the bomber force—particularly during the later part of this decade. By that time the Soviet Union could have a large number of missile-firing submarines on station within reach of most of our bomber bases.[23]

The Congress reluctantly accepted McNamara's reasoning with respect to the B-52's. It then expected him to continue the

Skybolt air-to-surface ballistic missile which purportedly would extend the life of the B-52. This McNamara refused to do. He gave his reasons when he presented the defense budget in 1963.

It has been argued that Skybolt would be able to extend the life of the B-52 force in an era of increasingly sophisticated enemy air defenses; that is, even if the B-52 were to have trouble penetrating enemy defenses, it could stand off at a distance and fire Skybolt. Viewed in this role, it was clear that Skybolt could not make a worthwhile contribution to our strategic capability since it would combine the disadvantages of the bomber with those of the missile. It would have the bomber's disadvantages of being soft and concentrated and relatively vulnerable on the ground and the bomber's slow time to target. But it would not have the bomber's advantageous payload and accuracy, nor would it have the advantages usually associated with a manned system. It would have the lower payload and poorer accuracy of the missile—indeed, as designed it would have had the lowest accuracy, reliability and yield of any of our strategic missiles—without the relative invulnerability and short time-to-target of a Minuteman or a Polaris.

These characteristics make Skybolt unsuited to either category of primary strategic targets. On the one hand, Skybolt would not have been a good weapon to use against Soviet strategic airbases, missile sites or other high-priority military targets because it would take hours to reach its target, while a Minuteman could reach it in 30 minutes. On the other hand, Skybolt would not have been a good weapon for controlled, countercity retaliation. Aside from its relative vulnerability to antiballistic missile defenses, it has the important disadvantage that its carrier, the B-52, must be committed to its targets, if at all, early in the war because it would be vulnerable on the ground to enemy missile attack. Common sense requires that we not let ourselves be inflexibly locked in on such a matter. And being "locked in" is unnecessary when we have systems like Polaris whose missiles can be withheld for days, if desired, and used at times and against targets chosen by the President. The Skybolt, therefore cannot be, and is not, justified as a weapon to be used against primary targets.

Skybolt's value, then, would depend upon its effectiveness in the only remaining important target category, "defense suppression";

that is, the destruction of the enemy's defenses in order to permit
the bombers to penetrate. But in this role Skybolt offered no unique
capability. Several other missiles could also be used to attack enemy
defenses: Minuteman and Hound Dog in particular. Skybolt offered
a special advantage in this role only as long as it was expected to
be significantly cheaper than alternative systems. Unfortunately, this
advantage disappeared.

The cost history of Skybolt is particularly poor. Although originally
estimated to be less, the Air Force early in 1960 estimated that Skybolt would cost $214 million to develop and $679 million to procure.
By early 1961, the estimated development cost had risen to $391
million. By December 1961, the estimated development cost had
risen to $492.6 million and the procurement costs to $1,424 million.
In its July 1962 program submission, the Air Force increased the
estimated procurement cost to $1,771 million. Thus, the latest Air
Force estimate to develop and procure Skybolt exclusive of warheads was $2,263.6 million [for 1,012 missiles].[24]

Even then, McNamara thought there were "compelling reasons
for believing that even these latest estimates are still very un-
realistic, and that the actual costs would be much higher."[25]

For example, the Skybolt development program was far behind
schedule on the program that was supposed to be completed for
$492.6 million. According to that program, there were supposed to
be seven flight tests by the end of 1962, when in fact, there were only
six. Moreover, the amount of flight time allowed in the Skybolt test
program was less than half the amount which was actually required
for Hound Dog, a much less complex development.

Just how much more would have been required to complete Skybolt is uncertain. I am sure that the full development and engineering test program would have ultimately cost at least $600 million and
might have cost substantially more. As for procurement, it is difficult
to see how the cost could have been less than $2 billion. Thus, the
Skybolt would very likely have become nearly a $3 billion program,
not counting the additional cost of warheads. And even then, there
was no assurance that the Skybolt development would result in a
reliable and accurate missile.

In effect, this meant that Skybolt had lost whatever cost advantage
it once promised. The cost per missile aboard an alert bomber—and

that is the most realistic way to reckon the cost—would approximate
$4 million per missile, very close to the incremental initial invest-
ment cost for a Minuteman missile, complete with its blast resistant
silo. In view of Minuteman's greater flexibility, reliability, accuracy,
its much lower vulnerability and faster time to target, it clearly
makes sense to meet our extra missile requirements by buying
Minuteman rather than Skybolt.

We propose, then, that to the extent ballistic missiles are required
for defense suppression, they be Minuteman. I can assure you, moreover, that the missile program I am recommending is fully adequate
to the defense suppression task.[26]

That sounded the death-knell of the Skybolt. Despite Mc-
Namara's assurances about the retention of the B-52 in the
force, and about its ability to penetrate enemy defenses with
the aid of Minuteman, Hound Dog, and other devices, many
members of Congress suspected that the days of the bomber
were numbered. They expressed deep concern, in particular,
about McNamara's unwillingness to proceed with the development of the RS-70 as a full weapon system. This concern
resulted in a classic analysis by McNamara of cost and effectiveness applied to a particular program. His long statement, released on March 15, 1962, acknowledged the controversy surrounding the subject.

Because of the great Congressional and public interest in the B-70
bomber and the RS-70 reconnaissance-strike programs, I have within
the last week furnished to interested members of the Congress our
latest analyses of these two aircraft. In line with our policy to keep
our citizens informed on major defense issues, I believe as much of
this information as security considerations permit should also be
made available to the general public.

The B-70, in its long-range bomber configuration, has been a matter of intense controversy for a number of years. In reviewing the
history of this project, I was impressed by the fact that the B-70
never enjoyed the full support of the President and his Scientific Advisory Committee, the Secretary of Defense and his principal civilian
advisers, or the Joint Chiefs of Staff as a corporate body. In fact, the
only consistent supporter of this program was the Air Force itself.

The secretaries and chiefs of the other services, whether under this Administration or the previous Administration never supported the B-70 for full weapon-system development or procurement and, indeed, many vigorously opposed it. So it is a matter of record that the B-70 has long been considered a very doubtful proposition with the weight of competent scientific, technical and military opinion against it for many years.

Nevertheless, I approached the B-70 problem with a completely open mind and without any preconceptions one way or the other. I carefully studied not only all the arguments pro and con but also the specific facts and figures upon which these arguments were based. I was particularly concerned, for example, with the cost and effectiveness of other ways of doing the job proposed for the B-70. And, I would like to emphasize at this point that, in selecting a weapon system to accomplish a particular military task, we are dealing not with absolutes but with comparatives. We must always take into account not only the planned capabilities of the proposed weapon system but also its full cost in comparison to the cost and effectiveness of other weapon systems which can do the same job, perhaps in somewhat different ways. I believe we can all agree that the common objective of both the legislative and the executive branches of our Government is to provide all of the forces we need for our security at the lowest possible over-all cost.[27]

McNamara pointed out that a careful study of an earlier B-70 proposal had concluded that it was really no more than a manned missile.

Indeed, a book about it was published under just such a title. The old B-70 system offered none of the advantages of flexibility generally attributed to manned bombers. It could not look for new targets nor find and attack mobile targets or targets of uncertain location. It offered no option but preplanned attack against previously known targets—a mission that can be effectively performed by missiles.

Moreover, the B-70 had important disadvantages when compared with ballistic missiles. It would have been vulnerable on the ground to surprise missile attack. It would not have been hardened and dispersed like Minuteman, or continuously mobile and concealed like Polaris. Rather it would have had to depend on warning and ground-alert response—a method of protection far less reliable, in an era where large numbers of missiles exist, than hardening and dispersal or continuous peacetime mobility.

In answer to this it was argued that the B-70, like other manned bombers, could be launched subject to positive control on the basis of ambiguous warning—a property not possessed by missiles. But the important point here is not that bombers can be launched under positive control in response to warning; rather it is that they have to be launched on the basis of warning because they are vulnerable and cannot ride out an attack. We don't care whether or not Polaris missiles, for example, can be launched subject to positive control because we are under no great compulsion to launch them until we are ready to make the final decision to destroy their targets.

Further, the B-70 is far less suitable than the B-52 for airborne alert measures. And attempts to maintain it on the ground in a widely dispersed posture and at a very high level of alert would have entailed all kinds of difficult and costly operating problems, problems that have effectively prevented the Air Force from operating any other of its bombers in this way.[28]

McNamara felt, moreover, that the B-70 would have a rather poor chance of penetrating enemy defenses. It would show up very clearly on radar screens, and the higher it flew the earlier it could be picked up by the radar.

Furthermore, the B-70 had not been designed for the use of air-to-surface missiles such as Hound Dog or Skybolt, and therefore could not attack while standing off several hundred miles, but would actually have had to fly into the target area to drop its bombs. Finally, the B-70 would have been an extremely expensive aircraft, particularly so in relation to its capability in the straight bomber version.

So, it is not surprising that previous Secretaries of Defense and the previous President have had very grave doubts as to the desirability of this particular weapon system. Even the Air Force is now no longer proposing the B-70 in a bomber configuration, implicitly admitting the correctness of many of these reasons.[29]

What the Air Force was now proposing and presenting to the Congressional committees was a new and different version of the B-70, namely, a reconnaissance-strike aircraft known as the RS-70. McNamara had difficulties with this version too.

While the RS-70, if feasible, would be of considerably greater value to our over-all strategic power than the B-70, it would still suffer from some of the same shortcomings, including very high costs; and, in addition, would introduce entirely new problems which we have yet to explore fully.

The B-70, as it was formerly envisaged, was already a more technically complex vehicle than any of the ICBM's we are now developing. Because of its great speed, it required a mass of electronic components for bombing-navigation, for communications and for controlling the environment within the aircraft. In contrast to an ICBM, these subsystems must operate with very high levels of reliability for periods of hours rather than minutes.

The RS-70 would introduce, in addition, another new set of subsystems, including reconnaissance sensors, processing systems, display systems, communication systems, all requiring human interpretation and decision within very short times, and air-to-surface missiles. Many of these new subsystems, it should be recognized, have yet to be developed. Indeed, our technical review of this proposal, to date, indicates that some of the key elements may well lie beyond what can be done on the basis of present scientific knowledge.

The most attractive aspect of the RS-70 is its proposed reconnaissance-strike capability in a post-attack environment. This capability would require, first, the development of an extremely high resolution radar system—a system which, in combination with an operator, could recognize targets from an altitude of 70,000 feet and out to a considerable distance. To appreciate what this involves, consider the fact that to separate visually two points in an area as large as this radar is supposed to observe would require a screen 15 feet by 15 feet to present a television-quality picture. This example is given only to illustrate the problem of display and is not, of course, a solution which anyone would consider.

At the present time we do not know how to specify a system which can gather, process and display the data at the rates and with the resolution necessary for the RS-70 mission, which involves firing a missile from an aircraft flying at thirty miles a minute before it moves out of missile range. To achieve the capability which would be required to "recognize" or to analyze damage on some important types of targets is beyond any known technique.

Let me try to illustrate the severity of this problem. Picture the RS-70 flying at 70,000 feet and moving at 2,000 miles per hour. The proposed mission would require the gathering of radar reconnaissance data on the presence of new targets—or known targets which may not have been destroyed or neutralized—and the prompt processing and analysis of these data in flight. The proposed radar, moving with the aircraft at 2,000 miles per hour would be seeing new area at the rate of 100,000 square miles per hour or 750 million square feet per second. We cannot state today with any assurance that satisfactory equipment to perform this processing and display function in an RS-70 can be made operational by 1970, let alone by 1967, on the basis of any known technology, or whether the human interpretation job required of the operator can ever be done.

Thus, it is clear that there are many very difficult technical problems yet to be solved—and, indeed, yet to be fully understood—before we can have any reasonable expectation that the reconnaissance capability required by the RS-70 can actually be developed and produced within the 1967–70 time period. We have started work on these problems and over $50,000,000 has been separately provided for this purpose in the 1963 budget, but we are two or more years away from even a flight test of the reconnaissance subsystems in a form from which operational specifications can be drawn, let alone blueprints for the production of hardware.[30]

The RS-70 would also have the capability of transmitting processed radar data on important target areas back to the home base.

This capability, if obtainable, would be useful in retargeting follow-up strikes by other manned bombers or by ICBM's. However, the assured rate of transmission over intercontinental ranges in a wartime environment would be only a minute fraction of the rate at which the data are being acquired and processed by the RS-70 radar.

The Air Force proposal would also require the development of new air-launched strike missiles. For use against hard targets, these missiles, because of their limited size and warhead yields, would have to be far more accurate than any strategic air-launched missile now in production or development. This requirement would entail yet another set of problems.

Finally, the deployment of the RS-70 will involve operating problems far more difficult than that of the B-52.

Although the Air Force has not yet stated the ultimate size of the RS-70 force, a force of about 200 B-70's was proposed at one time. Considering the capabilities the Air Force specifies for this aircraft, we can assume that a smaller number, say 150, would suffice. The Air Force estimates that the first wing of forty-five RS-70 aircraft would cost $5,000,000,000. A force of about 150 would probably cost in excess of $10,000,000,000—excluding the cost of the tankers and the annual operating costs.[31]

McNamara made five points on the basis of the analysis thus far:

1. The RS-70, as proposed by the Air Force, is very far from being ready for production or even full weapon-system development. The new subsystems which could provide the RS-70 with its damage assessment capability have been started in development, but we are not sure now that we know how to develop successfully the extremely high data rate, sharp resolution radar system required. Our best estimates now are that we could not have such a system early enough to produce an operational RS-70 force capable of useful reconnaissance strike before 1970.

2. The RS-70, without these subsystems, would be nothing more than a B-70, the production of which it is now agreed would not be warranted.

3. Until we know much more about the proposed system—its technical feasibility, its military effectiveness and its cost—we have no rational basis for committing this aircraft to weapon-system development or production.[32]

That was one part of the decision. There remained the question of whether or not the program would be worth the cost.

This question can be answered only in terms of the total job to be done and the various alternative ways of doing it in relation to their respective costs.

The 1963 and prior year budgets provide for over 1,000 Atlas,

Titan and Minuteman intercontinental ballistic missiles, plus forty-one submarines with over 650 Polaris missiles, plus more than 700 B-52 and B-58 bombers. By 1967 the alert portion of the force alone will have three times the destruction capability of the alert force we had last June [1961].

Now, how large a part of the enemy target system could this force be expected to destroy after absorbing an enemy surprise attack?[33]

McNamara reviewed the factors that entered the calculation: the number of warheads per vehicle, the survival rate of each type of weapon system, the reliability of the delivery vehicles, their ability to penetrate enemy defenses, and the accuracy and yield of the warheads. He concluded that:

Utilizing these factors and applying to them values which, on the whole, are thought to be quite conservative, we calculate that the strategic retaliatory forces programmed through 1967 could achieve practically complete destruction of the enemy target system—even after absorbing an initial nuclear attack. The addition of a force of either 200 B-70's, which was proposed last year by the Air Force, or the 150 RS-70's now being considered, either of which would cost about $10,000,000,000, would not appreciably change this result.[34]

This argument did not deal with the utility of the wartime reconnaissance capabilities of the RS-70. On that score, McNamara maintained,

we have other means of performing that function and with any adequate high-processing-rate radar system which may be developed, the B-52's and B-58's could have a considerable reconnaissance and bomb damage assessment capability incident to their principal mission. We think that the B-52's and B-58's, arriving after our missiles have suppressed the enemy's air defense, could penetrate as well, or almost as well, as the RS-70.

A decision by the Soviet Union to produce and deploy an anti-ICBM system could not significantly change this over-all picture, and in any event would be no less effective against the RS-70 and its missiles. To ensure that our missiles can reach their targets even then, we have included a substantial sum in the 1963 budget for a "penetration aids program." We also have the option of increasing the Minuteman program for which extra production capacity has already been provided.

It is clear, therefore, that the RS-70 program, as we see it now, would not add significantly to our strategic retaliatory capability in the period after 1967. Interestingly enough, at the very time the Air Force is urging the production of another aircraft system on the grounds that nuclear-armed missiles are not dependable, one theatre commander is requesting the production of a new nuclear-armed missile to replace his aircraft which he says are too vulnerable in a nuclear war environment. And while the Air Force, in pressing its case for a new bomber, has questioned the dependability of nuclear-armed missiles, it is at the same time urging an aircraft (the RS-70) which itself depends for its strike capability on highly sophisticated nuclear-armed missiles.[35]

What all these considerations added up to, as far as Mc-Namara was concerned, was that:

While I am fully convinced that it is entirely premature to make any kind of commitment to weapon-system development or production of the RS-70 in fiscal year 1963, I am not prepared to preclude such a commitment at a later date. By continuing our XB-70 program of three prototype aircraft at the cost of $1,300,000,000 and by proceeding with the exploratory development of the key subsystems of the proposed RS-70 for which funds have been included in the 1963 budget, we will have open to us the option of producing and deploying an RS-70 system at a later time if the need for such a system should become apparent. Since the key subsystems have yet to be developed, delaying the decision for one year would not postpone the real operational readiness of the first wing at all.[36]

Nearly two years later, the first XB-70 had not yet flown and the commitment remained only to the production of two prototype aircraft. Senator Symington was inclined to bemoan "our current tendency in military planning to move away from people into button pressing."[37] But McNamara refused to budge from his basic position. He was quite willing to consider developing other manned systems in addition to the RS-70, but as he saw the issue:

When we are talking of missiles and the difficulty of relying on missiles, I think it is important to recognize that the alternative is not the manned bomber as is normally conceived of.

The term "manned bomber," I think, properly connotes a launch platform for a free fall bomb.

Now, I think everyone would agree in the Defense Department, all that I have talked to, that strategic launch platforms for free fall bombs will be obsolete in the 1970's, without any question, and no one that I know of is proposing that we develop a new system or continue existing systems for launch platforms for free fall bombs in the 1970 period.

The only thing that has been proposed that is based on a manned aircraft is a launch platform for a missile.

So the alternative is not manned bombers, on the one hand, in the traditional sense or the proper sense, versus missiles, on the other. The alternatives are missiles launched from the sea, missiles launched from the land, or missiles launched from the air, and of those three modes of launch the missiles launched from the air are, by far, the most complex missiles, likely to be the most expensive and unreliable, and certainly would require the most advanced development.[38]

When challenged about the reliability of missiles versus bombers, McNamara replied:

I don't wish to leave the conclusion . . . that these reliability problems in the missiles are any different than the reliability problems in our manned aircraft systems. They are essentially the same. They require the application of the same technology to correct, and I believe it is fair to say that many of our missile systems today are as reliable as some of our aircraft systems today.

Furthermore, I have every reason to believe that with concentration on the missile systems which are just now coming into the inventory, the reliability problems can be corrected in a reasonable period of time. I recall very vividly being at Omaha a few months ago on a day when almost literally all of our B-58 bombers were unavailable for alert status because of mechanical failures.

Mechanical systems have deficiencies and these deficiencies are not limited to missile systems. They apply equally well to manned aircraft.[39]

Although the Congressional committees engaged in the bomber-missile controversy with declining zest, they did not abandon it altogether, despite McNamara's arguments. Nor did they surrender their interest in the development of the new and more exotic systems. Many members, having witnessed the seemingly endless outpouring of new weapons during the 1950's, appeared to expect the process to go on forever. They were troubled by McNamara's caution with respect to all the bright new possibilities that stood just over the horizon. One such possibility was the 100-megaton weapon. The Soviet Union had it; why should not the United States follow suit? McNamara tried to explain.

I believe we must recognize the possible psychological effects of a statement by the Soviets that they have, or will have, such a weapon and are prepared to launch it against this Nation, or that they have the capability of launching it against this Nation. Because we must take account of that possibility, I believe we must continue the work that would make it possible for us to develop a weapon of that type should we later decide that is desirable.

But . . . I do not personally hold to the view that the greater the yield of the weapon, the greater the terror. I think a more proper standard of evaluating the degree of terror associated with a potential threat is the magnitude of destruction which that threat, when implemented, can bring about.

I believe the public can recognize that point, in which case the psychological impact of an announcement that a 100-megaton weapon is available and can be launched against this country would be no greater than the psychological impact of a statement that we are prepared to survive any first strike by the Soviets against this country with sufficient power, literally, to destroy the Soviet Union.[40]

More or less in contrast to the interest in the 100-megaton weapon was the fascination with the antiballistic missile system. The Army had been working on the Nike-Zeus ABM for some time, but neither the Eisenhower nor the Kennedy Administration had authorized its procurement in quantity. Was that not a dereliction of duty? McNamara thought not. The problem, as he described it, was "not to hit one bullet with a bullet," which has become the popular analogy, but to "choose among the thousand bullets the one that is the real bullet as opposed to the false bullets."[41] For that problem, according to McNamara, the Nike-Zeus was quite inadequate.

During the past year we have gained a much broader understanding of the technical problems involved in developing an effective system of ballistic missile defense. It is now generally agreed that the Nike-Zeus system currently being tested would not be effective against a sophisticated threat in the late 1960's and early 1970's. A thorough review of the available technical possibilities leads us to the conclusion that there are four major improvements which could be made in the present Nike-Zeus system.

(a) The use of the Zeus discrimination radar as a high volume, lower accuracy target tracker.

(b) The modification of the Zeus missile to reduce the minimum altitude at which an incoming warhead can be intercepted.

(c) The development of a new high-acceleration missile (Sprint) which, because of its greater acceleration, would increase the time available for discrimination of targets.

(d) The development of a new advanced radar which could simultaneously acquire, evaluate, and track a large number of objects.

In developing the program which we are now proposing, we considered three major alternatives.

(a) The first alternative envisioned the continued development and test of the present Nike-Zeus system and a separate limited development of the new advanced radar.

(b) The second alternative called for proceeding with all four major improvements with initial deployment of a system incorporating initially only the first two improvements.

(c) The third alternative envisioned skipping the first two improvements and proceeding on an urgent basis with the development of the more advanced system (Nike-X), incorporating the Sprint missile and advanced radars, and deferring the decision to deploy the system.

After thorough consideration of the alternatives, we propose to adopt the third. It incorporates the improvements which are best in the long run and will yield the most effective system which it is possible to visualize at the present time. The first alternative was rejected because it would not yield a system which would be effective against the kind of an attack we could be faced with by the time the system could be built. The second alternative would lead to a final system which is very similar to the Nike-X in both time and performance, but with an initial configuration only slightly better than that furnished by alternative 1. It was considered that the marginal protection offered by the early limited capability would not be sufficient to offset the additional costs which would be involved.

We recognize that there are some reasons why it might be desirable to proceed immediately with the production and deployment of such an antiballistic missile system, even one with a limited capability. Such a system might reduce U.S. casualties in the case of a small or medium Soviet attack on our urban areas. Further, it would complicate the design of and tactics for the attacker's offensive weapons.

But there are even better reasons why we should not proceed at this time with actual deployment of a system:

(a) We still have a great deal to learn about reentry phenomena and techniques for discriminating between real warheads and decoys.

(b) We also have a great deal to learn about the effects of a nuclear detonation from one of our intercepting missiles on other elements of the defensive system.

On balance, therefore, we believe that it is premature at this time to commit ourselves to the production of any system and certainly not to an interim system with admittedly limited capabilities. Instead, we propose to proceed with the greatest urgency in the development of the Nike-X system, retaining the option to move ahead with actual production and deployment of such a system, if the capabilities of the system and the circumstances should warrant such a decision at some later time. I believe that the matter of antimissile defense is so important that we must make every effort to develop an effective system, even if we cannot now make a decision to procure and deploy it. Accordingly, over $450 million is included in the 1964 budget to initiate the Nike-X development and continue the Nike-Zeus test program and related work under project Defender.

One final point: The effectiveness of an active ballistic missile defense system in saving lives depends in large part upon the existence of an adequate civil defense system. Indeed, in the absence of adequate fallout shelters, an active defense might not significantly increase the proportion of the population surviving an all-out nuclear attack. For this reason, the very austere civil defense program recommended by the President . . . should be given priority over any major additions to the active defenses.[42]

Another source of Congressional uneasiness—greater even than the concern about the antiballistic missile—arose from the military space program. McNamara found this uneasiness somewhat puzzling, although he admitted: "We are behind in certain space developments, particularly those associated with large booster capabilities." His point was that the Administration was spending about "a billion and a half, $1,513,000,000 within the Defense Department for military programs associated with space. That billion and a half is just about three times the amount spent on military space projects in 1961."[43] The effort, thus, was increasing, and McNamara prided himself that it was doing so in an orderly way. As he described the program within the Department, it fell into three major categories.

The first is a series of programs for which there is a clear military requirement and these would include satellites for such purposes as mapping, communications, navigation, nuclear tests detection, and weather forecasting. In each of these fields, we see very clearly a military need which we can meet by designing and launching into space certain satellite systems and receiving back from them information bearing on our military requirements.

A second category of projects relates to development work that is being carried on in relation to future probable military requirements, such as missile warning systems, additional communications requirements, and certain other clear military needs of the future.

In all of these cases in the second category, it is anticipated that the potential military requirement of the near future can most likely be met by unmanned space satellites.

A third category of research and development work sponsored by the Defense Department relates to the development of certain capa-

bilities which would be required were we subsequently to find it
necessary to put a man into space in conjunction with some military
requirement that might arise in the future. In this connection we
have a series of projects underway of which the largest by far is
Dynasoar; Titan III also falls into this category even though it will
also provide future launch capability for categories 1 and 2.

Here we are dealing with an uncertain military requirement, specifically the need for manned space vehicle operations but a requirement which, if it develops suddenly, cannot be met quickly unless
we are today carrying out the development work on large boosters,
on space environment systems that will facilitate the existence of a
man, and certain other techniques that would allow a man to operate
effectively in space and carry out certain assumed military missions.[44]

The first two categories, from McNamara's standpoint, established a clear foundation for a budget request. "The third category, that is to say the development of techniques and technology that will support the launch into space and the maintenance in space of a man carrying out military functions, the
requirement for that development in the future is perhaps more
questionable. It is also by far the most expensive."[45] Given the
uncertainties and the costs, McNamara was eager to avoid
parallel national programs to put men in space. The Department of Defense had already started work on the Dynasoar
space-glider and the Titan III solid-fueled booster. The National Aeronautics and Space Administration, for its part, was
engaged in the Gemini program which would place a two-man
capsule in orbit. To reduce duplication, McNamara joined with
James Webb, of NASA, in an agreement of January 21, 1963.

Under its terms we agreed that a joint planning board comprised
of representatives of NASA and the Defense Department would be
set up to plan the content and coverage of the Gemini program, to
insure that the requirements of the Defense Department for potential operation of a man in space and the requirements of NASA for
that same purpose were met by this single program, thereby avoiding the duplication that was implicit, for example, in the Air Force
request for its own manned space program.[46]

The idea that the Air Force would suffer because of this arrangement, as some members of Congress were suggesting, McNamara thought unwarranted.

The total research and development program of the Air Force is up about 40 percent in fiscal year 1964 over that of fiscal year 1962 so that the development work as such has not leveled off. The major part of that addition is associated with space developments of one type or another. . . .[47]

Moreover, Titan III and Dynasoar continued in the Air Force program despite the agreement on Gemini. Titan III could serve as booster for Dynasoar; it might also be a building block toward a future space weapon system, even though McNamara was unable "to describe any space weapon system that appears to offer greater potential for military use than a weapon that is land-based, sea-based, or airborne."[48] The case for continuing with Dynasoar looked, if anything, somewhat weaker. As McNamara admitted:

The NASA program provides for an unmanned launch of Gemini in the latter part of this year [1963], and a manned launch, one or more manned launches, in 1964.

The Dyna-Soar program, if I recall the figures correctly, does not provide for manned launches until 1966, roughly 2 years after the manned launch of Gemini.

So insofar as our objective is to acquire knowledge relating to the capabilities of a manned vehicle operating for military purposes in space, we can acquire that much earlier and, as a matter of fact, much more extensively from Gemini; this because the Gemini will have the capability of staying in orbit about 14 days, and my recollection is that Dyna-Soar will not have a capability for orbiting for more than 3 days and, therefore, Gemini is both earlier and will provide a more extensive experimental laboratory, if you will.

On the other hand, Dyna-Soar has certain characteristics that are unique to it, characteristics not possessed by Gemini. Specifically it will have the capability or is proposed to have the capability to control its selection of recovery area to a far greater degree than can the Gemini.

The Gemini is planned to allow land recovery in contrast to the Mercury which has been recovered at sea.

But Dyna-Soar goes quite a bit beyond that and it is planned to allow recovery at specified points on land, and it achieves this greater control . . . over reentry and point of recovery by a greater lift-to-drag ratio which allows it to control its flight, its return flight through the atmosphere.

But whether that is enough to warrant the huge expenditures that are unique to the Dyna-Soar, expenditures which in total would approximate $800 million in addition to the $800 million-plus required for Gemini is the question that the Air Force is presently examining.[49]

Dynasoar was clearly headed for cancellation. But the total research and development budget for the Department of Defense still stood at $5,938 million, about 40 percent higher than it had been two years earlier under the Eisenhower Administration. McNamara was quite prepared to admit that he had not proliferated new projects in the abundant way of his predecessors. He had even cancelled some. But he remained convinced that the country's security would not suffer from a lack of basic and applied research. The record, in his view, suggested ample effort in this area.

Congressional concern about the role of nuclear weapons in American strategy, about bombers and missiles, and about the adequacy of the research and development program was matched by anxiety about the relationship between the civilians and the military in the Pentagon and the role that each group was coming to play. More specifically, this anxiety expressed itself in the fear that the Secretary of Defense and his civilian aides were usurping the traditional functions of the Services and the Joint Chiefs of Staff. Chairman Vinson of the House Armed Services Committee expressed the basic apprehension most succinctly to McNamara.

We have today the Joint Chiefs of Staff system, a Joint Staff, and four separate services. One of the basic reasons why we have four services and four separate Chiefs who are responsible for their service and for their viewpoints as members of the Joint Chiefs of Staff, is to be very sure that we do not have one single type of defense thinking. We want, and the law expects, divergent views on defense planning. The whole purpose is to present this type of planning to the Joint Chiefs of Staff, and to you, in order that the collective wisdom of the four services and the four service chiefs may be brought together in order that intelligent defense plans may result.

I sincerely hope that unified planning does not contemplate the elimination of the separate views of the four separate services, nor any reduction in their capability to present these four divergent views to the Joint Chiefs of Staff, to you, and to the President.[50]

McNamara assured Vinson that unified planning did not contemplate any such result, and noted that he subscribed "fully to the objective you laid out."

And as a matter of fact, I think the approach that we are taking will assure achievement of that objective. It is certainly not my purpose to in any way eliminate the views of the services, but rather to insure that once the service view has been expressed and a service program approved, that it is properly balanced and fits in with the pattern of views and decisions relating to the other services.[51]

McNamara cited one illustration of the problem that confronted him.

The question is: what size Army do we require? The size of the Army that we require depends to some degree on the amount of airlift that we will have available. There is no sense in developing an Army that is bigger than we can move by sea or air.

So when you say to the Air Force, develop your budget for fiscal year 1963 designed to give us optional response, the Air Force cannot do that by itself. It must integrate its proposal into some kind of a plan that takes account of what the Navy is proposing to do, and the Army as well.[52]

McNamara's argument was hard to refute, but Chairman Vinson still wondered whether the planning-programming-budgeting system would lead, in fact, to a single service and the abandonment of the diversity inherent in the four Services and the Joint Chiefs. McNamara asserted that "it indicates the opposite."

And I say that because our objective certainly is . . . to obtain a unification of effort. There are two ways to obtain a unification of effort. The first is to develop a single service. That is certainly one way. But I think a far better way, at least as I visualize it today, is to take the organizational structure we have and unify the effort by considering the activities of one service which are related to another in the form of a program cutting across service lines. And this is what we have tried to do.

I think thereby we will unify the effort without the need for major organizational changes which might conceivably have resulted in the requirement for a single service.[53]

The Congressional committees had difficulty in finding fault with this position, but some members doubted that McNamara was paying sufficient attention to his military advisers. Congressman Hébert gave expression to the doubt when he said to McNamara:

This is what is concerning me, Mr. Secretary. It is as though a layman is put in charge of a great hospital to administer it—you are the administrator of the Defense Department—this man is put in charge of a great hospital and he consults with his doctors and then consults with a group of lawyers and makes a decision in favor of what the lawyers thought instead of what the doctors thought.

When I am sick, I go to see a doctor. When I want to fight a war, I go to see people who have fought wars and have the background and knowledge to do so.

I don't know about the RS-70; I don't know about the weapons, but I rely on them. If a doctor gives me medicine, I take it.[54]

McNamara's reply was brief: "The doctors disagreed here."[55] That represented the crux of the problem. It did not mean, however, that he was ignoring his military advisers. As he explained in 1961:

Since January 20th, I do not believe there has been any change in the reliance that I have placed on the advice and counsel of the Joint Chiefs. Since that date I have met with the Chiefs frequently, at least once a week every week, 2:30 on Monday afternoon. In most weeks, several times during the week, as a group, we have met together. Individually, I have met with them almost, literally, hundreds of times during the weeks, and there has been frequent telephone consultation between us. . . . I think Tom Gates, more than any other Secretary in recent years, did much to establish a close relationship with the Chiefs. I have endeavored to do just exactly what General Lemnitzer says he believes I have done, expand upon that relationship, drawing it closer and closer together.[56]

McNamara also wanted to see greater use made of the four-hundred-man Joint Staff. Again, in 1961, he said:

The Joint Staff, being composed of experienced officers from all military services, has the potential of becoming a most valuable asset to the Department of Defense, as a whole.

I am attempting to realize this potential by strengthening the participation of the Joint Staff in Department of Defense strategic deliberations.

Of the special studies I have initiated since taking office, 35 of the most important were assigned to the Joint Chiefs of Staff and thus to the Joint Staff for analysis. I intend to rely on the Joint Staff even more extensively in the future.[57]

Despite these efforts, differences between the Secretary and the Chiefs inevitably remained. McNamara, speaking of the defense budget for fiscal year 1964, estimated that there were "several hundred major decisions of the Chiefs and myself incorporated in the budget in which we are in complete agreement. There are a handful, maybe three or four major decisions, in which one or more of the Chiefs might differ from my recommendation. I don't recall any major decision in which there is a complete difference of view."[58]

McNamara described quite candidly the procedure that he followed in presenting and resolving these issues.

I start by trying to anticipate, 6 or 9 months in advance, the controversial issues that relate to the following year's program. Having tried to anticipate those, I request the Chiefs to address themselves to them, not that they wouldn't have done so otherwise, but specifically I request them to address themselves to them so that I may have their advice and counsel.

And in preparation of the 1964 budget I asked General Lemnitzer many months ago to establish a series of special studies relating to many of these controversial issues and requested him to have these studies prepared under the direction of either himself or the Chiefs, and subsequently reviewed by the Chiefs, after which I asked that they send their recommendations on the issues. These, I then studied myself. In most instances I found it necessary after reading the written report and recommendations from the Chiefs to return to the Chiefs and ask that we discuss the matter orally, so that I, by exchanging questions and answers with them, could better understand their views or the opposing views, if there were splits on the issue.

After the oral discussion, I then study the matter myself, arrive at my own conclusion, prepare a written report outlining my views, frequently in the form of a memorandum to the President, since most of these issues are so important that they require that I present my recommendations to the President rather than making the final decision myself.

If in this memorandum which I prepare to try to outline my own conclusions, my conclusions differ from those of the Chiefs, I will also include the views of the Chiefs, and if they are split, I include the split views of the Chiefs, and the reasons for these views in contrast to the reasons for my own recommendation. And usually, because these are very important matters, I will then, before discussing my own position and recommendations with the President, submit a draft of my memorandum back to the Chiefs and ask that they review it to insure that I have properly presented the problem.

Because even though I have views—and in most instances strong views—on most of these issues, and even though I have no hesitancy whatsoever in presenting a recommendation to the President that may differ from the views of the Chiefs, whether they be unanimous or split, I think it extremely important that the final decision-maker, whether it be me or the President, make that decision with full understanding of the views of opposing parties. And for that reason, I normally will submit any important memorandum, that I may be planning to submit to the President, back to the Chiefs in order that they may review it to insure that it does properly state their positions.

Then I will discuss the matter with the President, having presented to him in advance of the discussion the memorandum so he may acquaint himself with the issues before we discuss them. And

normally, in the event that there is a split between me and the
Chiefs or between me and some of the Chiefs on one side and some
of the other Chiefs on the other side, the President will wish to discuss the matter with all parties present.

That, then, is the decision-making process.

I think it is a very appropriate one. I think it provides for a very
complete examination of the problem. And I think it leads to responsible decision-making.[59]

Such a process hardly bypassed or downgraded the Joint
Chiefs. Still, there remained the fact that McNamara had
strong views, as he himself admitted, and did not hesitate to
express them. Where did they come from? Congressman Hébert
suspected the "lawyers" in his analogy of the hospital. A col-
league, Congressman Bob Wilson, raised the specter of computers. He said:

I'm just a little bit disturbed—while I'm not against progress, I like
computers and Univacs, and so forth, but I don't think you can crank
all the basic information into a Univac or a computer that will get
you the right answer.

Sometimes it takes a little bit of flying by the seat of your pants. I
will have to take the word of Mr. Vinson who has been sitting here
for 40 years listening to a lot of experts, and listening to the words
of a young expert that may know a lot about different things, but
doesn't have the broad experience that is necessary.

The Univac can be wrong. I can remember when it said the Re-
publicans were ahead in the election. And this was early in the
returns.[60]

McNamara thought Congressman Wilson would be "happy
to know that I have reduced requested appropriations from
the services for electronic equipment for fiscal year 1964."[61]
The joke was lost. Congressman Bray suggested that "we have
gone pretty far afield when we absolutely ignore the thinking
of men who came up the hard way from second lieutenant on
up to wearing a galaxy of stars on their shoulders," in favor of
those "who believe we can settle all by a computer or a slide
rule."[62] The concern, in short, was about the role of the civilian

analysts in the Pentagon. Members of Congress wondered whether they might not be replacing the military as the principal advisers of the Secretary.

One of the analysts, Alain Enthoven, faced the issue squarely. He pointed out that the "problems of selecting strategies and choosing weapon systems today are quite unlike anything that existed before the Second World War."

Although the change has been gradual, the Second World War seems as good a place as any to locate the watershed. Before that time military technology changed relatively slowly in relation to the average length of a military or political career. Both soldiers and statesmen could learn most of what they needed to know about military power and the relationship of weapon systems and forces to national security from their own direct experience and by reading history books. The direct personal experience of both military and civilian leaders, combined with the collective experience accumulated over centuries of warfare was sufficiently relevant to contemporary affairs so that the problem of interpreting their experience by the careful rules of scientific method had not become a major one. Of course, this is not to say that there were no important failures to adapt to new military technology. History is full of examples of military successes and failures attributable to successful innovation, or to a lack of adaptation, and the beginnings of both World Wars were full of surprises on this account alone.

But something new has been happening in the past twenty years. Science and technology have gone through a "take-off" and they are now in a period of rapid, accelerating, and apparently self-sustaining growth. Nuclear weapons, nuclear power, computers, large-scale rockets, and space flight are but the most spectacular examples of a revolution which has been led by both military men and civilian scientists. Before World War II, we did not plan on technological change; we merely adjusted to it. Now we are planning on it. We are debating whether inventions can be scheduled, and we have weapon systems that are being called obsolescent while still in production.[63]

According to Enthoven, the new situation had two important implications.

First, rampant technological change is producing not only better weapons of familiar kinds, it is also producing for us the possibility of many new kinds of weapons. Consider long-range bombardment. The progression from the B-17 to the B-29 to the B-36 was straight-forward and apparently obvious. But now we have the possibility before us of literally dozens of distinctly different strategic nuclear delivery systems, not to mention the endless array of other kinds of weapon systems and forces. And the number of possibilities is expanding almost daily. There are air breathing vehicles and ballistic vehicles that can be based and launched from fixed land bases, mobile land bases, platforms on the surface of the sea, under the sea, and in the air. There are missiles launched from aircraft, aircraft launched from missiles, missiles launched from submarines, and so on in endless progression. Although we have not tried to develop all of these possibilities, we have tried to develop many of them. In fact, within the past several years, the United States has had in development or production more than a dozen different long-range strategic nuclear delivery systems, including three different bombers (the B-52, the B-58, and the B-70), four different ICBM's (Atlas, Titan, Fixed Minuteman, and Mobile Minuteman), three IRBM's (Thor, Jupiter, and Polaris), two air-breathing intercontinental missiles (Snark and Navaho), and three air-launched missiles (Hound Dog, Skybolt, and Rascal). A similar development is taking place in almost every kind of warfare.

But in the face of the expanding number of systems that we could buy, we have not escaped the ancient necessity for choice arising out of the scarcity of available resources. Whether we like it or not, in the United States today, we have only a limited amount of goods and services available at any one time. Our gross national product, though large, is limited. We have only a finite number of man hours available for all forms of productive activity. If we attempted to develop and procure a dozen or more distinctly different strategic nuclear delivery systems, not to mention the three or four dozens that one might be able to conjure up in an evening's discussion, we doubtless would end up squandering our resources and not doing a good job on any of them. Therefore, we have to choose.[64]

Enthoven emphasized the inescapable nature of resource scarcity and the necessity for choice "because many people seem to believe that the scarcity of resources and the resulting limits in our Defense budgets are really the invention of the Bureau of the Budget, the Comptroller's Office, or the Appropriations Committees."

They are not. The limitation on our national resources is a fact of life, like the laws of physics or aerodynamics. There are other needs and demands for those resources besides the demands of defense and of expanding science and technology. There are such needs as feeding, clothing and housing our population, educating our children, and fighting disease, in almost endless number. Therefore, only a limited amount of resources are available for defense. And it is our responsibility . . . military and civilians working together, to get the most out of our limited resources by facing up to the hard choices and helping those who must make the decisions to make the right ones.[65]

Another implication of rapid technological change, in addition to the necessity for choice, according to Enthoven, was that current weapons differed more and more from the weapons used in World War II and Korea.

Although it is difficult to know exactly how and to what extent, this does mean that some aspects of earlier experience in combat are probably out of date. And peacetime experience with military operations, however valuable, does not completely make up for this. The wars of the future will differ in some important details from the wars of the past. If, therefore, we are to prepare for the next war rather than the last one, we must address these changes in a systematic way and do all we can to understand their implications for the choice of weapon systems and strategy. As I remarked earlier, this problem is not unprecedented. The machine gun reduced some of the tactical planning preceding the first World War to irrelevance. Armored warfare made a mockery of some of the assumptions on which the Maginot Line was based. The development of naval aviation dealt the battleships such a decisive blow that the defenders of battleships have become the symbol of adherence to outmoded thinking. But the problem is of greater proportions today than ever before.

To deal with it, the Office of the Secretary of Defense is trying to encourage, stimulate, and contribute to the development of a new analytical approach or discipline for synthesizing many of the factors that go into defense planning. It is clear that both the Secretary of Defense and our senior military leaders are being forced by present circumstances to place increasing reliance on such analysis rather than placing exclusive reliance on their experience and judgment. This development has become controversial. It has been described by some as "downgrading the military" or "excessive reliance on young and temporary civilians" and other such epithets. But such a characterization misses the point. It is not a matter of upgrading some people and downgrading others. That is neither the intent nor is it a necessary consequence of the development and reliance on improved methods of analysis. Rather, the problem is one of making a sensible adjustment in our ways of thought to deal with rapid changes in technology and in international circumstances, an adjustment that is appropriate for both military and civilian leaders.[66]

It was Enthoven's view that, to the extent that controversy existed, it was inaccurate to describe it as civilian versus military.

One can find both military and civilians on all sides of this issue. Rather, it is a conflict between new and old ways of thinking about national security problems. In fact, the reforms now taking place have their roots in many places, both military and civilian. They are not purely a civilian invention. All of the Services make extensive use of operations analysis. It was the Navy that created the Operations Evaluation Group, and the first important applications of operations analysis included anti-submarine warfare. The Air Force sponsored the RAND Corporation. General Maxwell Taylor, in his book, called for the development of explicit quantitative standards of adequacy, something we are working hard to do now. But it is appropriate that the broader application of the analytical approach be led by the Secretary of Defense because an important part of his job is to stimulate innovation and reform.[67]

The issue, thus, was not numbers or computers or civilians versus words or judgment or the military.

The real issue is one of clarity of understanding and expression. Take, for example, the statement "Nuclear power for surface ships offers a major increase in effectiveness." Precisely what does that mean? Does it mean 10 per cent better or 100 per cent better? When that sort of question is asked a frequent answer is, "It can't be expressed in numbers." But it has to be expressed with the help of numbers. Budgets are expressed in dollars, and nuclear power costs more than conventional power. If nuclear power costs, say 33 per cent more for some ship type, all factors considered, then, no matter what the budget level, the Navy and the Secretary of Defense have to face the choice of whether to put the nation's resources into four conventional or three nuclear ships, or for a large budget, eight conventional or six nuclear ships, and therefore whether by "major increase" is meant more than 33 per cent, about 33 per cent, or less than 33 per cent. Because the Secretary of Defense has to make the decision in these terms, the statement "major increase" is not particularly helpful. It must be replaced by a quantitative analysis of the performance of various missions, leading to a conclusion such as, "Nuclear power for surface ships offers something between X and Y per cent more effectiveness per ship. Therefore, $1 billion spent on nuclear powered ships will provide a force somewhere between A and B per cent more or less effective than the same dollars spent on conventionally powered ships.[68]

That, precisely, was the kind of advice McNamara sought. Being eclectic, he would take it from the military and the civilians alike. It was the quality of the counsel rather than the apparel of the counselor that he valued. Members of Congress, however, found it difficult to believe that the military and the civilians, working together, could produce advice equal or superior to that of the military alone. Thus, when McNamara seemed to overrule his military advisers, as in the case of the TFX, he produced the biggest controversy of all.

If the Congressional hearings on the experimental tactical fighter known as TFX have not produced much in the way of light, they have certainly generated a great deal of heat. Bitter and unsubstantiated charges of favoritism and conflict-of-interest abound. Yet the central fact remains that McNamara heard a great deal of military and civilian advice about the TFX during a period of nearly two years, and that he developed powerful arguments to support both the concept of a single fighter for all the Services and his award of the contract for the aircraft to the General Dynamics Corporation.

One argument had to do with the general problem of weapon system costs.

In the past, the actual costs of major weapon systems have commonly increased from 300 to 500 percent over the cost estimated when the program started, and in some instances more. Some of the reasons for such overruns have been:

1. We have insisted that weapon systems meet performance standards that go far beyond essential military requirements.

2. We have accepted unrealistically optimistic cost estimates at the beginning of a program, only to find costs multiplied many times during the program.

3. We have not sufficiently defined at the outset what it is we are asking our contractors to develop. Here we have discovered that it is frequently helpful to work with more than one contractor in what we call a program definition phase before the development contract is awarded.

4. We have too often employed inadequate and unsatisfactory procedures to select major contractors, putting insufficient weight on seasoned experience in the design and production of similar weapons.

5. We have relied too much on cost-plus contracts and other contracting procedures which do not provide incentives to reduce cost.[69]

A second argument presented by McNamara concerned the costs of operating different weapon systems for similar purposes.

The disadvantages of operating many different weapon systems can be observed in the Navy and in the Air Force today. The Navy currently has a rate of aircraft out of operation for lack of parts which is altogether too high. The Air Force is maintaining a better operational rate but at a cost of excessive spare parts inventories. With the present rapid rate of technological change, the Air Force has acquired a $2.2 billion inventory of spare parts that are already obsolete and practically worthless.[70]

One way to reduce costs and increase reliability, McNamara noted, "is to insist that weapon systems be developed that can be used by more than one service, where this can be accomplished without degradation of essential military requirements."

The advantages of one weapon system over two are obvious. They result in substantial savings not only in the development, test and production stages, but throughout the life of the system in terms of logistic support, maintenance, training programs and operations.[71]

In fact, there already existed a multiservice tactical fighter. Whereas the Navy and the Air Force had been producing the F4H and the F-105, a comprehensive analysis of the two production programs in 1961 convinced McNamara "that one aircraft, the F4H, could meet the need of the Air Force as well as the Navy, and do it better than the F-105."

Accordingly, further procurement of the F-105 has been terminated and the F4H, now designated the F-4, will be bought for both the Air Force and the Navy. In addition, I have assigned supply management responsibilities for all spare parts and components peculiar to the F-4 aircraft to the Department of the Air Force and I have asked the Air Force and the Navy to develop and submit to me, for my approval, joint plans for the maintenance of this aircraft.[72]

With the experience of the F-4 in mind, McNamara believed that one tactical fighter could be developed to meet the future requirements of both the Navy and the Air Force. He agreed that the concept of a major multiservice weapon system had met with opposition.

I would be less than candid . . . if I did not admit that the majority of experts in the Navy and Air Force said it couldn't be done. As late as the 22nd of August, 1961, after the Navy and the Air Force had been working together for almost 8 months, it was reported to me by both services that development of a single TFX aircraft to fulfill stated requirements of both services was not technically feasible.

While this attitude, based on years of going separate ways, was understandable, I did not consider it was a realistic approach, considering the versatility and capabilities that could be built into a modern aircraft because of advances in technology. I was also convinced that, if we could achieve a single tactical fighter, we would save at least $1 billion in development, production, maintenance, and operating costs. In short, after study and review, I believed that the development of a single aircraft of genuine tactical utility to both services in the projected time frame was technically feasible and economically desirable. I directed that we continue to work toward this objective.[73]

McNamara received confirmation of his belief some fourteen months later, after an extensive competition between the Boeing Company and the General Dynamics Corporation, when evaluation officers of the Navy and the Air Force concluded:

(1) Both contractors have the capability to successfully design and produce this weapon system.

(2) Both designs are acceptable as initial development design configurations to the using agencies involved—TAC and the Navy.

(3) Both designs will require further design refinement, and changes can be expected during the development period.

(4) When fully developed, the operational tactical aircraft will markedly improve the capability of the Tactical Air Command in carrying out its assigned missions, especially in limited war.

(5) Similarly, the Navy version, when fully developed, and when configured with the new long-range air-to-air missile, will markedly improve existing fleet air-defense capability.[74]

The evaluation report, the fourth of its kind, did not indicate a preference for either the Boeing or the General Dynamics proposal, but suggested that there was little to choose between them. General LeMay and Admiral Anderson certified that both proposals met the military requirements. Both wanted Boeing as the contractor. McNamara preferred General Dynamics.

My examination of the facts, in consultation with my advisers, convinced me that, as compared with the Boeing proposal, the General Dynamics proposal was substantially closer to a single design, requiring only relatively minor modifications to adapt it to the different requirements of the Navy and the Air Force, and that it embodied a more realistic approach to the cost problem. Accordingly, I decided to select General Dynamics as the development contractor, since I concluded that it was best qualified to design the most effective airplane that could be produced at the least cost, in the least time, to meet our military requirements.[75]

In further explanation of his decision, McNamara made these points:

In this case we are faced with a situation in which judgments are pyramided upon judgments. First, we have the judgments of the competing contractors that an aircraft of particular design can be built at a given cost within a specific time-frame. Next, we have the judgments of the Evaluation Group regarding feasibility, and the degree to which the designs would or would not satisfy the stated requirements. Then the Source Selection Board, using factors weighted by judgment, made a recommendation which appeared to place greater emphasis on potential bonus factors in certain operational areas, rather than on dependability of development and predictability of costs. This recommendation, understandably, was seconded by the Navy and Air Staffs, since these officers are most vitally interested in obtaining the ultimate in performance in individual weapon systems. On occasion, this desire leads to the establishment of characteristics for weapon systems which cannot be met within the time or funds available, and it has frequently resulted in lowering operational effectiveness.

There is only one way I know to minimize the compounding of error that can occur through this pyramiding of judgment, and that way is to apply the judgment of the decision-maker not only to the final recommendation, but also to the underlying recommendations and facts. This I did to the best of my ability. In doing so, I found it necessary to balance the promises held out by competing contractors, against the hopes and aspirations of military officers, and the limiting realities of economics and technology.

That I attach great importance to the principle of free competition is, I believe, demonstrated by my insistence that competition continue through the program definition phase of the TFX project. That I attach great importance to the fulfillment of established military requirements is, I believe, demonstrated by my refusal to terminate the program definition phase until I was satisfied that the military requirements of both the Navy and Air Force had been met. That I attach great importance to the recognition of economic and technological limiting conditions is, I believe, demonstrated by my selection of General Dynamics as the contractor that most clearly recognized the effects of these limitations on the task to be achieved.

I do not feel that this is a case which presents a civilian-military conflict but rather one of placing emphasis where it must be placed. In the final analysis, judgments differed. In reaching my decision, I considered the recommendations of my various military and civilian advisers as well as other available evidence, but I had the final responsibility.[76]

McNamara could do no more than show reason, responsibility, and dedication in defense of his decisions. Thereafter, the Congress would have to pass judgment on TFX and all the other matters in dispute. But Congress was not the only judge. The crucial test of McNamara's policies lay elsewhere, in the harsh realities of the international arena.

CHAPTER 7

Tests of Effectiveness

THE FORCE STRUCTURE and contingency war plans of the United States come under constant and critical scrutiny from a variety of sources. McNamara and his aides have subjected them to the test of inspection, analysis, and exercise. The Joint Chiefs, the Joint Staff, and the Services, besides making them up, have been free to criticize them and argue for their change. The great diversity of the defense establishment, in fact, has continued to be an invaluable asset in this respect and McNamara has encouraged its preservation. The Congress, in its dialogue with the Secretary, the Chiefs, and the Service Secretaries, and in its special investigations, has also reviewed almost every aspect of the programs recommended and implemented by McNamara. But the great test of effectiveness for any defense posture lies in its performance as the basic guardian of American interests.

The relative effectiveness of the multiple options approach is difficult to determine by this crucial standard. For one thing, there is no clear-cut alternative with which to compare it. Although the approach of the Eisenhower Administration sounds strikingly different—and the force structure accompanying it did differ in certain important respects—it is probably fair to say that in his last two years of office, President Eisenhower was groping toward something approximating the approach of multiple options. Perhaps the principal difference between the Eisenhower and Kennedy eras—force structure aside—is that Eisenhower and his aides, in their declarations if not in their actions, continued to insist on the early use of nuclear weapons in any confrontation with the Soviet Union. Kennedy and McNamara eschewed so stark a position.

Making comparisons is not the only difficulty. There is also the problem that, in a rapidly shifting international environment, the modern defense posture has two related functions to perform; the deterrence of conflict and the conduct of successful military operations if deterrence fails to work. The two functions are related because, as McNamara has pointed out, the force which is politically usable, and effective in combat, is likely to have the most powerful deterrent effect. But it is by no means clear exactly how to measure the performance of a defense posture under conditions which do not correspond precisely to a state of war or peace. War itself provides the final and obvious test; the cold war does neither. Yet it is the cold war in a particularly virulent form, with its recurring crises and low-level conflicts, which marked the thirty-four months of the Kennedy Administration. How much difference a change in defense plans and programs has made in the incidence and severity of these events does not lend itself to easy resolution. About the best one can do in the circumstances is to examine the effects that the introduction of the multiple option approach had on certain key controversies between East and West.

One of these controversies is very strange and superficially harmless. It takes the form of a dialogue or argument between the United States and the Soviet Union about the state of the strategic nuclear balance. It is characteristic of the postwar period that nuclear weapons in general and strategic nuclear capabilities in particular have riveted the attention of the major powers. There are obvious reasons why they should. Although the struggle between East and West has matched non-

military and non-nuclear instruments of power against one
another, the existence of strategic nuclear capabilities in the
background of every confrontation since 1945 has no doubt influenced the calculations and the actions of the major con-
testants in a number of important ways. The objectives of current foreign policy may resemble the goals of nations in earlier
periods of history; the rules of the political-military game, as
now played, appear to have altered radically as the possibility
of thermonuclear war has become linked with the threat or use
of force. The continuing dialogue about the state of the strategic nuclear balance thus has significance as a reflection, however distorted, of the estimates by the two greatest powers concerning the freedom and degree of risk with which they can
pursue their objectives. But the dialogue probably contains more
than simply Soviet and American claims about their respective
positions in the strategic nuclear balance. Although in this
Aesopian age the language is all nuclear, the two principal
antagonists seem to be comparing the total military capabilities
of the two sides as well. In other words, by this interpretation,
the strategic nuclear dialogue has become symbolic of the
Soviet-American estimate of the over-all military balance—
nuclear and non-nuclear. In the light of claims that American
determination and power diminished during the years of the
Kennedy Administration, it is interesting to observe how this
ominous and esoteric dialogue has proceeded.

When James Reston interviewed Khrushchev in 1957, shortly
after the first sputnik had gone into orbit, the latter said to him
confidingly:

I think I will not be revealing any military secret if I tell you that
we now have all the rockets we need: long-range rockets, intermediate-range rockets and close-range rockets. Of course, these are
not the limits of what can be achieved, for engineering is not marking time, but these means fully insure our defense.[1]

Toward the end of 1959, Khrushchev had embroidered on this
view to the point where he told a group of press representatives:

We do not want to scare anyone, but we can tell the truth—in saying that we have now stockpiled so many missiles and so many atomic and hydrogen devices that, if we were attacked, we could wipe all our probable enemies off the face of the earth. . . . In one year a plant that we visited produced 250 missiles with hydrogen warheads on the assembly line.[2]

By early 1960, Khrushchev had converted this claim into the flat assertion that "the Soviet Union is now the world's strongest military power."[3]

A little more than a year later the Kennedy Administration had come to power, McNamara somewhat artlessly dismissed the missile gap, and the supplements to the Eisenhower defense budget began to appear. Khrushchev found it necessary, in these circumstances, to announce that Kennedy had "said during our talks in Vienna that a balance of power had now been established between the two world camps and that a direct clash between the USSR and the United States must be prevented because such a clash would have the most disastrous consequences."[4] Khrushchev no longer argued Soviet military superiority. Rather he praised Kennedy for this "sober view" which "displayed definite realism."[5] The only trouble, in his opinion, was that the President refused to act reasonably. A few months later, the Chairman sounded an even more defensive note. He said, "We believe that now the forces of socialism . . . are mightier than the aggressive imperialist forces. But even if we should agree with the United States President, who quite recently stated that our forces were equal, even then it is plainly unreasonable to use the threat of war."[6]

During the last months of 1961 and the beginning of 1962, the Kennedy Administration unleashed a barrage of appraisals about the nuclear balance. Deputy Secretary of Defense Gilpatric expressed his confidence in the overwhelming strength of American retaliatory power. The President himself, in response to questions about the strength of the United States relative to the Soviet Union, indicated that he "would not trade places with anyone in the world."[7] And McNamara was beginning to stress "the fact of U.S. nuclear power, which is able to survive a nuclear surprise attack and strike back with sufficient power to destroy the enemy target system."[8] To all this, Marshal Malinovskii, the Soviet Defense Minister, replied somewhat weakly: "Since our forces are equal, the American leaders should draw the correct conclusions and pursue a reasonable policy."[9] Such a claim was a far cry from Khrushchev's assertion in 1960 that "the Soviet Union is now the world's strongest military power."

Even more interesting was the Soviet discussion of the nuclear balance in the wake of the Cuban missile crisis. According to a distinguished American authority, a pamphlet by Marshal Malinovskii, which appeared in 1962, "contained repeated assurances that Soviet military power was in excellent shape and superior to that of the West. In fact, variations on the theme of Soviet military superiority were dominant throughout the pamphlet."[10] However, the claim was to qualitative rather than quantitative superiority, and Malinovskii admitted that "real reasons exist that force the government and the Communist Party to strengthen the Soviet armed forces."[11] Khrushchev was substantially more candid in a speech he gave in January, 1963. He announced that "foreign scientists and military experts estimate that the United States has at the present time approximately 40,000 nuclear bombs and warheads. As is known, the Soviet Union, too, has more than enough of this stuff."[12] He also said that, despite the withdrawal of the Soviet medium-range missiles from Cuba, he still had the United States covered, and talked somewhat ambiguously about "80, probably 120 missiles."[13] That was hardly the stuff of nuclear superiority.

The nuclear dialogue will continue, and its terms will surely shift about as they have done in the past. No doubt controversies will also continue about the validity of the dialogue as a test of American strength and purpose. But several aspects of the Soviet side of the argument are worth noting. Although some critics of McNamara's policies claim that the United

States has been undergoing a gradual process of unilateral nuclear disarmament, Khrushchev does not seem to share this view. In fact, if the dialogue means anything at all, it is that Khrushchev found it far less plausible to assert the superiority of Soviet arms in 1963 than he did in 1961. Moreover, the Soviets—unlike critics in the United States—do not appear to regard the increase in American conventional power since 1961 as having weakened the effectiveness of the Western deterrent. On the contrary, at the same time that the non-nuclear build-up has proceeded, Khrushchev and his minions have expressed increasing concern that, despite the supposed "balance of forces," the United States might refuse to be deterred. By this test, then, McNamara and his multiple options have passed with flying colors.

The Soviets have provided other and more severe tests than this strange and shadowy dialogue. Berlin is an outstanding example. It is also a familiar test. Every postwar American Administration has had to take it, and Khrushchev determined early in 1961 that President Kennedy and his advisers should prove no exception. The problem of Berlin must be familiar to all Americans. It is not only that the city is exposed, vulnerable, and high on the list of American vital interests. It is also that the Soviets can interfere with the rights of the three protecting powers—the United States, Britain, and France—in such a way as to force the West to take offensive action for the maintenance of those rights. The Eisenhower Administration met this problem in two ways: by threatening the use of nuclear weapons if the Soviets interfered with Allied rights, and by offering to negotiate about the status of Berlin. For reasons which remain obscure, Khrushchev initiated a Berlin crisis in 1958 and then abandoned it in early 1960 without having put the Eisenhower strategy to a very severe test. Many students of the problem thereupon concluded that the Eisenhower strategy had in fact been successful, that nuclear deterrence would work in the future, and that the purchase of insurance in the form of additional non-nuclear capabilities would actually under-

mine the strategy by weakening the credibility of the nuclear
deterrent.

Kennedy and McNamara subscribed to a quite different
view. They feared that the Soviets might simply ignore the nuclear threats and exploit one or more of Berlin's many vulnerabilities. At that point the nuclear threats would be meaningless
as such and action would be required. For a contingency of this
character, they argued, the United States and its allies should
have available a significant non-nuclear option. Even further,
they asserted that the prior availability of the non-nuclear option would decrease rather than increase the chances of Soviet
action. Their premise was that the threat of non-nuclear operations would be initially more credible to the Soviets than a gen-
eralized nuclear threat, and that, consequently, Khrushchev
would act, if at all, with great caution. The problem of Berlin
thus contained the potential of affording a very sharp test of
opposing theories and of the multiple option approach.

Khrushchev, although his motives were hardly scientific,
seemed eager to start the experiment. On June 15, 1961, he
announced that "the conclusion of a peace treaty with Germany cannot be postponed any longer. A peaceful settlement in
Europe must be attained this year."[14] Six days later he donned
the uniform of a lieutenant-general, his wartime rank, and made
a speech in which he offered the status of a free city to West
Berlin. If the West would not negotiate to that end, he threatened, the Soviet Union and the other peace-loving states would
be forced to sign a peace treaty with East Germany by the end
of the year.[15] The implication was clear. Unless Soviet terms
were accepted, the Western Allies would lose their wartime
rights in Berlin and would have to negotiate any future arrangements with East Germany. As if to underline the threat, the
East Germans announced that, after August 1, all air traffic to
and from Berlin would have to be registered with the East
German authorities.[16] The expectation in the West now was
that Khrushchev might take action against the access routes
to Berlin in order to bring the Allies to heel.

The Kennedy response was to renew the pledge that the United States would defend Berlin, start an American non-nuclear build-up, and engage in contingency planning with Britain, France, and West Germany. The Air Force began the movement of sixteen tactical fighter squadrons to Europe. The Army underwent a major expansion. According to Elvis J. Stahr, then Secretary of the Army,

in late July, draft calls were expanded and actions begun to fill the Active Army divisions that had been training commands and to start their intensive training as combat units. In early September, accelerated shipments of over 40,000 Active Army troops were started to Europe to reinforce the 7th Army and its supporting forces. Concurrently, we began expansion of the training base . . . in order to accommodate the still further stepped-up inputs from Selective Service and volunteers. At the end of August 46,000 Ready Reservists—individuals and units—were called to active duty to report beginning in late September, largely to replace, in our strategic reserve, the units being shipped to Europe. On October 15, the 32d Infantry and 49th Armored Divisions from the National Guard, with supporting forces, a total of some 73,000 men, also reported for active duty. And on November 1, the 3d Armored Cavalry Regiment was shipped to reinforce further the 7th Army in Europe.[17]

Despite these efforts, the monstrous Wall dividing East Berlin from West Berlin went up on August 13, 1961. Thereafter, a number of dangerous incidents occurred, including a confrontation of American and Soviet tanks at the border of the divided city. But Allied rights in West Berlin and along the access routes remained intact. By the middle of October, Khrushchev was moved to announce that "if the Western powers show readiness to settle the German problem, the question of a deadline for the signing of a German peace treaty will not be of such importance. Then we shall not insist on the signing of the peace treaty before December 31, 1961."[18] Shortly thereafter the genial Chairman assured listeners at a Kremlin reception that "for the moment we shall wait. We still have patience. . . . It is not good for the time being to press one another."[19] Few

officials in Washington believed that the disappearance of the
deadline meant the last of the Berlin problem. As late as January, 1962, McNamara expressed the view that "what the Soviet Union seems to be seeking is a virtual surrender of West
Berlin as well as attempting to dictate the future shape of the
world."[20] But the immediate test had ended. What, if anything,
had it proved?

To those who favored a nuclear-dependent strategy, there
was the hateful Wall ostensibly to support their case. No one,
however, has yet succeeded in establishing any connection between the American non-nuclear build-up and the Soviet decision to build the Wall. On the other side of the argument
is a measure of evidence that the Soviets and their satellites did
indeed worry about the non-nuclear build-up, and that their decision to drop the peace treaty was influenced by it. But proof
in support of either argument is lacking. Khrushchev designed
a bad test.

It is interesting, nonetheless, to observe what happened to
General Curtis E. LeMay when, early in 1963, he defended the
thesis that the threat of nuclear war would by itself act as a deterrent to a broad spectrum of hostile acts. When questioned by
Congressman Ford on this score, General LeMay started by
saying:

As far as strategic superiority not preventing limited wars, it did
not prevent the limited war in Korea because we did not exercise
it like we did in Cuba. In Korea we did not say there will be no
limited war. We just said there will be no general war or we will
use our nuclear weapons. I think if we had said there will be no
limited war or there will be no war in Korea or we will use nuclear
weapons, there would not have been any.[21]

LeMay also indicated his belief that President Eisenhower's
statement to the effect that ground forces would not be used
to defend Berlin had deterred the Soviets in 1958. Congressman Ford then mentioned the landings in Lebanon and Le-
May described them as "another classic example of what you
can do if you have strategic superiority and then are able to

exploit any situation with your conventional forces without interference." In fact, he thought that "without nuclear and strategic superiority, I do not think we would have dared go into Lebanon."[22]

Congressman Flood entered the discussion at this point and wondered whether "any time we have an argument in the plaza with some Latin republic we do not like," we should say, "We are going to use nuclear weapons. You had better stop that street riot in Lima." LeMay denied that he had meant any such thing but went on to confess: "It just seems odd to me to think that you can stop a big war with nuclear weapons, but something less than that you cannot." After some further exchanges, Congressman Flood asked:

Then if we want to stop the trouble that is going on in Vietnam by half-past 9 tonight or in the next half hour, all we have to do is announce: "If you Reds do not get out of South Vietnam by half-past 10 tonight, we are going to strike at Cambodia, we are going to strike at North Korea, and we are going to strike at North Vietnam, where you are getting your supplies and munitions and aid." Is that what we are supposed to say? You can stop it?[23]

More argument followed, after which LeMay said: "Once a war starts and we are attacked, as in the case of Korea, where we were in there fighting, I think that could have been stopped by using nuclear weapons." He added somewhat lamely that he did not want "to settle every little border dispute around the world by threatening to use nuclear weapons."[24]

Exactly where he would have drawn the line, General LeMay did not specify. Nor did he indicate on which side harassing actions against Berlin and its access routes would have fallen. But it remains difficult to see how, even by his severe standards, the non-nuclear build-up of 1961 made Soviet aggression any more probable. Indeed, it is possible to argue that the build-up contributed positively to deterrence precisely because it pushed the nuclear decision further into the background and thus enabled the Alliance to present a united front to the Soviet Union. But that is speculation. Of only two points can we be sure. Not even General LeMay has suggested that the United States might actually increase the probability of deterring Soviet action by reducing its non-nuclear forces. Nor has anyone argued that Khrushchev's threats were any less plausible because he commenced a non-nuclear build-up of his own. Whether or not any kind of threat could have prevented the construction of the Wall, the approach of multiple options, even as early as 1961, appears to have passed the test of Berlin at least as well as the alternatives.

The guerrilla war in South Vietnam subjected the McNamara plans and programs to quite a different kind of test. Perhaps there are those who believe that the United States should not have come to the support of the Republic of Vietnam at all. Some might even take seriously Congressman Flood's ironic questions to General LeMay about threatening or actually engaging in nuclear strikes to end the insurrection. Others might prefer to see the commitment of major American units to the war in an effort to bring it to an early and successful conclusion. Most students of the problem would agree, however, that some degree of American intervention in South Vietnam was necessary. They would probably agree also that the multiple option approach facilitated intervention because of its emphasis on resources for countering insurgency, and that the magnitude of the intervention has been of approximately the right scale. In fact, the war in South Vietnam, if it has done nothing else, illustrates how the Military Assistance Program and an American military advisory group can produce an indigenous combat force of significant power with a relatively small commitment of American manpower. But the real test of South Vietnam is less of the Military Assistance Program than it is of the ability of the United States to deal effectively with all the related aspects of subversion and guerrilla warfare.

The guerrilla threat has existed in the Republic of Vietnam ever since the Geneva accords of 1954 separated the country from the Communist north of Ho Chi Minh. But it was not until 1959 that the guerrillas began seriously to challenge the regime of Ngo Dinh Diem. Since then, guerrilla forces have grown to more than 23,000 full-time military personnel and 100,000 local auxiliaries. Some of the more highly trained personnel come from North Vietnam; so does the more complex military equipment. But the guerrillas, or Viet Cong, rely primarily on the population of South Vietnam for recruitment of new members, and for weapons, ammunition, and supplies. The Viet Cong attempts to capture, maintain, and expand a number of local territorial bases. From these bases, it engages in subversion, terror, ambush, and more regular military operations up to battalion strength. The objective is not the immediate defeat of the regime, but rather the alienation of the population, the disruption of the economy, and the demoralization of the government and its forces. It is a cruel, destructive, and indiscriminate type of campaign.

President Diem's regime was not particularly well equipped to deal with the Viet Cong. Its army consisted of about 200,000 men, but it had been organized, trained, and deployed to defend against an open attack from North Vietnam. It had neither the doctrine nor the mobility to combat guerrilla attacks and terrorism. Moreover, Diem tended to view the Viet Cong as a threat created and sustained from the outside. In fact, as many as five hundred infiltrators a month were coming into South Vietnam near the Seventeenth Parallel, over the Ho Chi Minh trail through Laos, by way of Cambodia, and across the Gulf of Siam. But the main threat remained internal and to it Diem did not have an effective answer. He had launched a program of economic development but oriented it more to the urban than to the rural populace. Yet out of a population of 14,000,000, about 12,000,000 were villagers and peasants. It was from them that the Viet Cong drew its greatest support and upon whom it inflicted the greatest damage. By 1961, the Viet Cong was reportedly killing as many as five hundred villagers a month.

President Kennedy, in October, 1961, sent General Taylor to South Vietnam to determine what the United States could do to assist the Diem regime. Three weeks later, Taylor returned to Washington with a recommended course of action. Shortly thereafter, the United States embarked on a large-scale program of counterinsurgency in support of President Diem. The principal categories of assistance have been money—on the order of $400,000,000 a year—training, military and economic advice and advisers, and certain support functions for the Vietnamese armed forces such as the helicopter companies which have attracted so much attention. All told, more than fifteen thousand American military personnel are now in South Vietnam.

The goals of the United States, working through the regime, have been to maintain the independence and integrity of South Vietnam, win the loyalty of the population for the government and stamp out the Viet Cong. These goals have entailed a wide range of military, social, and economic measures all designed to separate the rural population from the Viet Cong, provide adequate protection to the villagers and peasants, and subject the Viet Cong to constant harassment and attrition. At the heart of this effort is the strategic hamlet program which ultimately may include some ten thousand fortified hamlets. They are the principal device for separating the rural populace from the Viet Cong and instituting social, economic, and political reform. Each hamlet may consist of about two hundred families. Many are fortified by barricades, trenches, bamboo spikes, and watchtowers. Anywhere from ten to twenty men are provided with carbines, shotguns, and a radio transmitter. After six weeks of training, they are expected to furnish the basic protection to the hamlet and to hold off intruders long enough for reinforcements to arrive. The inhabitants of the hamlet hold elections for a hamlet council which then becomes responsible for the local defense. The government, with American assistance, furnishes the hamlet a variety of economic and social services, including seeds and fertilizers; and civic action teams drawn from the Vietnamese and American armed forces engage in local development projects, provide medical assistance, and offer technical instruction useful to the villagers.

Military operations are closely related to the strategic hamlet program. The principal objective of the ongoing campaign is to expand the areas under government control by means of "clear and hold" actions, after which the strategic hamlets are constructed and protection is provided for them. In addition, the military campaign is directed toward sealing off the borders of South Vietnam and locating and destroying Viet Cong units and strongholds. If the Viet Cong can be cut off from the rural population and outside assistance, if it can be kept under constant attack and compressed into ever smaller pockets of territory, then effective control of the guerrillas will be in sight and their threat substantially eliminated.

The manpower requirements for such a campaign are considerable. It is a rule of thumb of counterinsurgency that the government must have superiority of ten-to-one in forces if it is to overcome a dedicated guerrilla effort. The regime does not have nearly that degree of superiority. In addition to the 200,000 men in the regular army, the government has organized a civil guard of 100,000 men and a self-defense corps of approximately 75,000 men which the Americans help to train. The regular army bears the principal responsibility for offensive action. The village self-defense corps and the province civil guard are intended to assume the protection of the strategic hamlets and the essentially static defense missions to which the army was formerly committed. These units, together with other special forces in the area, probably do not give the government more than a five-to-one advantage over the Viet Cong. However, it is hoped that the combination of American tactical advice, modern firepower, rapid communications, air support, and the growing mobility provided by armored personnel carriers and air transport will provide the needed margin of superiority.

As is always the case in counterinsurgency operations, the military campaign will have no more than a temporary or superficial success unless it gains the active support of the population. The peasants and villagers can become a vital source of intelligence about guerrilla movements and concentrations. They can resist depredations, levies of food, and efforts at recruitment. They can defend their hamlets. But they can also continue to assist the Viet Cong. A strategic hamlet may remain intact and guarded yet still constitute a source of supplies, arms, and manpower for the guerrillas. The Viet Cong can still melt into the tangled countryside of mountains, jungles, and swamps with the aid of the peasants, only to reappear once government forces have "cleared" the area. Counterinsurgency thus is a campaign for the loyalty of the population as well as a brutal battle against the guerrillas. The two must go hand-in-hand, and doubts about the ability of the Diem regime to gain the loyalty of its citizens, as well as questions about its ability effectively to prosecute the war, were what caused the United States to review its programs of assistance to South Vietnam and brought about Diem's downfall.

That there should have been doubts and questions rather than certainties is understandable. It remains unclear, for example, to what degree the dissatisfaction with the Diem regime, so manifest in the cities, had spread to the crucial battlefields of the countryside and made the campaign against the Viet Cong more difficult. Although it is possible to cite a number of cases where the late masters of Saigon had jeopardized or impaired military operations, proceeded too far too fast with the strategic hamlet program, and lagged in the implementation of economic and social reforms, there still must be some uncertainty as to whether Diem's successors will represent a significant improvement over the old regime. Above all, there remains genuine uncertainty about the actual progress of the war.

A counterinsurgency campaign proceeds simultaneously in a number of directions and on a great many different levels of activity. Owing to the character of guerrilla operations, the war is almost formless in character and the conventional means for judging progress are nonexistent. As a substitute for these means, a battery of indices has been developed to measure progress and test the effectiveness of alternative courses of action. Among the available measures are comparisons of casualties suffered by the Viet Cong and Vietnamese forces, the proportion of territory controlled by the two sides, the relative rates of defection from the two forces, the number of incidents initiated by the Viet Cong per month, and comparative losses of weapons. There are nonmilitary indices as well: the number of applications for licenses to start new businesses, the movement of goods and food by road and water, loans to farmers and fishermen, and the number of students in rural areas. Thus, it was reported in 1963 that 51 percent of the villages in South Vietnam were loyal to the government, while 41 percent remained uncommitted and 8 percent were in the hands of the Viet Cong. The Vietnamese forces were said to have suffered 12,000 casualties in 1962 as against 20,000 Viet Cong casualties for the same period. At the same time, Viet Cong strength appeared to remain constant. It was also noted that the rate of Viet Cong attacks had fallen from 120 to about 70 a week and that government forces had stepped up the pace of their attacks from 445 to 700 a month. However, defections from the Viet Cong reportedly dropped from 600 to 350 a month. Exactly what could be deduced from this mosaic of statistics in terms of either progress or efficiency becomes inevitably a matter of judgment.

McNamara expressed his judgment of the situation at regular intervals. In July, 1962, he said:

I am still encouraged by what I see there. The effectiveness of the U.S. assistance requested by the Vietnamese Government and provided to the Vietnamese Government has greatly increased over the past several months. The scope of the Viet Cong operations sponsored directly by the Communists in North Vietnam, if anything, has increased. But their effectiveness has declined, and this decline is measured in a much more favorable ratio of killed and captured, much more favorable to the Vietnamese. The decline is measured in a lesser number of incidents, a lesser number of attacks by the

Viet Cong, and the decline is measured in terms of smaller incidents, smaller forces, indicating their inability to consolidate and operate on a large scale because of the greater mobility and greater effectiveness of the South Vietnamese armed forces. But I wish to emphasize what I have emphasized before, that we can't expect a termination of a war—and it is a war—within a matter of months. It will be years before it is concluded, and I believe it will be concluded successfully.[25]

More than a year later, after the downfall of the Diem regime, McNamara sounded an even more cautious note.

Last September we had hoped we could bring sufficient pressure to bear on the Diem government to persuade it to abandon its oppressive measures against the Vietnamese people and get on with the task of winning the war against the Viet Cong. Although the military situation in the Delta region was still very bad, good progress had been made in the northern areas and especially noteworthy work had been done in the key coastal provinces where Viet Cong strength had once threatened to cut the country in half. In the central area and in the highlands, progress had been steady, though slower. The situation was still difficult in the provinces to the west and north of Saigon itself. Throughout the northern two-thirds of the country, the strategic hamlet program had developed very well and freedom of movement in the rural areas had grown steadily. We concluded then that top priority should be given to the Delta region which contains approximately 40 percent of the population. This region has traditionally resisted central authority. It is the center of Viet Cong strength, and the swampy nature of the terrain makes it the most difficult area to pacify.

The first step in that direction had already been taken by September when a third division was moved to the Delta. But we felt that additional measures were needed, particularly the consolidation, rather than the further spread, of strategic hamlets; the elimination of many fixed outposts; better hamlet defenses; and more trained hamlet militia. We also felt that the regular . . . Army units should be reserved for use in mobile actions and for "clear and hold" operations in support of the strategic hamlet program. . . .

Unfortunately, the Diem government did not choose to follow the advice we offered. In November that government was overthrown and replaced by a new government made up of military officers and civilians. The Viet Cong was quick to take advantage of the growing opposition to the Diem government and the period of uncertainty following its overthrow. Viet Cong activities were already increasing in September and continued to increase at an accelerated rate in October and November, particularly in the Delta area. And I must report that they have made considerable progress since the coup.[26]

Thus, the future course of the war in South Vietnam remained uncertain in 1963. But McNamara continued to believe in the necessity of defending Vietnamese freedom. Whether the counterinsurgency program instituted for that purpose would do the job still could not be determined. As to whether or not the United States should be developing a major counterinsurgency capability there can hardly be any doubt at all. Khrushchev's declarations of support for wars of national liberation and the instabilities that exist in Southeast Asia, Africa, and Latin America all indicate the vital importance of having this kind of capability. No doubt we have a great deal still to learn in this complicated area, and the problem is only partly military. The need to anticipate and, if possible, forestall the kind of breakdown that has occurred in South Vietnam is of equal importance. But where military action is required, there appears to be no adequate substitute for the types of capabilities that are committed to the campaign in South Vietnam. The approach of multiple options surely stands up well on that score.

Although the approach of multiple options has run the gantlet of the strategic dialogue, Berlin, and South Vietnam, its supreme test has come from Castro's Cuba. Indeed, the test has occurred in two parts: one before multiple options were more than a gleam in McNamara's eye; the other after the concept had undergone substantial implementation. Cuba thus provides some basis, however slight, for comparing the effectiveness of two essentially different defense postures.

Too much should not be made of the comparison. The attempt to overthrow Castro with the invasion at the Bay of Pigs in April, 1961, was a debacle from start to finish. None of the principal policy-makers connected with the disaster tried to pretend otherwise; none offered any extenuating circumstances for their mistakes. It is doubtful that the President or McNamara would even have argued that they might have acted differently in 1961 with the force structure of multiple options at their backs. At most they might have pleaded a lack of experience and an inadequate fund of skepticism about the feasibility of a plan which depended so critically for success on the coordinated occurrence of widely separated actions. It is interesting, nonetheless, to note that the President apparently did feel desperately short of usable military resources precisely at this time. Just as the date for the invasion of Cuba approached, so the crisis in Laos seemed to worsen. Thus, he faced the dilemma that if he committed American forces to Laos, he might have no reserves left for Cuba; and if he became involved in Cuba, he would have nothing remaining for action in Laos. The Chiefs of Staff, reportedly, heightened the dilemma by stressing that a move into Laos would require as many as twenty divisions or the limited use of nuclear weapons.[27] If that was the range of choice, it remains a wonder that the President took the gamble of the Bay of Pigs. It is less a wonder that, with so few resources and so many troubles, he should have refused to commit the United States to overt support of the invasion.

The situation in October, 1962, was different in several important respects. The missile crisis took place against the melancholy background of the Bay of Pigs and offered an opportunity to retrieve the disaster of the previous year. It also arose out of a direct and brazen challenge by the Soviet Union; as such, there was no turning back from it. And it occurred in an environment of significantly greater and more diversified American military power.

McNamara has described the development of the Soviet challenge in the following brief account.

Firm intelligence on the existence of offensive ballistic missiles was developed in this sequence:

First, from April to late September, a great volume of unconfirmed reports and rumors, principally from refugees and exile organizations, was received concerning the situation in Cuba. Many thousands of refugees were interviewed and several thousand specific written reports were produced, analyzed for intelligence value, and collated with other source material. Although a large number of these and other reports received in Washington related to the extensive military buildup, none could be equated to strategic weapons when carefully checked out. Actually, interpretation of the high altitude photographs taken before October 14, 1962, of the areas which refugee reports indicated as the most likely locations to contain missiles, either disproved the presence of missiles or linked the suspected activity to SAM [surface-to-air missiles] or cruise-type missiles that posed no offensive threat to the United States.

The second crucial stage of the story started in late September when a recently arrived Cuban refugee gave the first description of equipment that could be equated with a medium-range ballistic missile. Although raw and unevaluated, this report was an indication of the possible presence in Cuba of offensive ballistic missiles.

The third and final stage in our detection of strategic missiles resulted from careful evaluation of this refugee report, together with other intelligence. In conjunction with a suspicious pattern of deployment of SAM sites noted in the same general area—a pattern which could not be related to any known military installations—analysis of this single report resulted in the designation of a specific area as a suspect medium-range ballistic missile site. Photographic coverage was thereupon proposed, and on the 14th of October a military high-altitude reconnaissance aircraft flew a flight route specifically planned to cover this suspect MRBM area. This led to the discovery of the San Cristobal MRBM complex.[28]

Eventually, reconnaissance work demonstrated that the Soviets were deploying a total of 24 MRBM launchers and fixed launching facilities for 16 IRBM's. In addition, they shipped in 42 IL-28 light bombers with a combat radius of about 700 miles. The actual capability of the force was somewhat larger than the total number of vehicles, since at least the MRBM launchers could be reloaded and refired.

Exactly what the Soviets intended to do with these forces remains a matter of speculation. However, some months after the crisis, McNamara expressed the view that "our sharp confrontation of the Soviets in the Caribbean no doubt upset their agenda for Berlin."

Their stationing of nuclear armed ballistic missiles in Cuba was directly related to that agenda. The psychological if not the military threat that these missiles would have posed to our own homeland was apparently the trump card which Mr. Khrushchev intended to play in the next round of negotiations on the status of Berlin.[29]

The President and his immediate advisers had no intention of letting him play it. Within days of the first hard evidence of the ballistic missiles in Cuba, a massive array of forces began moving to combat stations. The Strategic Air Command immediately increased its alert forces. General Power put more of his B-52's on constant airborne status and set into operation his dispersal plan for the B-47's. "Within 48 hours after the order was passed," according to General LeMay, "tactical fighter and reconnaissance aircraft were moved to Florida bases and brought to full-scale alert status supplementing the tactical aircraft already in place."[30]

The Navy set itself to perform a wide variety of tasks. Admiral Anderson later reported that "some 180 ships were directly involved at the height of the Cuban operation."

At the same time, our naval forces elsewhere were vigilant and prepared. Ten battalions of Marines were afloat in the vicinity of Cuba. Three more Marine battalions manned Guantánamo defenses, backed up by air and surface support from ships of the fleet.

Our aircraft and ships were searching an area of some 3.5 million square miles for Russian merchant ships and submarines. They were engaged in the most extensive and, I might add, the most productive, antisubmarine warfare operations since World War II.[31]

The Army, with eight divisions now in its continental reserve, prepared for a major movement to the Florida coast. As General Wheeler described it, "The Army forces were alerted, brought up to strength in personnel and equipment, moved and made ready for the operation as part of the largest U.S.

invasion force prepared since World War II. The Cuban enterprise was the largest operation ever planned to be launched and supported direct from the United States."[32] Wheeler later admitted that he had "100,000 Army troops that would have gone ashore in Cuba, plus an additional 10,000 to 20,000 that would have been in support in the base area back in the United States."[33] Multiple options with a vengeance stood ready at the President's hand.

At 7 p.m. on October 22, 1962, Kennedy described the threat to a nationwide radio-TV audience and outlined the initial counteractions that he had ordered to be taken. Among the most important were "a strict quarantine on all offensive military equipment under shipment to Cuba" and "the continued and increased close surveillance of Cuba and its military build-up." The President also announced that "it shall be the policy of this nation to regard any nuclear missile launched from Cuba against any nation in the Western Hemisphere as an attack by the Soviet Union on the United States requiring a full retaliatory response upon the Soviet Union."[34]

During the five days that followed Kennedy's dramatic address, the Navy implemented the Presidential quarantine order, the Army poured men and matériel into Florida and Georgia, and the Air Force stood poised for a tactical strike against the Cuban missiles or the strategic nuclear offensive against the Soviet Union. The pressure proved too much for Khrushchev and, on October 28, he threw in his hand. His letter to the President, broadcast by Moscow radio and distributed by the Tass news agency, said in part:

I regard with great understanding your concern and the concern of the peoples of the United States of America in connection with the fact that the weapons you describe as offensive are formidable weapons, indeed.

Both you and we understand what kind of weapons these are.

In order to eliminate as rapidly as possible the conflict which endangers the cause of peace . . . the Soviet government, in addition to earlier instructions on the discontinuation of further work on

weapons construction sites, has given a ne~~~~ ~~~~ ~~~~lismantle the
weapons, which you describe as offensive, ~~~~ ~~~~ ~~n them to
the Soviet Union.[35]

One aftermath of Khrushchev's surrender w~~~~ ~~~~ ~~f controversy about whether the Administration had u~~~~ ~~~~ ~~mph
to exact sufficient terms from the Soviet Union. A~~~~ ~~~~ ~~er-
math was a considerable difference of view about~~~~ ~~~~ ~~d
caused Khrushchev to beat such a sudden and hast~~~~
General LeMay spoke for one school of thought when ~~~~
"I am convinced that superior U.S. strategic power, co~~~~
with the obvious will and ability to apply this power, was~~~~
major factor that forced the Soviets to back down."[36] Gener~~~~
Wheeler, however, was of another view. In his opinion,

the major lesson for the Army in the Cuban situation lies in the
demonstrated value of maintaining ready Army forces at a high state
of alert in order to equip national security policy with the military
power to make a direct confrontation of Soviet power. As Secretary
McNamara pointed out to the NATO ministers recently, ". . . perhaps most significantly, the forces that were the cutting edge of the
action were the non-nuclear ones. Nuclear force was not irrelevant
but it was in the background. Non-nuclear forces were our sword,
our nuclear forces were our shield." I wholeheartedly agree with
this statement.[37]

Since the Soviets have not as yet opened their archives to
historians of the Cuban missile crisis, no one can say with certainty whether General LeMay or General Wheeler was right.
Perhaps they both were. Khrushchev did, after all, have open to
him alternatives to surrender. As McNamara pointed out, one of
them was the familiar testing ground of Berlin. That he chose
not to expand the crisis by counteraction in Europe may be
interpreted as support for the theories of either LeMay or
Wheeler. It may simply be a compliment to both.

On the other hand, the knowledge that he commanded large
non-nuclear as well as nuclear resources certainly facilitated action by the President. Unlike the situation in early 1961, he
could cope with the threat in Cuba and still dispose of reserves

for contingencies elsewhere. Although the shadow of nuclear war hung over every major decision, he no longer carried the awful weight imposed by the possibility of having to initiate the use of nuclear weapons. Khrushchev, it would appear, was now bearing more of that hateful burden. In the crunch of those five days in October, it may have become too much. We can probably never be sure.

Despite these uncertainties, the confrontation over Cuba, together with the other tests to which the Kennedy Administration was subjected, give some grounds for believing that the availability of multiple options has several distinct merits. It makes force more nearly the servant than the master of American objectives. If the Cuban experience is any guide, it would appear to strengthen deterrence by putting readily usable force at the President's disposal and forcing the opponent to share more equitably the responsibility for nuclear war. And if deterrence should fail, it offers the hope that force can still be used in a controlled and deliberate way. In an era of transition and danger, it is doubtful that any alternative defense strategy can offer much more than that.

CHAPTER 8

Agenda for Action

As THE SUMMER AND AUTUMN of 1963 sped
by, the President and McNamara had reason to believe that
they were approaching a more stable period of international relations than had marked the previous two years. The great tests
to which Khrushchev had subjected the defense posture of the
United States and its allies seemed to have satisfied him at last
that a change of Administration in this country did not mean
any weakening in the power and resolve of the West. The
President and McNamara, for their part, could hope and pray
that actions as reckless and compulsive as had characterized
the crises of Berlin and Cuba would not be repeated now that
Khrushchev had taken the measure of their determination and
capabilities. But both recognized the uncertainty of the future
and the need to keep up the nation's defenses. The maintenance
of sufficient military power for the protection of vital American
interests thus continued to be a matter of primary concern to
them. But neither was prepared to stop there. However effective the approach of multiple options had proved, the President
and McNamara did not consider their work at the Pentagon
anywhere near completed. They had accomplished a great deal
in less than three years; much still remained to be done.

Some of the problems that awaited McNamara's attention

were related specifically to, and in many instances had grown out of, the changes that he had already instituted. Despite the pace at which he had proceeded, despite the flood of questions and answers that connected the office of the Secretary with the Joint Chiefs and the military departments, the complexities of defense were such that thirty months or so had not nearly sufficed to shape every facet of the defense establishment to the emerging design. The revolution had been comprehensive, but there were depths that it still had to plumb. Consequently, the agenda for future action was sure to contain as many items as it had in 1961 when McNamara shook the Pentagon with his first ninety-six questions—known then as "McNamara's Ninety-Six Trombones" and remembered since in the staffs with fear and trepidation. Even some of the items would almost certainly prove familiar. Pentagon problems seemed reluctant to die, and many positively refused to fade away. Moreover, the fruits of technology and the kaleidoscope of the international environment ensured that new and frequently startling questions would arise. Not many observers would have thought in 1961 that the world of 1963 would find Khrushchev buying wheat from the West, signing a limited nuclear test ban, seeming to offer the moon to the United States, and quarreling with his Chinese comrades. The world of 1966 was likely to contain just as many surprises and just as many problems. The Department of Defense, despite the uncertainties, had to be prepared to meet them. The Pentagon, in these circumstances, promised to remain an exciting and rapidly changing place.

McNamara had enjoyed an extraordinary amount of freedom in dealing with his past problems. Despite the controversies with Congress and occasional differences with some of his military advisers, his record of success in obtaining what he sought had remained impressively high. Whether he could maintain a comparable record in the future, particularly if defense budgets stabilized at existing levels or actually began to decline, necessarily was a question. The going might prove harder if the resources became more scarce. On the other hand, some of

the forces that currently threatened to limit his freedom of
action might turn out to be quite transitory in character. The
concern about deficit spending could result in attempts to reduce defense expenditures below what McNamara regarded as
acceptable. But the Department of Defense had been traditionally less vulnerable to this kind of pressure than other
agencies of the government. The balance of payments problem
could also force actions that might not otherwise be taken,
even though the Department had already instituted policies,
many of them uneconomical, to help solve it. Indeed, Mc-
Namara continued to treat the deficit with the utmost gravity.
As he pointed out early in 1963:

During the 1958–60 period, total U.S. expenditures abroad (i.e.,
imports, oversea defense expenditures, foreign investments, etc.)
exceeded total U.S. earnings (i.e., exports, income from our foreign
investments, sales of services, etc.) by an average of $3.7 billion per
year. Although the size of the deficit was reduced last year, it was
still on the order of $2 billion.

Such a continuing deficit would concern us in any event since
it is usually the symptom of a fundamental economic imbalance. But
there is a second reason for our concern. For a long time, particularly
since the end of World War II, the dollar has been a world currency, held by many free world countries as backing for their own
money. Their willingness to hold dollar balances is directly related
to the convertibility of the dollar into gold upon demand. To the
extent that our payments deficit results in a continued outflow of
gold from our reserves, the position of the dollar as a fully con-
vertible world currency is imperiled.

In 1960, potential claims held by foreign countries against U.S.
gold in the form of short-term dollar balances rose above the $18
billion mark, and for the first time exceeded our total gold supply.
As of last September, the net deficit between our gold stocks and
potential foreign dollar claims had risen to $4.9 billion. While this
does not indicate any immediate danger to the position of the dollar,
continuation of a sizable deficit for several more years could greatly
damage international confidence in our currency.

National security expenditures overseas represents a significant percentage of recent deficits in our balance of payments.' In recent years, net U.S. defense expenditures entering the balance of payments have averaged $2.6 billion per year. Through economies in our own expenditures, and by arranging with our allies for their purchase of additional American equipment and services, we reduced that figure to about $2 billion for 1962, and it is our objective to bring it below the billion-dollar mark by 1966.[1]

Perhaps a more serious potential constraint for the future than the balance of payments was the intellectual climate in which McNamara might have to operate. He himself had warned against the danger of euphoria in the wake of the limited nuclear test ban. Much as he favored the treaty, he did not see it as a justification for major changes or reductions in the defense effort. Others might disagree and try to impose more limited budgets upon him. An even greater danger, which McNamara had not yet directly addressed, was that some of the habits of mind of the 1950's would persist and that military power would continue to be regarded as a function solely of nuclear weapons and novel strategic offensive and defensive systems. To a degree that kind of thinking persisted in the Congress of 1963. It took the form of concern about the maintenance of nuclear superiority without being very precise about what that meant or implied. The attitude also manifested itself in a desire for bigger bombs, faster aircraft, and more advanced missile or space systems without much regard for their utility or whether they were worth the cost. If this frame of mind gained widespread currency, McNamara could be forced into gross inefficiencies in the allocation of defense resources. He was determined to combat it.

If McNamara could hold his existing course, however, he wanted to concern himself as much with basic strategic concepts in the future as he had done in the past. In early 1963 he told a House subcommittee:

I can see 100 ways in which we could improve our operations. Time is required, however, to accomplish the improvements. We

have identified a number of these areas. We have programs underway to carry out these improvements.

Perhaps the most difficult problems we face lie not primarily
in the administration of the internal functions of the Department,
but in the formulation of defense policies relating to the relationships between this Nation and other nations throughout the world,
both those in the Communist bloc and those in the Western World.
These are problems of great difficulty, and the solutions to them
are not in all cases apparent to me at this time.[2]

McNamara did not mean by this that he had become any
less enthusiastic about the approach of multiple options. Bar-
ring some extraordinary technological change not apparently
in the cards, or a determination on the part of the Soviets to
place exclusive reliance on nuclear weapons, he wanted to
maintain the kinds of military choices that were currently available and to place main but not sole reliance on non-nuclear
weapons. But basic satisfaction with the appropriateness of the
approach to the current international environment did not im-
ply that problems were lacking. There remained, for example,
the task of articulating the approach not only to our allies but
also to our own major theater commanders. These commanders
have the principal responsibility for the development of contingency plans and the deployment, exercise, and employment
of the forces within their jurisdiction. Unless they are given to
understand fully the reasoning and preferences of the President and the Secretary, the danger exists that they will not be
able to meet completely and expeditiously the demands placed
upon them in a crisis. Declarations and explanations of policy
from Washington probably do not suffice in this respect. Effective implementation of the multiple options approach called
for a continuing review of existing plans and additional testing
of deployments and capabilities.

One of the still-unsolved issues of the multiple options approach which required clarification was the role that commanders should assign to their tactical nuclear capabilities. The

question may seem academic since the President, by law, controls the release of nuclear weapons. But an order to release nuclear weapons does not necessarily tell the designated commander how they should be used, or, if it does, it may not coincide with the plans and missions that the commander has developed. The need for doctrine about the tactical use of nuclear weapons thus was of considerable operational significance. McNamara had frequently indicated his doubts about the possibility of using nuclear weapons in a small-scale, local exchange. At the same time, he had felt it desirable to increase the nuclear capabilities available to the major theater commanders, particularly in Europe where the nuclear stockpile has increased by more than 60 percent during the past three years. He had also tried to inform himself on the range of choice available within the tactical nuclear option and the implications of implementing alternative types of plans. As he advised Senator Russell early in 1963,

the question . . . of whether the forces moving from the use of non-nuclear weapons to the use of tactical nuclear weapons can limit the nuclear conflict to the use of these smaller tactical weapons, is a question we have addressed ourselves to on several occasions. I set up a special group of officers reporting to the Chairman of the Joint Chiefs last year to examine this in great detail.

A major general was placed in charge of that; a series of studies were prepared by each of the services, and this group examined them and came up with rather inconclusive answers and therefore we are again examining it. We hope by the first of June of this year to be able to speak more authoritatively on it.[3]

June came and went, however, without authoritative answers. Perhaps there were none. The result was that the United States possessed a powerful tactical nuclear capability but still lacked an adequate rationale for it. Although the option existed, no one could yet say with confidence how it could be exercised with the greatest over-all effectiveness or what constituted the appropriate size and composition of the force. The Soviets, no doubt, had the same problem.

Consideration of multiple options could not, in fact, be separated from questions about force size and composition, and cost. When McNamara spoke of options he clearly meant more than enabling the nation to deter or engage in all the types of wars that modern technology has made possible. In effect, he was talking about options within these categories, and sought the ability, for example, to respond in one of several different ways with the strategic nuclear forces, or to handle a range of non-nuclear conflicts. But how much of these differing capabilities sufficed? That was perhaps the biggest single remaining question about the approach of multiple options. The answer, obviously, could not be fixed or precise. Much depended upon the international environment, the action of allies, and the decisions of the Soviet Union. And since there was a connection of some sort between what the United States and the Soviet Union did, difficult issues about the arms race arose and required consideration before further adjustments in force structure were made. The problem of sufficiency was complicated further by the fact that it is always easier to reduce forces than it is to build them up. The B-47's could be removed from the active inventory and placed in parking lots or sent to the scrap heap on very short notice. It takes years to create a major bomber or ICBM force. McNamara had tried to deal with these complexities in part by a judicious mixture of ready and reserve forces, stand-by production facilities, and a vigorous research and development program. He had bought insurance against a sudden increase in the range of threats at the same time that he avoided any dramatic initiative in the arms race. In the light of the forces that were already available, he had also attempted to judge where the greatest dangers might lie; and in this context, he tried to determine where the addition of resources would result in the greatest over-all increase in the nation's security. "In adding to a defense budget as large as the one we now have," he explained,

we begin to encounter the law of diminishing returns, where each additional increment of resources applied produces a smaller increment of overall defense capability. While the benefits to be gained from each additional increment cannot be measured with precision, careful cost-effectiveness analysis can greatly assist in eliminating those program proposals which clearly contribute little military worth in relation to the resource expenditures involved. We have applied this principle throughout our program and budget reviews.[4]

Despite these efforts, a number of issues remained concerning the force structure appropriate to the concept of multiple options. Some of these issues had to do with the relative merits of alternative systems, as in the case of the conventional versus the nuclear-powered attack aircraft carrier. Others were more directly related to the question of sufficiency. Perhaps the most difficult issue of all involved the size and composition of our capabilities for strategic nuclear war.

The problem here was esoteric and complex. To many it was too fantastic and macabre to warrant attention. Perhaps they were right. But McNamara and his advisers could not shirk the responsibility of trying to understand as fully as possible the character and implications of thermonuclear war. Unless that were done, McNamara could not define satisfactorily for the President the decisions he must make about such matters as the size and composition of the strategic offensive forces, the deployment of an antiballistic missile, or the magnitude of the civil defense program.

As McNamara examined this dark subject, he reached a number of conclusions about it which bore importantly on the question of how much was enough. Perhaps outstanding among them was his view that the strategic forces and related capabilities that were being planned and procured through fiscal year 1969 would, along with existing forces, suffice to provide a very powerful deterrent to a Soviet nuclear attack upon the United States or Europe. Secondly, there was no doubt that the Soviets were also improving their own forces in several significant ways. They had begun to protect their growing ICBM and MRBM capability, and they were enlarging their submarine-based missile forces. The consequence of these measures for the United States was that the cost of covering the Soviet target system was rising quite rapidly. There could be no certainty, moreover, that all important Soviet warheads—that is, those in bombers and missiles—could be eliminated by available offensive and defensive measures. In fact, McNamara tended to estimate that a significant fraction of these warheads would survive regardless of the efforts made by the United States. He also continued to assume that, at some point— whether at the outset or the end of such a war—the Soviets would direct warheads against American and European cities. This assumption, combined with his apparent confidence that the Soviets would be effectively deterred, and the high cost of gaining only a small increment of effectiveness, led McNamara to believe that present programs in this area were either about right or required little additional support. His views were evident in his description of a hypothetical war in which, at some unspecified point, the cities of the two sides came under attack. At that juncture, according to McNamara,

it is entirely possible—as a matter of fact I think probable—that the fatalities in Western Europe would approach 90 million, the fatalities in the U.S. would approach 100 million, and the fatalities in the Soviet Union would approach 100 million.

Now when you consider on the order of 300 million people dead in those areas, it is very difficult to conceive of what kind of military weapons, even if provided ahead of time, would continue to exist or if they existed how they might be used.

We have nonetheless faced that issue, and we have systems provided that we believe would survive. For example, certain elements of our Navy almost certainly would survive, and we have other elements of our forces that we believe would survive.

But it exceeds the extent of my imagination to conceive of how those forces might be used and of what benefit they would be to our Nation at that point.[5]

McNamara believed, in sum, that strategic offensive forces comprising more than 1700 ballistic missiles and 700 bombers sufficed for all imaginable purposes, and he was tempted at times to find a criterion for measuring force requirements that would keep the nuclear forces from growing still further.

General LeMay, with typical and admirable candor, expressed a somewhat differing point of view. In his opinion, "We have to have sufficient military power to knock out all of the targets that we know he has, or all the weapons that we know he has, and I would like to have a little cushion to take care of some that we might not know he has."[6] Thus, his difference with McNamara was "in the size of the force, of what constitutes a deterrent force. He thinks it can be done with something less than I think it can be done."[7] At another point, LeMay indicated his basis for wanting still larger forces.

Many people unfortunately measure the effectiveness of a proposed deterrent force by counting the number of enemy citizens to be brought under attack.

As you know, it doesn't take much of a nuclear force to destroy a large number of enemy cities. But the destruction of cities *per se* does not protect U.S. and Allied lives.

Only the destruction of his military force can do this. Therefore, an entirely different force capability is required to destroy those weapon systems posing a threat to U.S. and Allied populations.

To be credible, this deterrent force must have certain capabilities:

1. First, a capability to acquire that information necessary to attack effectively selected elements of enemy strength. For this, we rely on reconnaissance and comprehensive intelligence efforts.

2. Secondly, a capability to survive. For this, we rely on diversity, numbers, hardening, dispersal, ground and airborne alerts, early warning systems, and constant training.

3. Third, rapid response to an order to execute operational plans. For this, we rely on a high state of alert; and rapid, dependable, and survivable command and control.

4. Fourth, immediate response in full strength or with selectivity under continuous control. Alert manned aircraft and missile forces provide this capability.

5. Fifth, sustained effectiveness in portions of the force which may be withheld from initial attacks as uncommitted reserve, or for contingencies. Missiles which are dispersed, hardened, and mobile

and manned systems which are dispersible on the ground and in the air—as well as recoverable and reusable—give these capabilities.

6. Sixth, the ability in a portion of our forces to make swift and clearly recognizable moves to evidence U.S. resolve in the face of provocation. Manned systems provide this capability.[8]

Although the difference between McNamara and LeMay was not very great, it still seemed sufficient to promise a future of strenuous battles about force size and composition for strategic nuclear deterrence. McNamara, understandably, wanted to limit expenditures in an area where costs were high and the Soviets seemed adequately deterred. LeMay, also understandably, sought the forces required to achieve a higher level of effectiveness without much regard for cost. Both gave the appearance of taking up irreconcilable positions in the process. McNamara argued that the Soviets would act irrationally if a thermonuclear war occurred at all; LeMay talked as though complete destruction of the Soviet target system were feasible. As a consequence, neither considered, publicly at least, the intermediate cases where the Soviets might behave rationally, damage is high but related to past experience, each side retains important nuclear forces under control, great prizes such as Europe remain at stake, and there is a problem of ending the war on mutually acceptable terms. Yet until these perhaps bizarre cases were faced explicitly, our understanding of thermonuclear war would remain incomplete and the problem of sufficiency with respect to nuclear force size and composition would not be satisfactorily resolved. The agenda for the future could hardly avoid this issue.

McNamara faced a problem of equal magnitude in the Navy's four fleets or carrier task forces. The carrier task forces played an outstanding role during World War II in the drive across the Pacific against both the Japanese fleet and land-based Japanese air forces. Since that time, without an enemy fleet of major proportions to oppose, the Navy has had to find new roles for the attack carriers. It has justified a force of fifteen, with a requirement for the construction of a new carrier every other year, on the ground that they could make a vital contribution to the conduct of both a strategic nuclear war and a local non-nuclear conflict. McNamara, however, pointed out that "as we acquire larger forces of strategic missiles and Polaris submarines, the need for the attack carrier in the general war role will diminish." At the same time, he endorsed the attack carriers in the limited war role.

There are many potential trouble spots in the world where the attack carrier is and will continue to be the only practical means of bringing our air-striking power to bear. Carrier airpower can be employed, obviously, without involving third parties, without invoking treaties, agreements, or overflight rights. And, as has been demonstrated many times before, the carrier task force is a most effective means for presenting a show of force or establishing a military presence, which often has helped to maintain the peace and discourage hostilities.[9]

If there was no question about the basic utility of the attack carriers, doubts most certainly existed about the need for fifteen of them. The reasons for wondering how much was enough in this area were quite straightforward. On the one hand, modern technology promises to provide aircraft with very substantial ranges which can also take off from and land on small and relatively unprepared airstrips. Such aircraft—and the TFX may prove to be one—could offer a partial substitution for the attack carrier. On the other hand, the carrier task forces, as the Navy currently operates them, are enormously expensive enterprises. It takes four of the task forces to keep two on station, one in the Mediterranean and one in the Far East. In fact, it is rare that more than five of the fifteen carriers are actually on station at any given time. A task force containing two attack carriers (with perhaps two hundred aircraft on board) requires the protection and support of more than fifty ships, plus another task force in reserve and an almost equal number of vessels in maintenance. The initial cost of a two-carrier task force on station thus runs as high as $6 billion; the operating costs could amount to $1 billion a year. No one has yet invented a more expensive way of projecting air power to the far corners of the globe.

It is conceivable that the cost of the carrier task forces can be reduced. There may be ways of maintaining the same amount of air power on station with fewer carriers and supporting vessels. Possibly land-based aircraft can serve as substitutes in some parts of the world. Whatever the solution, however, it was clear that the carrier task forces and the number of attack carriers would be the object of critical scrutiny in the years to come.

McNamara had devoted a great deal of attention between 1961 and 1963 to the ground and air forces for non-nuclear war. It was here that the most marked improvement in American capabilities had taken place. It was also where more than half of the increased expenditures since 1961 had been invested. As a consequence, McNamara had opened up a number of interesting conventional options for the country. Even so, important questions remained with respect to these forces. The Army, having already reorganized its divisional structure twice in less than ten years, was now experimenting with an air-assault division to see whether its effectiveness could be increased commensurately with the high cost of larger complements of transport aircraft and helicopters. The issue was still in doubt. Meanwhile, tactical air power had received a new lease on life with modern equipment and ordnance and the possibility that it could continue to defeat active defenses by a combination of low-level tactics and the Shrike antiradar missile. If the ground-air team was to be strengthened further—in itself a major issue—it was a good question whether the bulk of any future resources should go to the ground or the air. Up to some point they complement one another; beyond that point, one probably can be substituted for the other. But the point itself is of unknown location and, to use the dreaded term, the cost-effectiveness of alternative combinations of ground and air remains a mystery. There was food for study here.

An even more difficult problem lay in how to maintain American commitments yet avoid tying American non-nuclear forces irrevocably to particular theaters. As McNamara characterized the problem:

> If large forces are deployed in forward areas they can respond quickly and the need for long-haul transportation is reduced. The drawbacks to this approach are that it requires very large numbers of men, great quantities of equipment, long periods of oversea service, and involves all of the uncertainties and difficulties associated with foreign bases, such as base rights, status-of-forces agreements, *et cetera*. It also reduces the flexibility of our military posture and considerably increases defense expenditures abroad, thereby adversely affecting our balance of payments.
>
> On the other hand, a mobile "fire brigade" Reserve, centrally located in the United States and ready for deployment to a threatened spot anywhere in the world, is basically a more economical and flexible use of military forces. Fewer men and less equipment can do the job and most of the problems involved in stationing large U.S. forces in foreign countries in peacetime could be avoided. However, to move the forces required with all of their heavy equipment from the continental United States and then to supply and support them overseas would require an enormous transport capacity. Furthermore, movements by sea from the continental United States [deleted] could take about 30 days. Therefore, the forces and their essential support during the first 30 days would have to come by air.[10]

The problem had been met thus far by committing roughly half the Active Army to duty in Hawaii, Korea, and Western Europe, by prepositioning heavy equipment for reinforcements in storage sites in Europe and floating depots in the Far East, and by increased airlift and sealift for the strategic reserve in the United States. But the balance of payments deficit could make this compromise deployment too costly to maintain. Future political developments might also require that the United States be able to dispose of its forces more freely than was then the case. But what combination of deployment, prepositioned stocks, and transport would satisfy our allies and improve our military posture remained to be determined.

Greater understanding of the relationship between air and ground forces and improved dispositions of existing forces could help the United States to handle a wider range of threats by conventional means than was feasible in 1963. They could not, by themselves, make feasible a major non-nuclear option in Europe. Yet the acquisition of that option remained as essential as ever to McNamara's scheme of defense. Indeed, the greatest challenge confronting him was the continuing refusal of the European allies to accept the logic of his position. How he could overcome that refusal was not obvious in the autumn of 1963. The massive American presence in Europe was more than adequate assurance that the Soviet Union could not possibly use nuclear weapons against one or more of the allies without suffering immediate retaliation. The revised estimates of Soviet conventional strength indicated that it was feasible to devise a major non-nuclear defense of Europe at reasonable cost. And past experience with the Berlin problem made it evident that the threat of nuclear weapons would not deter the Soviets from slicing away at Western interests. Yet the key European allies still seemed to cling to the belief that, somehow or other, the presence or possession of nuclear weapons in Europe would ward off all evil, however reluctant they might be actually to use these weapons. McNamara, clearly, had not yet found the right formula for disabusing them of this notion. Perhaps there was no such formula. Perhaps France and Germany and Italy could only learn for themselves how specialized is the power of nuclear weapons. Perhaps the multilateral nuclear force would suffice to satisfy the nuclear ambitions of its prospective members without distracting them from the main business at hand—the non-nuclear build-up—but the prospects were not encouraging.

It was tempting, in the circumstances, for the United States to abdicate all responsibility for leadership in Europe and accept a period of drift and indecision in the affairs of NATO. But the biggest single item on the agenda of the future remained the construction of a rational defense posture for Europe. Although the political prerequisites for the effort existed only in part, McNamara was determined to stick to the task and seek new ways of pressing home his point.

The great issues of force size and composition, including the problem of Europe's defense, necessarily occupied the bulk of McNamara's extraordinary span of attention. But they could not completely obscure another important piece of unfinished business—the reorganization of the Department of Defense. It was characteristic of McNamara that he had actually done far less than his predecessors by way of formal reorganization. Even so, the late James V. Forrestal, the first Secretary of Defense, would probably have found the Pentagon of Thomas Gates, with all its institutional changes, far more familiar than the environment created by McNamara. What was so different about the Pentagon now was not so much the organization chart as it was the locus of authority and the processes by which the major decisions were being made. Owing to the force of McNamara's personality and intellect, the Secretary of Defense was the master of his department in fact as well as in theory. The result had been called, disparagingly, the McNamara monarchy, but the monarchy was constitutional and the rule was the rule of reason.

It has also been said that the two main instruments of authority at the disposal of the Secretary are the power of appointment and the power of the purse. By themselves, however, they cannot direct the Pentagon to the desired ends. What McNamara had added, and what made the vital difference in the conduct of the department's business, was persistent questioning, increasing clarity of purpose, and detailed staff study. The two great symbols of this change were the planning-programming-budgeting system and the analyses done according to the joint criteria of cost and effectiveness.

The planning-programming-budgeting system had worked remarkably well in three different respects. It had provided the Secretary with a much clearer and more meaningful representation of the department's vital functions than was ever previously available, and it had enabled him to relate and compare competitive and complementary activities much more readily than by the examination of separate Service budgets drawn up according to the traditional accounts. The system also gave a sense of order and perspective to the annual budgetary cycle with its emphasis on a five-year plan and program change proposals. Above all, it provided a common format and language for the Services and obliged them to think in terms of major missions of interest to the department as a whole rather than simply of their own separate functions.

The fact that the system had performed so well in these respects did not mean that there was no room left for improvement. It had been charged that the Services, no longer feeling that they controlled their own budgets, had abdicated all responsibility for choice and had simply moved the decision to the Secretary by flooding his office with indiscriminate proposals for changes in the program. Whether the Services had actually abandoned the right to indicate the range and scale of their preferences was doubtful. But additional incentives were perhaps required to encourage them to be more explicit about these preferences. It was probably the case, also, that the current program packages could be broken down still further. The general purpose forces package, for example, contained most of the Army and the Navy, as well as the tactical air forces, and, owing to the dual capability of these forces, it mixed nuclear with non-nuclear systems. It might increase the Secretary's understanding and facilitate his decisions if the missions represented in this package could be sorted out and placed in separate and distinct groupings. However, the accomplishment of such a refinement necessarily awaited a better understanding of both the Navy's roles and the requirements for tactical nuclear war. Achievement of the requisite understanding meant, in turn, further study and analysis.

The Pentagon is not ordinarily thought of as a place of study. Yet study, analysis, and recommendations are its staples. The staffs of the Services, the Joint Staff, and many of the civilians in the department are engaged in hammering out policy on a wide range of issues; and, in the course of their efforts, they do a large amount of research. The Pentagon may indeed be the largest debating and research society in the world. It commands, in addition, the services of consultants drawn from all conceivable professions and it contracts for research from specialized organizations such as the RAND Corporation, from industry, and from the universities. Under previous Administrations, however, the Services and their Chiefs had been the principal repositories of the resulting knowledge, and used or discarded it as they saw fit.

McNamara changed this dispensation in several important ways. Frequently, instead of simply receiving opinion, he asked questions and sought information on which to make decisions. In these circumstances, it was not only the alternative courses of action that he wanted presented to him; he also insisted on seeing the data and reasoning on which the recommendations were based. What was perhaps even more unsettling, he found the cost-effectiveness approach entirely congenial and would wax enthusiastic over a study which compared alternatives in terms of their costs and some solidly based criteria of effectiveness. Worst of all, he scattered his "whiz kids" about the Pentagon and seemingly made use of them in competition with his military advisers.

The term "whiz kids" is actually inappropriate for the civilians who have made up this group. They range in age from the early thirties to the middle fifties. Furthermore, they have played a rather different role in the Pentagon than has been generally attributed to them. They are not alternatives or substitutes for McNamara's military advisers. Rather, as experienced practitioners of the kinds of studies that McNamara has found useful, they help to initiate, guide, and synthesize research in the many areas which are relevant to decisions by the Secretary. If military advice alone were all that McNamara required, these special research assistants might be expendable. But where economic, political, and technical considerations must also weigh in his decisions, he must include other sources of information and advice. And he must find ways of integrating this maze of information into a meaningful basis for choice. This his civilian aides have helped him to do. Military advice has not been downgraded; it has been formulated in such a way that it can be combined with all the other factors that must bear on the design and execution of defense policy.

The result of McNamara's efforts has been a substantial rise in the quality and relevance of the Pentagon's research. Indeed, it is no exaggeration to say that professional military advice has gained a higher standing than at any previous time in the brief history of the Department of Defense. But with the improvement have come problems. Some officers, feeling that they have lost status, have resisted the new dispensation. Others, who are basically sympathetic, resent what they regard as a failure to recognize their contributions. Still others fear that even where the work of the military staffs has improved dramatically, it will not receive due consideration and credit. Even if these feelings lack justification, they exist; and they could well delay or even prevent the institutionalization of the modes of research and analysis that McNamara has so assiduously fostered. This is not to say that the planning-programming-budgeting system is likely soon to disappear. But a major value of the system is that it challenges the Services to present their requirements and the justifications for them in the language of cost-effectiveness. With McNamara and his assistants at the Pentagon, the major staffs have been brought to meet the challenge with rising competence and ingenuity. But whether the trend will continue, once their presence is removed, must remain a matter of doubt. McNamara has undoubtedly recognized his obligation to wed the military staffs to this, the greatest of his innovations. It was difficult, in the autumn of 1963, to imagine a more delicate or complex task for his future agenda.

Articulation of basic strategic concepts, determination of force size and composition, and management of the Pentagon are not the only responsibilities that fall to the Secretary of

Defense. He also stands in the chain of command between the President and the Armed Forces. He must therefore play a role in the use of force under the President's direction. McNamara had interpreted this role to mean primarily the provision of options—to permit the President "to apply a fly swatter where a fly swatter is a proper weapon, instead of using a sledge hammer."[11] But where conditions permitted, he also favored the graduated application of military power. The Cuban missile crisis he regards as "a perfect illustration of the application of this strategy and this force structure."[12] Where nuclear weapons might have had to be used, he tried equally hard to provide for a controlled and deliberate application of force, even though he might not have pursued the implications of a controlled nuclear war to all their possible conclusions. It was with respect to guerrilla warfare and its prevention, however, that he apparently felt most strongly the need for greater skill and imagination. As far as the United States itself was concerned:

We have . . . made a good start on building up the specialized forces required to cope with covert military aggression, guerrilla warfare, and so forth, and we are pressing forward with the development of the specialized equipment and weapons required by such forces.

But, even more importantly, we must help the less developed and less stable nations of the free world to develop these same capabilities. This is the primary need in such countries as South Vietnam. We must help them, not only with the specialized weapons and equipment required, but also with training and on-the-spot advice. All of us in the free world have much to learn about counterinsurgency and guerrilla warfare operations, but learn we must if we are to meet successfully this particular aspect of the Communist threat.

Admittedly, it will take much more than military force alone to stamp out communism permanently in such places as South Vietnam. We must help these people to provide a more desirable alternative to communism, and to do this will require all the means at our disposal—political, ideological, technical, scientific, and economic, as well as military.[13]

Repeatedly, McNamara came back to this theme and referred to Khrushchev's speech on wars of national liberation. He reminded his listeners

that Mr. Khrushchev, in his speech of January 6, 1961, made it quite clear that he considered world wars and even local wars too dangerous for the Soviet Union; he favored wars of national liberation or popular revolts as the preferred method of armed aggression against the free world because it was, in his view, the safest.

It may well be that as long as we maintain the kind of forces which would make global nuclear war, and even local wars, unprofitable for the Soviet Union, we could deter them from starting such wars. But this still would leave us with the problem of guerrilla or sublimited wars. Indeed, to the extent we deter the Soviet Union from initiating these larger wars we may anticipate even greater efforts on their part in the sublimited war area. Conflict, as Mr. Molotov so rightly pointed out, is a cardinal tenet of Communist doctrine.

I think we can all agree that the Communists have a distinct advantage over the democracies in this area of conflict. They are not inhibited by our ethical and moral standards. Political assassination, robbery, arson, subversion, bribery—all are acceptable means to further their ends. They are quick to take advantage of any breakdown of law and order, or any resentment of people toward their government, or of any economic or natural disaster. They are masters of mass psychology and of propaganda, having had many decades of experience in these fields. We have a long way to go in devising and implementing effective countermeasures against these Communist techniques. But this is a challenge we must meet if we are to defeat the Communists in this third kind of war. It is quite possible that in the decade of the sixties the decisive struggle will take place in this area.[14]

No doubt there were other areas that would become of concern to McNamara. If the first thirty-four months provided any indication, he would continue to approach them, not as the technocrat of the public image, but as an enlightened and humane seeker for the complexities of truth. As he said of the controversy over the TFX development within the Pentagon:

I think there are differences of opinion and I think these are to be expected, frankly, because in that particular instance General LeMay and Admiral Anderson were looking at the problem from a somewhat narrower point of view than I was, and I think this was appropriate; that's their job. They are my military advisers, they're not my technical advisers, they're not my financial advisers. They are looking at the problem from the point of view of their individual service, and this leads to a difference in conclusion, a difference in opinion on a particular issue. So controversy develops out of such differences. Exchange of views, and forceful presentation of views, I think, tends to throw light on the truth and this is what I am seeking.[15]

Pursuit of the truth would also be accompanied by the determination to stimulate and lead that are his hallmarks. Pointing to the great General Pershing desk at the center of his office, McNamara has said that

there are two philosophies of management that every manager must choose between. One is what I would call the passive judicial role: You sit behind this desk—it's a large desk—the papers flow across it— and they'll flow across it because only you have the authority to make certain decisions and the decisions must come to you for signature, and there are boxes and boxes of pieces of paper. And one could spend a full day just sitting here and reading the paper and signing on the signature line.

This is, as I say, a judicial role—it's a passive role. I don't believe in that. My own strong belief is a manager should be an aggressive leader, an active leader, asking questions, suggesting alternatives, proposing objectives, stimulating progress. . . . And this is the role I'm trying to fill.[16]

The spirit of his leadership also remained one of cautious and restrained hope. Talking shortly after signature of the limited test ban treaty, McNamara remarked of recent Soviet behavior:

These probes for reductions of tensions may indicate a recognition by Khrushchev that he has to choose between two courses: he has to choose between a course directed toward world domination, directed toward extending the influence of the Communists

beyond the boundaries of the Soviet Union, a course that they appear to have been following over most of the last four decades. That
course, on the one hand, versus a course of action that's in the
interests of the Soviet people, a course of action that will lead to a
rising standard of living, to greater personal freedom.

I suspect that that rising standard of living and these hints that
there is some loosening of the fetters on personal liberty will in
themselves push the Soviet leaders some way away from world
domination toward a course of action that has the interests of the
Soviet Union and the interests of its people as its foundation. How
far they'll go, I don't know. . . . We must follow the President's
thought . . . "We must never negotiate from fear, but we should
never fear to negotiate." That seems to me to be the foundation of
our policy today and the road for the future. And, of course, there is
a corollary to that: such a policy depends on strength and, therefore,
we must continue to maintain and increase our military strength
and keep our powder dry.[17]

A questioner asked him: "But if somebody comes knocking
at the door with an olive branch, you don't want to shoot him?"
McNamara replied: "No, but I want to have a secure door between me and the carrier of the olive branch, until I see what
lies behind it."[18] The "secure door" was a cardinal tenet of his
attitude toward the nation's security. But he joined to it a
deeply held conviction that the United States, as befitted its
past, must embody a more positive ambition.

On November 11, 1962, McNamara went to Arlington National Cemetery and spoke his thoughts about that aspiration at
the annual Veterans Day ceremony. The Cuban missile crisis
was still ringing in his ears. He said:

This is a day when we honor silence above speech. Therefore, I
shall be brief.

We began the day by paying tribute to men whom we cannot
name. Yet our memory of their deeds is as fresh as the wreath we
laid on their graves and as enduring as the light of the torches
brought here from far away. The strength of this memory is the
measure of our obligation to every veteran, known and unknown.
We renew that obligation by this ceremony.

A year ago, speaking on this occasion, President Kennedy observed that "there is no way to maintain the frontiers of freedom without cost and commitment and risk." He added, "There is no swift and easy path to peace in our generation." The hard truth of his remarks has been demonstrated for all of us by the events of the last few weeks.

The men and women, living and dead, whom we honor here today learned that truth through their own experience. It is the mark of a civilized society that later generations profit from the experience of earlier ones. Today it may be the mark of a society that can survive to pass anything on to future generations. The margin for error is shrinking.

Let me tell you what I see as some of the lessons that can be derived from the experience of our veterans—lessons which we have tried to apply over the last few weeks.

The first lesson is the lesson of strength. Two World Wars have taught us that weakness, not strength invites war in a world which is still only beginning to see the possibility of a rule of law. We must be strong enough to defend ourselves, with our allies, against any nation that would try our strength, and the strength of the Alliance.

The second lesson is the lesson of resolve. We know that a nuclear holocaust would be a disaster of unimaginable proportions, but we know also that unless we are prepared to place everything at risk, we cannot hope to save anything from disaster. We must be resolute enough to commit ourselves to the ultimate test, if our adversaries put us to that test.

The third lesson is the lesson of restraint. Once we are prepared for a thermonuclear showdown, we can afford to use all our patience and all our ingenuity to avoid one—and we cannot afford to do otherwise. We must constrain ourselves to employ the least amount of force that is effective to determine the immediate issues between our adversaries and ourselves.

These lessons, like all the lessons of the soldier, are easy to forget in the heat of battle. They must be learned in advance, and deeply understood.

There is another lesson that every veteran has learned. Wars solve no problems by themselves. They only give us another chance to work on the problems that lead to wars. In fact, the problems of war and the problems of peace cannot be separated from each other.

Individual freedom is both a condition and an objective of a peaceful world, and inequality of opportunity is as much a source of international difficulties as it is an obstacle to domestic tranquility. We need better schools not only to train scientists and engineers for national defense, but also to produce experts who can find economical ways to turn salt water into fresh. And we need to educate humanists who can teach us to use less of our working time destroying each other and less of our leisure time destroying ourselves.

These problems are the greatest challenge that this occasion puts before us. It must not be said that those whose sacrifice we celebrate fought and died in vain.[19]

McNamara stood ready and eager to meet the challenge. And in the late autumn of 1963, he no doubt cherished the thought that the wisdom, grace, and wit of the President would continue to support him in the solution of his problems and the fulfillment of his credo. It seemed a comforting certainty in a world of great and perilous uncertainties.

Epilogue

At ARLINGTON NATIONAL CEMETERY, little more than a year after McNamara had spoken there, the nation bade President Kennedy a reluctant farewell. The loss of the President, incomparably tragic in itself, also cut off a unique relationship in the history of American defense policy. The collaboration between Kennedy and McNamara was a close one. The President allowed his Secretary of Defense remarkable latitude in the development of specific defense plans and programs while McNamara, for his part, sought consistently to attain the objectives that Kennedy had defined even before acceding to the Presidency. In so doing, McNamara actively solicited and received the President's final decision on every major defense issue. The Secretary and the Joint Chiefs proposed; the President disposed. For McNamara, the right was Kennedy's as much out of the wisdom of the President as out of the authority of the Presidency. Yet so linked were their thoughts that Kennedy rarely found it necessary to overrule his Secretary. Typically, when McNamara prepared a major address on defense policy, Kennedy not only reviewed the draft, but contributed to the drafting. When McNamara spoke, it was for the President in a very literal sense.

One of the last results of this most fruitful collaboration was a speech given by McNamara to the Economic Club of New York on November 18, 1963, just four days before the President's murder. It reflected, as usual, their shared views about the options, forces, and budgets required by the United States and its allies in the face of changing international conditions. The speech, with its inevitable statistics, is a tribute to what President Kennedy had already accomplished in the field of national security. It is also an expression of what he still sought to achieve.

At the outset, McNamara reminded his audience that the Administration would soon be presenting, once again, "the details of a proposed national defense budget for the consideration of the Congress and the public."

Given the importance of these matters, their complexities and uncertainties and the existence of real differences of opinion, a degree of controversy is inevitable, and even desirable.

Some controversies, however, reveal underlying differences in perspective that scarcely suggest the participants are living in the same world. Within the past few weeks, some critics have suggested that we have literally hundreds of times more strength than we need; others have accused us of risking the whole future of the nation by engaging in unilateral disarmament. I would like to believe that criticisms bracketing our policy in that fashion prove it to be rational and sound. But a discrepancy of that order cannot be reassuring. Rather, it indicates that we have failed to convey to some part of our audience even the broadest outlines, as we see them, of the problems that our military strategy and force structure are meant to address. I believe we should be able to move from controversy on that scale toward consensus in military affairs, not always on details or components of our policies, but at least on an appreciation of the major national security problems confronting us, on the broad alternative paths to their solution and on the dominant goals, obstacles, costs and risks affecting choice. My purpose in speaking to you this evening is to help move in this direction.

As a prelude, then, to the coming season of debate, I should like to identify and discuss some basic matters on which a considerable degree of consensus seems to me both possible and desirable, although by no means assured.

These include those over-all comparative strengths and weaknesses of the opposing military alliances that form the bold relief in the strategic environment. In short, they are the considerations that seem to have relatively long-term significance compared to the annual budget cycle.

Matters of that degree of permanence tend to be stamped on our minds as being unchanging and unchangeable, the unquestioned framework of daily and yearly policy-making. Yet these factors of which I shall speak do change: more swiftly and more profoundly than our picture of them tends to change. Indeed, I believe it is just the fact that over the last decade this topography has changed—while many maps have not—that accounts for some apparently irreconcilable controversies.

Let me recall the earlier period briefly, for comparison. The strategic landscape at the outset of the 'Fifties was dominated by two outstanding features. One was the practical U.S. monopoly of deliverable, strategic nuclear weapons. The other was the Soviet Union and Communist China's virtual monopoly of ground force on the continents of Europe and Asia.

Both of these determinants of Western military policy had changed considerably by the end of the Korean War. The Soviets had produced atomic explosions and had created a sizable nuclear delivery capability against Europe, while NATO ground forces had expanded rapidly, and military operations in Korea had greatly tarnished the significance of Chinese Communist superiority in numbers. But the old notions of monopoly persisted as short-cut aids to thinking on policy matters. And they were not so misleading as they came later to be. Soviet armed forces approaching five million men still heavily outweighed the NATO forces in Europe; and Soviet delivery capability against the U.S. was dwarfed by that of SAC. Moreover, tactical nuclear weapons were being heralded as a new nuclear monopoly for the West.

Even as these earlier notions of monopolies grew obsolete, ideas about the feasibility of alternative policies continued to reflect them. So did ideas about how wars might be fought. Nuclear operations, both strategic and tactical, by the U.S. in response to Soviet aggression against our allies were considered to be virtually unilateral. Hence it was supposed the problem of credibility of the U.S. response would scarcely arise, even in the case of relatively limited Soviet aggressions. Western reliance upon nuclear weapons, in particular strategic systems, both to deter and to oppose non-nuclear attack of any size seemed not only adequate but also unique in its adequacy.

That sort of situation is convenient for policy-makers. It makes policy easy to choose and easy to explain. Perhaps that is why throughout most of the 'Fifties, while the Soviets under various pressures decreased their ground forces and the NATO allies built theirs up, and while the Soviets acquired a massive nuclear threat against Europe and laid the groundwork for a sizable threat against the U.S., the picture underlying most policy debate remained that appropriate to 1949. It was a picture of a Communist Goliath in conventional strength facing a Western David, almost naked of conventional arms but alone possessed of a nuclear sling.

Toward the end of that decade, the prospect that the Soviets would acquire intercontinental ballistic missiles at a time when our strategic forces consisted almost entirely of bombers focused our attention and our budget even more sharply than before upon our strategic forces. The urgency of the problem of deterring the most massive of attacks was a new reason for thinking that the West could spare neither resources nor thought to deal more specifically with lesser threats. The most urgent task was to provide for deterrence of massive aggression by assuring the survival under any attack of forces at least adequate, in the calculations of a potential attacker, to destroy his society in retaliation. It was now not the assurance of continued nuclear superiority that preempted the attention of policy-makers but, on the contrary, the struggle to maintain it.

But it is time to change the maps by which policy is charted and justified. The old ones, which assumed a U.S. nuclear monopoly, both strategic and tactical, and a Communist monopoly of ground combat strength, are too far removed from reality to serve as even rough guides. Neither we nor our allies can afford the crudities of maps that tell us that old policies are still forced upon us, when a true picture would show important new avenues of necessity and choice.

What most needs changing is a picture of ourselves and of the Western Alliance as essentially at bay, outmanned and outgunned except for nuclear arms no longer exclusively ours. We should not think of ourselves as forced by limitations of resources to rely upon strategies of desperation and threats of vast mutual destruction, compelled to deal only with the most massive and immediate challenges, letting lesser ones go by default. It would be a striking historical phenomenon if that self-image should be justified. We are the largest member of an Alliance with a population of almost 450 million people, an aggregate annual product which is fast approaching a trillion dollars, and a modern and diverse technological base without parallel, facing the Soviet Union and its European satellites with their hundred million fewer people and an aggregate output no more than half that of the West.

And quite apart from ignoring the underlying strengths of the West, the outdated picture I have described takes no account of the military capabilities in being that our investment over the last decade, and specifically in the last few years, have bought for us. If new problems put strong claims on our attention and our resources today, it is very largely because we have come a large part of the way that is feasible toward solving some old ones.

Let me summarize the current status of the balance of strategic nuclear forces, that part of the military environment that has preoccupied our attention for so long. In strictly relative numerical terms, the situation is the familiar one. The U.S. force now contains more than 500 operational long-range ballistic missiles—Atlas, Titan, Minuteman, Polaris—and is planned to increase to over 1700 by 1966. There is no doubt in our minds and none in the minds of the Soviets that these missiles can penetrate to their targets. In addition, the U.S. has Strategic Air Command bombers on air alert and over 500 bombers on quick reaction ground alert. By comparison, the consensus is that today the Soviets could place about half as many bombers over North America on a first strike. The Soviets are estimated to have today only a fraction as many intercontinental missiles as we do. Furthermore, their submarine-launched ballistic missiles are short-range, and generally are not comparable to our Polaris force. The Soviets pose a very large threat against Europe, including hundreds of intermediate and medium-range ballistic missiles. This threat is today and will continue to be covered by the clear superiority of our strategic forces.

The most wishful of Soviet planners would have to calculate as a certainty that the most effective surprise attack they could launch would still leave us with the capability to destroy the attacker's society. What is equally pertinent is that the relative numbers and survivability of U.S. strategic forces would permit us to retaliate against all the urgent Soviet military targets that are subject to attack, thus contributing to the limitation of damage to ourselves and our allies.

Deterrence of deliberate, calculated attack seems as well assured as it can be, and the damage-limiting capability of our numerically superior forces is, I believe, well worth its incremental cost. It is a capability to which the smaller forces of the Soviet Union could not realistically aspire. That is one reason, among others, why I would not trade our strategic posture for that of the Soviets at any point during the coming decade.

But given the kind of force that the Soviets are building, including submarine-launched missiles beyond the reach of our offensive forces, the damage which the Soviets could inflict on us and our allies, no matter what we do to limit it, remains extremely high.

That has been true for our allies ever since the middle and late 'Fifties. Soviet acquisition of a sizable delivery capability against the U.S., and more significantly their acquisition of relatively protected forces, submarine-launched or hardened, has been long and often prematurely heralded. Its arrival at last merely dramatizes the need to recognize that strategic nuclear war would under all foreseeable circumstances be bilateral—and highly destructive to both sides.

Larger budgets for U.S. strategic forces would not change that fact. They could have only a decreasing incremental effect in limiting somewhat the damage that the U.S. and its allies could suffer in a general nuclear war. In short, we cannot buy the capability to make a strategic bombing campaign once again a unilateral prospect.

That must, I suggest, be accepted as one of the determinants affecting policy. Another is that the same situation confronts the Soviet leaders, in a way that is even more intensely confining. In fact, enormous increases in Soviet budgets would be required for them to achieve any significant degree of damage-limiting capability. The present Soviet leaders show no tendency to challenge the basis of the U.S. strategic deterrent posture by such expenditures.

In the last two years alone, we have increased the number of nuclear warheads in the strategic alert forces by 100%. During that period we have more than doubled the megatonnage of the strategic alert forces. The fact that further increases in strategic force size will at last encounter rapidly diminishing returns—which is largely an effect of the very large investments the U.S. has made in this area—should be reflected in future budgets. The funding for the initial introduction of missiles into our forces is nearing completion. We can anticipate that the annual expenditure on strategic forces will drop substantially, and level off well below the present rate of spending. This is not to rule out the possibility that research now in progress on possible new technological developments, including the possibility of useful ballistic missile defenses, will require major new expenditures. In any event, there will be recurring costs of modernization.

In the field of tactical nuclear weapons, the picture is in important respects similar. The U.S. at present has in stockpile or planned for stockpile tens of thousands of nuclear explosives for tactical use on the battlefield, in anti-submarine warfare and against aircraft. They include warheads for artillery, battlefield missiles, demolition munitions, bombs, depth charges, air-to-air missiles and surface-to-air missiles. The consensus is that the U.S. is presently substantially superior in design, diversity and numbers in this class of weapons.

This is an indispensable superiority, as we can readily understand if we consider how our problems of strategic choice would be altered if the tables were reversed and it were the Soviet Union which held a commanding lead in this field. Nevertheless, what we have is superiority, not monopoly, and even if tactical nuclear warfare can be limited, below some ill-defined threshold of strategic exchange, the key fact is that if the West initiates such warfare in the future, it must be expected to be bilateral, in any theater which engaged the Soviet Union. Again, we cannot buy back a monopoly, or the assurance of unilateral use.

Finally, there is the area of what we call our general purpose forces. Within the last two years, we have increased the number of our combat-ready Army divisions by about 45%, from 11 to 16. There has been a 30% increase in the number of tactical air squadrons; a 75% increase in airlift capabilities; and a 100% increase in ship construction and conversion to modernize the fleet.

But it is not only force size that matters. The key to the effective utilization of these forces is combat readiness and mobility.

The most recent demonstration of our ability to reinforce our troops presently stationed in Europe occurred last month in Operation Big Lift, the first of a series of planned large-scale, world-wide exercises. For the first time in military history, an entire division was airlifted from one continent to another. That movement could never have been accomplished without a massive increase in our airlift capability, which is still being expanded. (It will have risen 400% between 1961 and 1967.) It required the development of new techniques to preposition combat equipment, of which we have two extra division sets now in Europe. It called for new techniques in military training and administration to make sure that units are really ready to move out on a moment's notice. This exercise, in which some 16,000 airmen and soldiers and more than 350 planes took part, is directly relevant to the needs of Europe, where it brought a seventh division to join the six that are to remain in place. It is also relevant to the ability of the U.S. to fulfill its policy commitments world-wide, swiftly and in effective strength.

But, it might be asked, what is the significance of all this for the realistic security problems of the United States and its allies? To what contingencies are these forces expected to contribute, and how effective might they be, measured against the strength of opposing forces? How meaningful is it to talk of 16 or 20 or 30 divisions in opposing the ground armies of the Soviet Union and Communist China?

Such questions are often meant to be merely rhetorical, in view of the supposed masses of Communist troops. The fact is that they are serious, difficult questions, to which I shall suggest some tentative answers. But it is difficult to encourage realistic discussions of specific contingencies so long as the shadow of the Communist horde hangs unchallenged over the debate. The actual contingencies that seem to be to me most likely and most significant are not those which would involve all, or even a major part, of the Soviet Bloc or Chinese Communist armed forces, nor do they all involve Europe. Hence, aggregate figures of armed strength of NATO and the Warsaw Pact nations are not immediately relevant to them. But it is useful to make these over-all comparisons precisely because misleading or obsolete notions of these very aggregates often produce an attitude of hopelessness toward any attempt to prepare to meet Communist forces in ground combat, however limited in scope.

The announced total of Soviet armed forces for 1955 was indeed a formidable 5.75 million men. Today that figure has been cut to about 3.3 million; the Warsaw Pact total including the Soviets is only about 4.5 million. Against that, it is today the members of NATO whose active armed forces number over five million. The ground forces of NATO nations total 3.2 million, of which 2.2 million men are in Europe, as against the Soviet ground combat forces total of about 2 million men, and a Warsaw Pact total of about 3 million. Both the Soviet Union and the U.S. forces of course include units stationed in the Far East. In Central Europe, NATO has more men, and more combat troops, on the ground than does the Bloc. It has more men on the ground in West Germany than the Bloc does in East Germany. It has more and better tactical aircraft, and these planes on the average can carry twice the payload twice as far as the Soviet counterparts.

These facts are hard to reconcile with the familiar picture of the Russian Army as incomparably massive. The usual index cited to support that picture is numbers of total active divisions, and the specific number familiar from the past is 175 divisions in the Soviet Army.

This total, if true, would indeed present a paradox. The Soviet ground forces are reliably estimated to be very close to two million men, compared to about one million for the U.S. How is it that the Soviets can muster ten times the number of active, combat-ready, fully-manned divisions that the United States has manned, with only twice as many men on active duty? The answer is simply that they do not. Recent intensive investigation has shown that the number of active Soviet divisions that are maintained at manning levels anywhere close to combat readiness is less than half of the 160–175 figure.

What remains is a large number, but even that is misleading. For one thing, U.S. divisions have about twice as many men in the division unit and its immediate combat supporting units as comparable Soviet divisions. A U.S. mechanized division has far more personnel in maneuvering units, far more in armored cavalry, far more engineers, far more signals, far more light armored personnel carriers, and far more aircraft available in support than Soviet divisions. In addition to longer staying power, much of the U.S. manpower and equipment margin is muscle that would make itself felt on D-Day. If, on the other hand, we were to reorganize along Soviet lines, we could display far greater numbers of divisions comparable to those of the Soviets.

The Soviet combat-ready force remains a formidable one. Moreover, the Russians do have a powerful mobilization capability; in particular, they have a large number of lightly manned or cadre divisions to be filled out on mobilization. Still, this reality remains strikingly different from our accustomed maps of it.

I do not wish to suggest that such aggregate comparisons are by themselves a valid index to military capabilities. But they are enough to suggest the absurdity, as a picture of the prevailing military strengths on which new efforts might build, of David and Goliath notions borrowed from 1949.

None of this is to say that NATO strength on the ground in Europe is adequate to turn back without nuclear weapons an all-out surprise non-nuclear attack.

But that is not in any case the contingency toward which the recent and future improvements in the mobility and capabilities of U.S. general purpose forces are primarily oriented. Aggression on that scale would mean a war about the future of Europe and, as a consequence, the future of the U.S. and the USSR. In the face of threats of that magnitude, our nuclear superiority remains highly relevant to deterrence. The Soviets know that even non-nuclear aggression at that high end of the spectrum of conflict so threatens our most vital interests that we and our allies are prepared to make whatever response may be required to defeat it, no matter how terrible the consequences for our own society.

The probability that the Soviet leaders would choose to invoke that exchange seems to me very low indeed. They know well what even the Chinese Communist leaders must recognize upon further reflection, that a nuclear war would mean destruction of everything they have built up for themselves during the last 50 years.

If we were to consider a spectrum of the possible cases of Communist aggression, then, ranging from harassment, covert aggression and indirect challenge at one end of the scale to the massive invasion of Western Europe or a full scale nuclear strike against the West at the other end, it is clear that our nuclear superiority has been and should continue to be an effective deterrent to aggression at the high end of the spectrum. It is equally clear, on the other hand, that at the very low end of the spectrum a nuclear response may not be fully credible, and that nuclear power alone cannot be an effective deterrent at this level in the future any more than it has been in the past.

The fact is that at every level of force, the Alliance in general, and the U.S. Armed Forces in particular, have greater and more effective strength than we are in the habit of thinking we have—and with reasonable continued effort we can have whatever strength we need. I have spoken already of strategic weapons, where the great superiority of the United States is the superiority also of the Alliance. In tactical nuclear weapons a parallel superiority exists—and while many of our Allies share with us in manning the systems which would use these tactical warheads in the hour of need, it is not unfair to point out that, even more than in the strategic field, the tactical nuclear strength of the Alliance is a contribution of the United States. That strength has been increased, on the ground in Europe, by more than 60% in the last two years. Today the thousands of U.S. warheads deployed on the continent for the immediate defense of Europe have a combined explosive strength more than 10,000 times the force of the nuclear weapons used to end the Second War. Tactical nuclear strength the Alliance has today, and we have provided it.

But neither we nor our Allies can find the detonation of such weapons—and their inevitable bilateral exchange—an easy first choice. At the lower end of the spectrum, therefore, we also need strong and ready conventional forces. We have done our part here and we continue to believe it just—and practicable—for our partners to do theirs.

The most difficult questions arise over the best means for meeting a variety of dangerous intermediate challenges in many parts of the world: those which threaten the possibility of sizable conflict while still not raising the immediate issue of the national survival of ourselves or of any member of our alliances. Conflicts might arise out of Soviet subversion and political aggression backed up by military

measures in non-NATO areas in Europe, Latin America, the Middle
East and Africa. There is a range of challenges that could arise from
Communist China and its satellites in the Far East and in Southeast
Asia. Most dangerously, approaching the upper end of the spectrum,
there is the possibility of limited Soviet pressures on NATO territory itself, along the vast front running from Norway to Greece
and Turkey. Both the flanks and the center contain potential targets.
And always, of course, there are the contingencies that could arise
in relation to Berlin.

It is difficult to say just how probable any of these circumstances
might be, although they must be regarded as more likely than still
larger aggressions. What one can say is that if any of these more
likely contingencies should arise, they would be highly dangerous.
Inaction, or weak action, could result in a serious setback, missed
opportunity or even disaster. In fact, if either a nuclear exchange or
a major Soviet attack should occur, it would most likely arise from
a conflict on a lesser scale, which Western capabilities had failed to
deter and which an inadequate Western response had failed to curb
in time.

Since World War II, the expansionist impulse of the Communist
Bloc is clear, but equally clear is its desire to avoid direct confrontation with the military forces of the free world. In Greece, in
Berlin, and in Cuba, Communists have probed for military and
political weakness but when they have encountered resistance, they
have held back. Not only Communist doctrine has counselled this
caution, but respect for the danger that any sizable, overt conflict
would lead to nuclear war. It would follow that no deterrent would
be more effective against these lesser and intermediate levels of
challenge than the assurance that such moves would certainly meet
prompt, effective military response by the West. That response could
confront the Soviets with frustration of their purposes unless they
chose themselves to escalate the conflict to a nuclear exchange, or to
levels that made nuclear war highly probable—a choice they are
unlikely to make in the face of our destructive power.

The basis for that particular assurance cannot be systems in development, or weapons in storage depots, or reserves that must be
mobilized, trained and equipped, or troops without transport. We
need the right combination of forward deployment and highly
mobile combat-ready ground, sea and air units, capable of prompt

and effective commitment to actual combat, in short, the sort of capability we are increasingly building in our forces.

This capability requires of us—as of our Allies—a military establishment that is, in the President's words, lean and fit. We must stop and ask ourselves before deciding whether to add a new and complex weapon system to our inventory, whether it is really the most effective way to do the job under the rigorous conditions of combat. We must examine constantly the possibilities for combining functions, particularly in weapons that could be used by two or more Services. Given this tough-minded sense of reality about the requirements of combat readiness, it should be possible for the United States not only to maintain but to expand this increased strength without over-all increases in our defense budget. As our national productivity and our gross national product expand, the defense budget therefore need not keep pace. Indeed, it appears likely that measured in relative—and perhaps even absolute—terms, the defense budget will level off and perhaps decline a little. At the same time, we are continuing the essential effort to reduce the impact of Defense spending on our balance of payments. We have already brought this figure down from $2.7 billion in FY 1961 to $1.7 billion for FY 1963, and we shall continue to reduce it, without reducing the combat ground forces deployed in Europe, and while strengthening our over-all combat effectiveness.

And it must be our policy to continue to strengthen our combat effectiveness. I do not regard the present Communist leaders as wholly reckless in action. But recent experience, in Cuba and, on a lesser scale, in Berlin, has not persuaded me that I can predict with confidence the sorts of challenges that Communist leaders will come to think prudent and profitable. If they were again to miscalculate as dangerously as they did a year ago, it would be essential to confront them, wherever that might be, with the full consequences of their action: the certainty of meeting immediate, appropriate, and fully effective military action.

All of our strengths, including our strategic and tactical nuclear forces, contributed last year, and they would contribute in similar future situations to the effectiveness of our response, by providing a basis for assurance that the Soviets would not dangerously escalate or shift the locale of the conflict. But above all, in order to fashion that response, and to promise the Soviets local defeat in case of actual ground conflict, we had to use every element of the improvements in combat readiness and mobility that had been building over the preceding year and a half, including combat divisions, air transport, and tactical air. And the last ingredient was also there: the will to use those forces against Soviet troops and equipment.

Let us not delude ourselves with obsolete images into believing that our nuclear strength, great as it is, solves all of our problems of national security, or that we lack the strengths to meet those problems that it does not solve. In the contingencies that really threaten—the sort that have occurred and will occur again—we and our allies need no longer choose to live with the sense or the reality of inferiority to the Soviet Bloc in relevant, effective force. Let us be fully aware of the wide range of our military resources, and the freedom they can give us to pursue the peaceful objectives of the free world without fear of military aggression.[1]

President Kennedy himself had decided to sound many of the same themes on his visit to Texas. In Fort Worth, he proudly recited the increases in American military power that had occurred under his Administration and noted: "Without the United States, South Vietnam would collapse overnight. Without the United States, the SEATO Alliance would collapse overnight. Without the United States, the CENTO Alliance would collapse overnight. Without the United States there would be no NATO, and gradually Europe would drift into neutralism and indifference."[2]

Then the President went to Dallas. The speech he proposed to deliver there was intended for the nation as well as the Dallas Citizens Council. It is an appropriate valedictory. Characteristically, he was concerned that ignorance and misinformation could, "if allowed to prevail in foreign policy, handicap this country's security."

In a world of complex and continuing problems, in a world full of frustrations and irritations, America's leadership must be guided by the lights of learning and reason—or else those who confuse rhetoric with reality and the plausible with the possible will gain the popular ascendancy with their seemingly swift and simple solutions to every world problem.

There will always be dissident voices heard in the land, expressing opposition without alternatives, finding fault but never favor, perceiving gloom on every side and seeking influence without responsibility. Those voices are inevitable.

But today other voices are heard in the land—voices preaching doctrines wholly unrelated to reality, wholly unsuited to the sixties, doctrines which apparently assume that words will suffice without weapons, that vituperation is as good as victory and that peace is a sign of weakness.

At a time when the national debt is steadily being reduced in terms of its burden on our economy, they see that debt as the greatest single threat to our security. At a time when we are steadily reducing the number of Federal employes serving every thousand citizens, they fear those supposed hordes of civil servants far more than the actual hordes of opposing armies.

We cannot expect that everyone, to use the phrase of a decade ago, will "talk sense to the American people." But we can hope that fewer people will listen to nonsense. And the notion that this nation is headed for defeat through deficit, or that strength is but a matter of slogans, is nothing but just plain nonsense.

I want to discuss with you today the status of our strength and our security because this question clearly calls for the most responsible qualities of leadership and the most enlightened products of scholarship. For this nation's strength and security are not easily or cheaply obtained—nor are they quickly and simply explained.

There are many kinds of strength and no one kind will suffice. Overwhelming nuclear strength cannot stop a guerrilla war. Formal pacts of alliance cannot stop internal subversion. Displays of material wealth cannot stop the disillusionment of diplomats subjected to discrimination.

Above all, words alone are not enough. The United States is a peaceful nation. And where our strength and determination are clear, our words need merely to convey conviction, not belligerence. If we are strong, our strength will speak for itself. If we are weak, words will be no help.

I realize that this nation often tends to identify turning-points in world affairs with the major addresses which preceded them. But it was not the Monroe Doctrine that kept all Europe away from this hemisphere—it was the strength of the British fleet and the width of the Atlantic Ocean. It was not General Marshall's speech at Harvard which kept Communism out of Western Europe—it was the strength and stability made possible by our military and economic assistance.

In this Administration also it has been necessary at times to issue specific warnings that we could not stand by and watch the Communists conquer Laos by force, or intervene in the Congo, or swallow West Berlin or maintain offensive missiles on Cuba.

But while our goals were at least temporarily obtained in those and other instances, our successful defense of freedom was due—not to the words we used—but to the strength we stood ready to use on behalf of the principles we stand ready to defend.

This strength is composed of many different elements, ranging from the most massive deterrents to the most subtle influences. And all types of strength are needed—no one kind could do the job alone. Let us take a moment, therefore, to review this nation's progress in each major area of strength.

First, as Secretary McNamara made clear in his address last Monday, the strategic nuclear power of the United States has been so greatly modernized and expanded in the last 1,000 days, by the rapid production and deployment of the most modern missile systems, that any and all potential aggressors are clearly confronted now with the impossibility of strategic victory—and the certainty of total destruction—if by reckless attack they should ever force upon us the necessity of a strategic reply.

In less than three years, we have increased by 50 per cent the number of Polaris submarines scheduled to be in force by the next fiscal year—increased by more than 70 per cent our total Polaris purchase program—increased by 50 per cent the portion of our strategic bombers on 15-minute alert—and increased by 100 per cent the total number of nuclear weapons available in our strategic alert forces.

Our security is further enhanced by the steps we have taken regarding these weapons to improve the speed and certainty of their response, their readiness at all times to respond, their ability to survive an attack and their ability to be carefully controlled and directed through secure command operations.

But the lessons of the last decade have taught us that freedom cannot be defended by strategic nuclear power alone. We have, therefore, in the last three years accelerated the development and deployment of tactical nuclear weapons—and increased by 60 per cent the tactical nuclear forces deployed in Western Europe.

Nor can Europe or any other continent rely on nuclear forces alone, whether they are strategic or tactical. We have radically improved the readiness of our conventional forces—increased by 45 per cent the number of combat ready army divisions—increased by 100 per cent the procurement of modern army weapons and equipment—increased by 100 per cent our ship construction, conversion and modernization program—increased by 100 per cent our procurement of tactical aircraft—increased by 30 per cent the number of tactical air squadrons—and increased the strength of the Marines.

As last month's Operation Big Lift—which originated here in Texas—showed so clearly, this nation is prepared as never before to move substantial numbers of men in surprisingly little time to advanced positions anywhere in the world. We have increased by 175 per cent the procurement of airlift aircraft—and we have already achieved a 75 per cent increase in our existing strategic airlift capability. Finally, moving beyond the traditional roles of our military forces, we have achieved an increase of nearly 600 per cent in our special forces—those forces that are prepared to work with our allies and friends against the guerrillas, saboteurs, insurgents and assassins who threaten freedom in a less direct but equally dangerous manner.

But American military might should not and need not stand alone against the ambitions of international Communism. Our security and strength, in the last analysis, directly depend on the security and strength of others—and that is why our military and economic assistance plays such a key role in enabling those who live on the periphery of the Communist world to maintain their independence of choice.

Our assistance to these nations can be painful, risky and costly—as is true in Southeast Asia today. But we dare not weary of the task. For our assistance makes possible the stationing of 3.5 million allied troops along the Communist frontier at one-tenth the cost of maintaining a comparable number of American soldiers. A successful Communist breakthrough in these areas, necessitating direct United States intervention, would cost us several times as much as our entire foreign aid program—and might cost us heavily in American lives as well.

About 70 per cent of our military assistance goes to nine key countries located on or near the borders of the Communist bloc—nine countries confronted directly or indirectly with the threat of Communist aggression—Vietnam, free China, Korea, India, Pakistan, Thailand, Greece, Turkey and Iran. No one of these countries possesses on its own the resources to maintain the forces which our own chiefs of staff think needed in the common interest.

Reducing our efforts to train, equip and assist their armies can only encourage Communist penetration and require in time the increased overseas deployment of American combat forces. And reducing the economic help needed to bolster these nations that undertake to help defend freedom can have the same disastrous result. In short, the $50 billion we spend each year on our own defense could well be ineffective without the $4 billion required for military and economic assistance.

Our foreign aid program is not growing in size—it is, on the contrary, smaller now than in previous years. It has had its weaknesses —but we have undertaken to correct them—and the proper way of treating weaknesses is to replace them with strength, not to increase those weaknesses by emasculating essential programs.

Dollar for dollar, in or out of Government, there is no better form of investment in our national security than our much-abused foreign aid program. We cannot afford to lose it. We can afford to maintain it. We can surely afford, for example, to do as much for our 19 needy neighbors of Latin America as the Communist bloc is sending to the island of Cuba alone.

I have spoken of strength largely in terms of the deterrence and resistance of aggression and attack. But, in today's world, freedom can be lost without a shot being fired, by ballots as well as bullets. The success of our leadership is dependent upon respect for our mission in the world as well as our missiles—on a clearer recognition of the virtues of freedom as well as the evils of tyranny.

That is why our information agency has doubled the shortwave broadcasting power of the Voice of America and increased the number of broadcasting hours by 30 per cent—increased Spanish-language broadcasting to Cuba and Latin-American readers—and taken a host of other steps to carry our message of truth and freedom to all the far corners of the earth.

And that is also why we have regained the initiative in the exploration of outer space—making an annual effort greater than the combined total of all space activities undertaken during the fifties—launching more than 130 vehicles into earth orbit—putting into actual operation valuable weather and communications satellites—and making it clear to all that the United States of America has no intention of finishing second in space.

This effort is expensive—but it pays its own way, for freedom and for America. For there is no longer any fear in the free world that a Communist lead in outer space will become a permanent assertion of supremacy and the basis of military superiority. There is no longer any doubt about the strength and skill of American science, American industry, American education and the American free enterprise system. In short, our national space effort represents a great gain in, and a great resource of, our national strength—and both Texas and Texans are contributing greatly to this strength.

Finally, it should be clear by now that a nation can be no stronger abroad than she is at home. Only an America which practices what it preaches about equal rights and social justice will be respected by those whose choice affects our future. Only an America which has fully educated its citizens is fully capable of tackling the complex problems and perceiving the hidden dangers of the world in which we live. And only an America which is growing and prospering economically can sustain the worldwide defense of freedom, while demonstrating to all concerned the opportunities of our system and society.

It is clear, therefore, that we are strengthening our security as well as our economy by our recent record increases in national income and output—by surging ahead of most of Western Europe in the rate of business expansion.

And the margin of corporate profits—by maintaining a more stable level of prices than almost any of our overseas competitors—and by cutting personal and corporate income taxes by some $11 billion, as I have proposed, to assure this nation of the longest and strongest expansion in our peacetime economic history.

This nation's total output—which three years ago was at the $500 billion mark—will soon pass $600 billion, for a record rise of over $100 billion in 3 years. For the first time in history we have 70 million men and women at work. For the first time in history average factory earnings have exceeded $100 a week. For the first time in history corporation profits after taxes—which have risen 43 per cent in less than 3 years—have reached an annual level of $27.4 billion.

My friends and fellow citizens: I cite these facts and figures to make it clear that America today is stronger than ever before. Our adversaries have not abandoned their ambitions—our dangers have not diminished—our vigilance cannot be relaxed. But now we have the military, the scientific and the economic strength to do whatever must be done for the preservation and promotion of freedom.

That strength will never be used in pursuit of aggressive ambitions —it will always be used in pursuit of peace. It will never be used to promote provocations—it will always be used to promote the peaceful settlement of disputes.

We in this country, in this generation, are—by destiny rather than choice—the watchmen on the walls of world freedom. We ask, therefore, that we may be worthy of our power and responsibility—that we may exercise our strength with wisdom and restraint—and that we may achieve in our time and for all time the ancient vision of peace on earth, good will toward men. That must always be our goal —and the righteousness of our cause must always underlie our strength. For as was written long ago: "Except the Lord keep the city, the watchman waketh but in vain."[3]

Notes

Chapter 1: Prelude to Revolution

1. Charles J. V. Murphy, "The Education of a Defense Secretary," *Fortune*, May, 1962, p. 102.
2. Joseph Kraft, "McNamara and His Enemies," *Harper's Magazine*, August, 1961.
3. *Department of Defense Appropriations for 1964*, Hearings before a Subcommittee of the Committee on Appropriations, House of Representatives, Part I (Washington, D.C., 1963), p. 237.
4. Kraft, *op. cit.*
5. Stewart Alsop, "Master of the Pentagon," *The Saturday Evening Post*, August 5, 1961.
6. *United States Strategic Bombing Survey*, Summary Report (Pacific War), 1 July 1946 (Washington, D.C., 1946), p. 32.
7. *Survival in the Air Age*, A Report by the President's Air Policy Commission (Washington, D.C., January 1, 1948), p. 6.
8. Robert E. Osgood, *NATO: The Entangling Alliance* (Chicago: University of Chicago Press, 1962), p. 391, fn. 98.
9. Warner R. Schilling, Paul Y. Hammond, and Glenn H. Snyder, *Strategy, Politics, and Defense Budgets* (New York: Columbia University Press, 1962), p. 439, fn. 92.
10. John Foster Dulles, "The Evolution of Foreign Policy," *Department of State Bulletin*, Vol. XXX, No. 761.
11. Samuel P. Huntington, *The Common Defense* (New York: Columbia University Press, 1961), p. 51.
12. *Ibid.*, p. 160.

13. Schilling, Hammond, and Snyder, *op. cit.*, p. 390.
14. Huntington, *op. cit.*, p. 80.
15. General Maxwell D. Taylor, *The Uncertain Trumpet* (New York: Harper and Brothers, 1960), p. 82.
16. *Organizing for National Security*, Subcommittee on National Policy Machinery, Committee on Government Operations, U.S. Senate (Washington, D.C., 1961), I, 795.
17. Huntington, *op. cit.*, p. 222.
18. *Organizing for National Security*, I, 797.
19. *Ibid.*, pp. 787–788.
20. Dulles, *op. cit.*
21. Richard P. Stebbins, *The United States in World Affairs, 1957* (New York: Harper & Brothers, 1958), p. 51.
22. Charles H. Donnelly, *The United States Guided Missile Program* (Washington, D.C., 1959), p. 26.
23. John Foster Dulles, "Challenge and Response in United States Policy," *Foreign Affairs*, October, 1957, p. 31.
24. *Facts on File*, Vol. XIX, No. 959, March 12–18, 1959, p. 81.
25. Dean Acheson, "The Practice of Partnership," *Foreign Affairs*, January, 1963, pp. 251–252.
26. Charles H. Donnelly, *United States Defense Policies in 1958* (Washington, D.C., 1959), p. 17.
27. Taylor, *op. cit.*, pp. 82–83.
28. *Organizing for National Security*, I, 769.
29. Robert S. McNamara, Address before the American Society of Newspaper Editors, Washington, D.C., April 30, 1963.
30. *Ibid.*
31. Robert S. McNamara, Testimony before the Subcommittee on Defense Procurement of the Joint Economic Committee of Congress, March 28, 1963.
32. Charles H. Donnelly, *United States Defense Policies in 1957* (Washington, D.C., 1958), p. 83.
33. *Organizing for National Security*, I, 780.
34. Charles H. Donnelly, *United States Defense Policies in 1959* (Washington, D.C., 1960), p. 39.
35. Huntington, *op. cit.*, pp. 158–159.
36. *Public Papers of the Presidents of the United States: Dwight D. Eisenhower, 1960–61* (Washington, D.C., 1961), p. 1038.
37. Huntington, *op. cit.*, p. 146.
38. *Organizing for National Security*, I, 794.

39. Huntington, *op. cit.*, p. 101.
40. *The New York Times,* January 14, 1961.
41. *Inquiry into Satellite and Missile Programs,* Preparedness Investigating Subcommittee, Committee on Armed Services, U.S. Senate (Washington. D.C., 1958), Part 3, p. 2414.
42. Donnelly, *United States Defense Policies in 1959,* p. 12.
43. *Organizing for National Security,* I, 778.
44. John F. Kennedy, *The Strategy of Peace,* ed. Allan Nevins (New York: Harper and Brothers, 1960), p. 184.
45. *Ibid.,* p. 226.
46. *Ibid.,* p. 34.
47. *Ibid.,* pp. 37–38.
48. *Ibid.,* p. 39.
49. *Ibid.,* p. 184.
50. *Ibid.,* p. 5.
51. *Ibid.,* p. 42.
52. *Ibid.,* p. 184.
53. *Ibid.,* p. 185.
54. *Ibid.,* pp. 185–186.
55. *Ibid.,* p. 42.
56. *Ibid.,* p. 100.
57. *Ibid.,* p. 25.
58. *Business Week,* February 11, 1961.
59. *Ibid.*

Chapter 2: The Search for Options

1. John F. Kennedy, *Inaugural Address,* January 20, 1961.
2. John F. Kennedy, *State of the Union Address,* January 30, 1961.
3. *Hearings on Military Posture,* Committee on Armed Services, House of Representatives (Washington, D.C., 1962), p. 3162.
4. Robert S. McNamara, Press Conference, February 2, 1961.
5. *Department of Defense Appropriations for 1964,* Subcommittee of the Committee on Appropriations, House of Representatives (Washington, D.C., 1963), Part 1, p. 331.
6. Robert S. McNamara, Press Conference, June 23, 1961.
7. Robert S. McNamara, Testimony before the Committee on Armed Services, House of Representatives, February 23, 1961.
8. *Hearings on Military Posture,* House Armed Services Committee, 1962, p. 3226.
9. Robert S. McNamara, Testimony before the Senate Subcommittee on Department of Defense Appropriations, April 18, 1961.

10. The Harvard *Crimson*, October 30, 1961.
11. Robert S. McNamara, Testimony before the Committee on Government Operations, House of Representatives, August 1, 1961.
12. Robert S. McNamara, Testimony before the Senate Subcommittee on Department of Defense Appropriations, April 18, 1961.
13. *Ibid.*
14. Robert S. McNamara, Testimony before the Senate Foreign Relations Committee, June 14, 1961.
15. Robert S. McNamara, Address before the Governors' Conference, Hershey, Pennsylvania, July 2, 1962.
16. *Hearings on Military Posture,* House Armed Services Committee, 1962, p. 3251.
17. *Facts on File,* Vol. XXI, No. 1075, June 1–7, 1961, p. 198.
18. *Ibid.,* Vol. XXI, No. 1077, June 15–21, 1961, p. 221.
19. Roswell L. Gilpatric, Address before the Business Council, Hot Springs, Virginia, October 10, 1961.
20. Robert S. McNamara, Testimony before the Senate Armed Services Committee, July 27, 1961.
21. *Ibid.*
22. Robert S. McNamara, Address before the White House Conference on National Economic Issues, May 22, 1962.
23. *Facts on File,* Vol. XXI, No. 1093, Oct. 5–11, 1961, p. 372.
24. Robert S. McNamara, Address in Atlanta, Georgia, November 11, 1961.
25. Robert S. McNamara, Address before the Fellows of the American Bar Foundation, Chicago, Illinois, February 17, 1962.
26. Robert S. McNamara, Testimony before the House Armed Services Committee, January 30, 1963.
27. Robert S. McNamara, Address before the Governors' Conference, Hershey, Pennsylvania, July 2, 1962.
28. *Hearings on Military Posture,* House Armed Services Committee, 1962, p. 3167.
29. Robert S. McNamara, Press Release, December 4, 1962.
30. *Hearings on Military Posture,* House Armed Services Committee, 1962, pp. 3477, 3486.
31. Paul H. Nitze, Address before the Cleveland Council on World Affairs, Cleveland, Ohio, March 2, 1963.
32. *The Economist,* August 17, 1963.
33. Cyrus R. Vance, Address before the Southern Governors' Conference, White Sulphur Springs, West Virginia, August 20, 1963.
34. Robert S. McNamara, Testimony before the House Armed Services Committee, January 30, 1963.

35. *Ibid.*
36. *Hearings on Military Posture,* Committee on Armed Services, House of Representatives (Washington, D.C., 1963), p. 332.
37. *Ibid.,* p. 571.
38. *Ibid.,* p. 308.
39. Robert S. McNamara, Testimony before the House Armed Services Committee, January 30, 1963.
40. *Department of Defense Appropriations for 1964,* House Subcommittee of the Committee on Appropriations, Part 1, pp. 340–341.
41. *Hearings on Military Posture,* House Armed Services Committee, 1963, p. 415.
42. *Department of Defense Appropriations for 1964,* House Subcommittee of the Committee on Appropriations, Part 1, p. 224.
43. Robert S. McNamara, Testimony before the House Armed Services Committee, January 30, 1963.
44. *Department of Defense Appropriations for 1964,* House Subcommittee of the Committee on Appropriations, Part 1, p. 515.
45. Robert S. McNamara, Testimony before the Subcommittee on Military Airlift, Committee on Armed Services, House of Representatives, July 29, 1963.
46. *Hearings on Military Posture,* House Armed Services Committee, 1963, p. 437.
47. *Ibid.,* p. 428.
48. Robert S. McNamara, Testimony before the House Foreign Affairs Committee, April 8, 1963.
49. *Department of Defense Appropriations for 1964,* House Subcommittee of the Committee on Appropriations, Part 1, p. 236.
50. Robert S. McNamara, Testimony before the House Armed Services Committee, January 30, 1963.

Chapter 3: Dialogue with NATO

1. John F. Kennedy, Address before the Senate and House of Commons of Canada, May 17, 1961.
2. *Facts on File,* Vol. XXI, No. 1079, June 29–July 5, 1961, p. 237.
3. *Department of Defense Appropriations for 1964,* Subcommittee of the Committee on Appropriations, House of Representatives, 88th Congress, First Session (Washington, D.C., 1963), Part I, p. 223.
4. Paul H. Nitze, Remarks to the Institute for Strategic Studies, London, England, December 11, 1961.
5. Robert S. McNamara, Press Conference, November 17, 1961.
6. *Hearings on Military Posture,* Committee on Armed Services, House

of Representatives, 87th Congress, Second Session (Washington, D.C., 1962), p. 3244.

7. Robert S. McNamara, Address before the Fellows of the American Bar Foundation, Chicago, Illinois, February 17, 1962.
8. Robert S. McNamara, Address at the Commencement Exercises, University of Michigan, Ann Arbor, Michigan, June 16, 1962.
9. *Ibid.*
10. *Ibid.*
11. *Ibid.*
12. *Ibid.*
13. *Ibid.*
14. *Ibid.*
15. *Hearings on Military Posture,* Committee on Armed Services, House of Representatives, 88th Congress, First Session (Washington, D.C., 1963), pp. 296–297.
16. *Ibid.*, p. 297.
17. *Ibid.*, pp. 297–298.
18. *Ibid.*, p. 298.
19. *Ibid.*
20. *Ibid.*, pp. 298–299.
21. *Ibid.*, pp. 299–300.
22. Paul H. Nitze, Address before the Cleveland Council on World Affairs, Cleveland, Ohio, March 2, 1963.
23. *Ibid.*
24. *Ibid.*
25. *Ibid.*
26. *Ibid.*
27. *Ibid.*
28. *Ibid.*
29. Cyrus R. Vance, Secretary of the Army, Address before the Southern Governors' Conference, White Sulphur Springs, West Virginia, August 20, 1963.

Chapter 4: The Long View

1. *Hearings on Military Posture,* Committee on Armed Services, House of Representatives, 88th Congress, First Session (Washington, D.C., 1963), p. 306.
2. *Ibid.*
3. John T. McNaughton, Address before the International Arms Control Symposium, University of Michigan, Ann Arbor, Michigan, December 19, 1962.

4. *Ibid.*
5. *Ibid.*
6. *Ibid.*
7. *Ibid.*
8. *Ibid.*
9. *Ibid.*
10. *Ibid.*
11. *Ibid.*
12. *Ibid.*
13. *Ibid.*
14. *Ibid.*
15. Robert S. McNamara, Press Conference, July 6, 1962.
16. Stewart Alsop, "Our New Strategy: The Alternatives to Total War," *The Saturday Evening Post,* December 1, 1962.
17. *Ibid.*
18. Robert S. McNamara, Statement before the Senate Foreign Relations Committee, *The New York Times,* August 14, 1963.
19. *Ibid.*
20. *Ibid.*
21. *Ibid.*
22. *Ibid.*
23. *Ibid.*
24. *Ibid.*
25. *Ibid.*
26. *Ibid.*
27. *Ibid.*
28. *Ibid.*
29. *Ibid.*
30. *Ibid.*
31. *Ibid.*
32. *The New York Times,* October 5, 1963.

Chapter 5: Cost and Effectiveness

1. *Organizing for National Security,* Subcommittee on National Policy Machinery, Committee on Government Operations, U.S. Senate (Washington, D.C., 1961), I, 1197.
2. Alain C. Enthoven, Address before the American Economic Association, Pittsburgh, Pennsylvania, December 29, 1962.
3. Joseph Kraft, "McNamara and His Enemies," *Harper's Magazine,* August, 1961.
4. *Hearings on Military Posture,* Committee on Armed Services, House

of Representatives, 88th Congress, First Session (Washington, D.C., 1963), p. 373.

5. *Ibid.*, p. 501.

6. Alain C. Enthoven, Address before the American Economic Association, December 29, 1962.

7. Charles J. Hitch, The Planning-Programming-Budgeting System, June 21, 1963.

8. *Ibid.*

9. *Hearings on Military Posture,* Committee on Armed Services, House of Representatives, 87th Congress, Second Session (Washington, D.C., 1962), p. 3161.

10. Charles J. Hitch, The Planning-Programming-Budgeting System, June 21, 1963.

11. *Ibid.*

12. *Ibid.*

13. *Ibid.*

14. *Hearings on Military Posture,* House Armed Services Committee, 1963, p. 286.

15. Charles J. Hitch, The Planning-Programming-Budgeting System, June 21, 1963.

16. *Hearings on Military Posture,* House Armed Services Committee, 1962, p. 3328.

17. *Ibid.*, p. 3171.

18. *Ibid.*, p. 3243.

19. *Hearings on Military Posture,* House Armed Services Committee, 1963, p. 429.

20. *Ibid.*

21. *Ibid.*, p. 440.

22. *Ibid.*

23. *Ibid.*, p. 441.

24. Robert S. McNamara, Press Conference, February 28, 1963.

25. *Hearings on Military Posture,* House Armed Services Committee, 1963, p. 462.

26. Robert S. McNamara, Testimony before the Subcommittee on Defense Procurement of the Joint Economic Committee of Congress, March 28, 1963.

27. *Hearings on Military Posture,* House Armed Services Committee, 1963, p. 462.

28. *Ibid.*, p. 287.

29. *Hearings on Military Posture,* House Armed Services Committee, 1962, p. 3329.

30. *Ibid.*, p. 3295.

31. *Ibid.*, p. 3298.
32. *Organizing for National Security*, I, 1187.
33. *Hearings on Military Posture*, House Armed Services Committee, 1962, p. 3298.
34. *Ibid.*, p. 3296.
35. *Ibid.*
36. *Ibid.*
37. *Ibid.*
38. Robert S. McNamara, Address before the White House Conference on National Economic Issues, May 22, 1962.
39. *Hearings on Military Posture*, House Armed Services Committee, 1962, p. 3298.
40. *Ibid.*
41. Robert S. McNamara, Testimony before the Subcommittee on Defense Procurement of the Joint Economic Committee of Congress, March 28, 1963.
42. Robert S. McNamara, Memorandum for the President, July 5, 1962.
43. Robert S. McNamara, Press Conference, July 6, 1962.
44. *Ibid.*
45. Robert S. McNamara, Testimony before the Subcommittee on Defense Procurement of the Joint Economic Committee of Congress, March 28, 1963.
46. Robert S. McNamara, Press Conference, July 11, 1963.
47. Robert S. McNamara, Press Conference, July 6, 1962.
48. Robert S. McNamara, Testimony before the Subcommittee on Defense Procurement of the Joint Economic Committee of Congress, March 28, 1963.
49. *Ibid.*
50. Robert S. McNamara, Memorandum for the President, Department of Defense Cost Reduction Program, July 8, 1963.
51. *Ibid.*
52. *Ibid.*
53. *Ibid.*
54. *CBS Reports*, September 25, 1963.
55. Robert S. McNamara, Memorandum for the President, July 8, 1963.
56. *Ibid.*
57. *Ibid.*
58. *Ibid.*
59. *Ibid.*
60. *Ibid.*
61. *The New York Times*, July 13, 1963.

Chapter 6: Capitol Controversies

1. *CBS Reports,* September 25, 1963.
2. *Hearings on Military Posture,* Committee on Armed Services, House of Representatives, 87th Congress, Second Session (Washington, D.C., 1962), p. 3306.
3. *Ibid.,* p. 3345.
4. *Hearings on Military Posture,* Committee on Armed Services, House of Representatives, 88th Congress, First Session (Washington, D.C., 1963), p. 623.
5. *Department of Defense Appropriations for 1964,* Subcommittee of the Committee on Appropriations, House of Representatives (Washington, D.C., 1963), Part 1, p. 341.
6. *Ibid.,* p. 333.
7. *Ibid.* p. 312.
8. *Ibid.*
9. *Military Procurement Authorization, Fiscal Year 1964,* Committee on Armed Services, Senate, 88th Congress, First Session (Washington, D.C., 1963), p. 89.
10. *Ibid.,* p. 109.
11. *Ibid.,* p. 106.
12. *Ibid.,* p. 380.
13. *Hearings on Military Posture,* House Armed Services Committee, 1963, p. 277.
14. *Military Procurement Authorization,* Senate Armed Services Committee, 1963, p. 313.
15. *Ibid.,* p. 275.
16. *Ibid.,* pp. 298–299.
17. *Ibid.,* p. 159.
18. *Ibid.,* p. 161.
19. *Ibid.,* p. 162.
20. *Hearings on Military Posture,* House Armed Services Committee, 1962, p. 3174.
21. *Hearings on Military Posture,* House Armed Services Committee, 1963, p. 310.
22. *Ibid.,* p. 314.
23. *Ibid.*
24. *Ibid.,* p. 312.
25. *Ibid.*
26. *Ibid.*

27. *The New York Times,* March 16, 1962.
28. *Ibid.*
29. *Ibid.*
30. *Ibid.*
31. *Ibid.*
32. *Ibid.*
33. *Ibid.*
34. *Ibid.*
35. *Ibid.*
36. *Ibid.*
37. *Military Procurement Authorization,* Senate Armed Services Committee, 1963, p. 333.
38. *Ibid.,* p. 76.
39. *Ibid.,* p. 96.
40. *Department of Defense Appropriations for 1964,* Part 1, p. 238.
41. *Military Procurement Authorization,* Senate Armed Services Committee, 1963, p. 120.
42. *Hearings on Military Posture,* House Armed Services Committee, 1963, pp. 324–325.
43. Robert S. McNamara, Press Briefing, August 21, 1962.
44. *Department of Defense Appropriations for 1964,* Part 1, p. 368.
45. *Ibid.,* p. 369.
46. *Ibid.*
47. *Ibid.,* p. 404.
48. *Military Procurement Authorization,* Senate Armed Services Committee, 1963, p. 321.
49. *Ibid.,* pp. 154–155.
50. *Hearings on Military Posture,* House Armed Services Committee, 1962, p. 3307.
51. *Ibid.*
52. *Hearings on Military Posture,* House Armed Services Committee, 1963, p. 374.
53. *Hearings on Military Posture,* House Armed Services Committee, 1962, p. 3316.
54. *Hearings on Military Posture,* House Armed Services Committee, 1963, p. 361.
55. *Ibid.*
56. Robert S. McNamara, Press Conference, May 26, 1961.
57. *Organizing for National Security,* Subcommittee on National Policy Machinery, Committee on Government Operations, U.S. Senate (Washington, D.C., 1961), I, 1187.

58. *Hearings on Military Posture,* House Armed Services Committee, 1963, p. 407.
59. *Ibid.,* p. 334.
60. *Ibid.,* p. 386.
61. *Ibid.*
62. *Ibid.,* p. 623.
63. Alain C. Enthoven, Address before the Naval War College, Newport, Rhode Island, June 6, 1963.
64. *Ibid.*
65. *Ibid.*
66. *Ibid.*
67. *Ibid.*
68. *Ibid.*
69. *TFX Contract Investigation,* Permanent Subcommittee on Investigations, Committee on Government Operations, U.S. Senate (Washington, D.C., 1963), Part 2, pp. 375–376.
70. *Ibid.,* p. 376.
71. *Ibid.*
72. Robert S. McNamara, Testimony before the Subcommittee on Defense Procurement of the Joint Economic Committee of Congress, March 28, 1963.
73. *TFX Contract Investigation,* Part 2, pp. 376–777.
74. *Ibid.,* pp. 374–375.
75. *Ibid.,* p. 375.
76. *Ibid.,* pp. 387–388.

Chapter 7: Tests of Effectiveness

1. *The New York Times,* October 10, 1957.
2. Charles H. Donnelly, *United States Defense Policies in 1959* (Washington, D.C., 1960), p. 10.
3. V. D. Sokolovskii, ed., *Soviet Military Strategy,* The RAND Corporation Translation (Englewood Cliffs, N.J.: Prentice-Hall, Inc., 1963), p. 166.
4. *Facts on File,* Vol. XXI, No. 1084, August 3–9, 1961, p. 278.
5. *Ibid.*
6. *Facts on File,* Vol. XXI, No. 1094, October 12–18, 1961, p. 377.
7. *Facts on File,* Vol. XXI, No. 1099, November 16–22, 1961, p. 430.
8. Robert S. McNamara, Address before the Fellows of the American Bar Foundation, Chicago, Illinois, February 17, 1962.
9. V. D. Sokolovskii, *op. cit.,* p. 26.
10. Thomas W. Wolfe, *A Postscript on the Significance of the Book*

"*Soviet Military Strategy*," RM-3730-PR, The RAND Corporation, July, 1963, p. 29.

11. *Ibid.*, pp. 30–31.
12. V. D. Sokolovskii, *op. cit.*, p. 336, fn. 4.
13. *Ibid.*, p. 24, fn. 26.
14. *Facts on File*, Vol. XXI, No. 1077, June 15–21, 1961, p. 221.
15. *Facts on File*, Vol. XXI, No. 1078, June 22–28, 1961, p. 229.
16. *Facts on File*, Vol. XXI, No. 1079, June 29–July 5, 1961, p. 238.
17. *Hearings on Military Posture*, Committee on Armed Services, House of Representatives, 87th Congress, Second Session (Washington, D.C., 1962), p. 3354.
18. *Facts on File*, Vol. XXI, No. 1094, October 12–18, 1961, p. 377.
19. *Facts on File*, Vol. XXI, No. 1097, November 2–8, 1961, p. 407.
20. *Hearings on Military Posture*, House Committee on Armed Services, 1962, p. 3165.
21. *Department of Defense Appropriations for 1964*, Subcommittee of the Committee on Appropriations, House of Representatives, 88th Congress, First Session (Washington, D.C., 1963), Part 2, p. 503.
22. *Ibid.*, pp. 503–504.
23. *Ibid.*, p. 504.
24. *Ibid.*
25. Robert S. McNamara, Press Conference, July 6, 1962.
26. Robert S. McNamara, Statement to the House Armed Services Committee, January 27, 1964.
27. Charles J. V. Murphy, "Cuba: The Record Set Straight," *Fortune*, September, 1961, pp. 94–95.
28. *Hearings on Military Posture*, Committee on Armed Services, House of Representatives, 88th Congress, First Session (Washington, D.C., 1963), p. 235.
29. *Ibid.*, p. 300.
30. *Military Procurement Authorization, Fiscal Year 1964*, Committee on Armed Services, U.S. Senate, 88th Congress, First Session (Washington, D.C., 1963), p. 891.
31. *Hearings on Military Posture*, House Armed Services Committee, 1963, p. 897.
32. *Ibid.*, p. 692.
33. *Military Procurement Authorization, Fiscal Year 1964*, Senate Committee on Armed Services, 1963, p. 579.
34. *Facts on File*, Vol. XXII, No. 1147, October 18–24, 1962, p. 361.
35. *Facts on File*, Vol. XXII, No. 1148, October 25–31, 1962, p. 375.
36. *Military Procurement Authorization, Fiscal Year 1964*, Senate Committee on Armed Services, 1963, p. 896.

37. *Hearings on Military Posture,* House Armed Services Committee, 1963, p. 692.

Chapter 8: Agenda for Action

1. *Hearings on Military Posture,* Committee on Armed Services, House of Representatives, 88th Congress, First Session (Washington, D.C., 1963), p. 305.
2. *Department of Defense Appropriations for 1964,* Subcommittee of the Committee on Appropriations, House of Representatives, 88th Congress, First Session (Washington, D.C., 1963), Part 1, pp. 242–243.
3. *Military Procurement Authorization, Fiscal Year 1964,* Committee on Armed Services, U.S. Senate, 88th Congress, First Session (Washington, D.C., 1963), p. 159.
4. *Hearings on Military Posture,* House Armed Services Committee, 1963, p. 287.
5. *Ibid.,* p. 392.
6. *Ibid.,* p. 1226.
7. *Ibid.*
8. *Ibid.,* p. 1162.
9. *Hearings on Military Posture,* Committee on Armed Services, House of Representatives, 87th Congress, Second Session (Washington, D.C., 1962), p. 3258.
10. *Ibid.,* p. 3269.
11. *CBS Reports,* September 25, 1963.
12. *Ibid.*
13. *Hearings on Military Posture,* House Armed Services Committee, 1962, p. 3167.
14. *Ibid.,* p. 3245.
15. *CBS Reports,* September 25, 1963.
16. *Ibid.*
17. *Ibid.*
18. *Ibid.*
19. Robert S. McNamara, Remarks at the Annual National Veterans Day Ceremony, Arlington National Cemetery, November 11, 1962.

Epilogue

1. Robert S. McNamara, Address before the Economic Club of New York, Waldorf-Astoria Hotel, New York, N.Y., November 18, 1963.
2. John F. Kennedy, Text of an Address Delivered in Fort Worth,

Texas, November 22, 1963; *The New York Times,* November 24, 1963.

3. John F. Kennedy, Text of an Address Prepared for Delivery before the Dallas Citizens Council, Dallas, Texas, November 22, 1963; *The New York Times,* November 24, 1963.

Index

ABM, 156–158, 162
Acheson, Dean, 106
Africa, 62, 90, 268
Air Force Logistics Command, 191
Air Material Command, 191
Air Policy Commission, 6
Air Research and Development Command, 191
Airborne Command Post, 143
Alsop, Stewart, 2, 148
Anderson, George W., 248, 271, 296
Andrews, George W., 2
antiballistic missile, 156–158, 175–176, 229–231
Armed Forces Supply Center, 193
arms control, 136, 138, 145, 148–149, 163, 166, 167, 212–213
arms race, 52, 146–147, 209, 281
Army, Navy, Air Force Journal, 2
Army Reserve, 63–64
Atlas missiles, 35, 78, 152, 195, 225–226, 304
atmosphere tests, 161, 162–163
atomic bombs, 9, 10

B–47, 205, 217, 281
B–52, 121, 182, 216, 217–218, 220, 222, 226
B–58, 217, 226
B–70, 195, 220–223, 225–227
balance of payments, 136, 277–278, 288

"balance of terror," 36, 148
Baldwin, Hanson, 36
Ballistic Missile Early Warning System, 35
ballistic missiles, 20
Basic National Security Policy, *see* BNSP
Bay of Pigs, 268–269
Berlin, 65, 66, 68, 73, 80, 88, 91, 96, 106, 108, 110, 112, 131, 134, 136, 147, 256, 257–259, 260, 261, 268, 271, 289, 311, 312
See also East Germany *and* West Berlin
Berlin Wall, 96, 258, 259, 261
"block obsolescence," 185
Bluestreak missile, 121
BNSP, 21–22, 23, 24, 33–34, 38, 87
Boeing Company, 248
Bradley, Omar, 14
Bray, William G., 206–207, 240
budget, *see* Defense budget
See also planning-programming-budgeting

Cambodia, 260, 262
Castro, Fidel, 61, 268
CENTO Alliance, 313
CEP, 181
China, *see* Communist China; free China
Churchill, Winston, 166

Cold War, 115, 252–253
command and control system, 143–144
Common Market, 122
communism, 77, 90, 107, 122, 316
Communist China, 88–91, 161, 164, 302, 307, 309, 311
Communists, 15, 60 ff., 95, 96, 100, 131, 266, 294–295, 296–297, 311, 315, 317, 318
competitive procurement, 198–199, 202
Congo, 65
controlled response, 145
cost-effectiveness studies, 180, 181, 188, 282, 287, 290, 292, 293
cost-plus-fixed-fee contracts, 194, 199, 202
cost reduction program, 193 ff.
Cuba, 61, 65, 88, 90, 96, 134, 136, 137, 210, 213, 255, 259, 268 ff., 294, 297, 317
Cuban missile crisis, 88, 90, 91, 96, 136, 210, 213, 255, 259, 269–275, 294, 297

Davy Crockett missile, 15
Decker, George H., 82, 87
Defense budget, 19, 20, 21, 25, 48, 54, 67, 73, 74, 77–79, 85, 88, 97, 116, 119, 135, 136, 166, 169, 170, 176, 178, 225, 238, 291, 302, 306, 312
    See also planning-programming-budgeting
Defense decision-making, 2, 3, 31, 170, 172–175, 177, 180, 186–188, 236, 240
    See also planning-programming-budgeting
deficit spending, 277–278
de Gaulle, Charles, 105, 120, 126
Denfeld, Louis, 19
Department of Defense
    organization, 5, 6, 19, 23, 173, 189–191, 201
    reorganization, 23, 31, 38, 81, 189–193
deterrence, 11, 13, 52, 53, 59, 66, 69, 72, 92, 95–97, 103, 108, 116, 118, 130, 146, 282–284, 305, 317
    credibility of, 68, 74, 75, 76, 106, 107, 109, 165, 257, 284, 303

deterrence (continued)
    failure of, 51
    local, 14
    of limited war, 43
    of nuclear war, 10, 15, 16, 26, 37, 42, 60, 65, 66, 68, 75, 106, 128, 131, 256
DEW line, 35
Diem, Ngo Dinh, 261–263
disarmament, 43, 136–138, 147, 212–213, 214, 256
Distant Early Warning line, 35
Dulles, John Foster, 17–18, 25–26, 35
Dynasoar, 233, 234–235

East Germany, 91, 131, 257, 258, 308
Economist, The, 85–86
Eisenhower, Dwight D., 21, 22, 23, 25, 37, 104, 105, 251–252, 259
Enthoven, Alain, 170–171, 173, 241–245
escalation, 66–67, 72, 73, 76, 82, 83, 129, 131, 146, 214, 215, 216
European Economic Community, 104, 126

F4H, 30, 247
F-105, 30, 247
fallout, 55–56, 144, 163
Five-Year Force Structure and Financial Plan, 175–179
flexible response, 24, 51–52, 53–56
Flood, Daniel J., 2, 260, 261
Ford, Gerald R., Jr., 259
Ford, Henry II, 45
Ford Motor Company, 44, 45
Foreign Affairs, 25
foreign aid, 316–317
Forrestal, James V., 20, 290
France, 126, 133, 164, 256
free China, 317

Gaither Committee, 32
Gates, Thomas S., Jr., 32, 34, 39, 44, 238, 290
Gavin, James M., 40–41, 43
Gemini program, 233, 234–235
General Dynamics Corporation, 248–249, 250
Germany, 65, 133
    See also East Germany; West Germany

Gilpatric, Roswell L., 65–66, 108, 139–140, 166, 178, 179, 213, 254
"gold-plating," 197–198, 202
Governors' Conference (Hershey), 80
Great Britain, 4, 17, 37, 121–126, 133, 166, 256, 258
Greece, 17, 99, 311, 317
Gromyko, Andrei A., 109
guerrilla warfare, 17, 42, 59, 77, 99, 261, 294, 295, 314

Hébert, F. Edward, 237, 240
Herter, Christian A., 26, 37, 105
Hitch, Charles J., 172, 174–178, 180
Ho Chi Minh, 261, 262
Home, Sir Alec Douglas, 109
"Hot Line," 144
Hound Dog missile, 70, 125–126, 219, 220, 222

ICBM's, 35, 39, 50, 53, 54–55, 89, 94, 108–109, 158, 182, 223, 281, 283
illegal tests, 160–162
India, 317
Iran, 317
IRBM, 270

Johnson, Louis, 20
Joint Chiefs of Staff, 19, 23
Joint Committee on Atomic Energy, 58, 213–214
Joint Economic Committee, 30
Joint Strategic Objectives Plan, 22, 173, 177
JSOP, 22
Jupiter missiles, 30, 213–214

Kennedy, John F., 40–41, 42–44, 45, 57, 60–61, 66, 69, 77, 106–107, 109, 121, 125–126, 129, 137, 147, 164–166, 201, 252, 254, 256, 257, 258, 262–263, 269, 272, 273, 297–301, 313
Khrushchev, Nikita S., 17, 60, 65, 68, 73–75, 91, 108–110, 210, 213, 255 ff., 268, 271–276, 295, 296–297
Killian, James R., 32
Korea, 259, 260, 317

Laos, 61, 65, 269
Lebanon, 259

LeMay, Curtis E., 13, 248, 259–261, 271, 273, 284, 285, 296
Lemnitzer, Lyman L., 32, 238–239
limited war, 24, 27, 59, 67
Lovett, Robert, 192

McElroy, Neil H., 31, 39, 44
McNamara, Robert S.
  background, 44
  character traits, 49
  hobbies, 45
  management philosophy, 171, 172, 188, 189, 296
  political affiliations, 45
  speeches at:
    Ann Arbor, 114–121, 124, 147
    Arlington National Cemetery, 297
    Athens, 114
    Atlanta, 69
    Chicago, 73
    Economics Club of New York, 301
    Hershey, Pa., 80
McNaughton, John T., 138 ff.
M-88 tank recovery vehicle, 196
Macmillan, Harold, 121, 125–126, 129
Mahan, Alfred Thayer, 6, 7, 9
Mahon, George, 2
Malinovskii, Rodion Y., 86, 255
manned bomber, 228
Marshall, George C., 315
massive retaliation, 12, 24, 25, 35, 37, 41, 172
medium-range ballistic missiles, see MRBM
Mercury program, 235
Minuteman missile, 53, 54, 69, 78, 121, 142, 144, 151, 152, 155–156, 170, 181, 182, 216–217, 218, 219, 220, 221, 225–227, 304
missile gap, 38, 39, 40–41, 44, 47, 49–50, 65, 107–109, 254
Molotov, V. M., 295
MRBM, 36, 37, 187–188, 270, 282
multilateral nuclear force, 127, 133, 289
multiple options, 47 ff., 167, 202, 251–252, 256, 261, 268, 269, 272, 274, 275, 279–282, 287, 289

NASA, 233–235
Nassau Pact, 121, 124–126
National Aeronautics and Space Administration, 233–235

National Guard, 63, 81, 183
NATO, 2, 8, 36, 37, 42, 43, 65, 71,
    76, 83, 84, 87, 100, 102 ff., 204,
    213, 214, 289, 302, 307, 308, 309,
    311, 313
  central front, 106, 110, 112, 120
  changing relationships, 122
  command and control, 123
  comparative strengths, 122, 132
  contingency planning, 130-131
  conventional forces, 43, 102, 106-
    115, 119-121, 127, 128, 131, 134,
    208
  diversity of views, 103, 104, 107,
    111, 128, 133
  force structure, 107, 110-112, 120,
    134, 213
  forward defense, 105, 132
  gross national product, 102
  military strategy, 115, 120, 130,
    131, 133
  military strength, 115
  nuclear strategy, 115, 118
  population, 102
  strategic nuclear forces, 122
  U.S. commitment, 211
  U.S. contribution, 107, 124, 129,
    132
Near East, 90-91
New York Times, The, 201, 202
Nike missiles, 30
Nike-X, 176, 230, 231
Nike-Zeus missile, 175-176, 178, 195,
    229-230, 231
Nitze, Paul H., 18, 84, 108-110, 129-
    133, 214
Norstad, Lauris, 36-37, 103, 106, 110-
    111
North Atlantic Treaty Organization,
    see NATO
North Korea, 15-16, 260
North Vietnam, 260, 262
NSC-68, 18-21

operating costs, 176
Operation Big Lift, 307, 316
options, *see* multiple options
"overkill," 208-209, 301

Pakistan, 317
parity, 210-211, 212

Parker, T. W., 183
Pentagon, 168, 291-292
Pershing missile, 15
pipeline requirements, 196
planning - programming - budgeting,
    188-189, 194, 202-203, 236,
    290-291, 293
Polaris missiles, 35, 50, 53-54, 69, 78,
    121, 124, 126-127, 142, 144, 151,
    152, 156, 170, 173, 181, 182, 207,
    213, 214, 216-217, 218, 221, 222,
    226, 286, 304, 315
Power, Thomas S., 271
program packaging, 174-179, 186-
    188, 291

Quarles, Donald A., 35-36

RAND Corporation, 244, 292
Research and Development, 175-176,
    186
Reserve Forces Act (1955), 26
Reserve Forces, 80-82, 98, 132, 183,
    191, 281, 288
Reston, James, 253
Ridgway, Matthew B., 24
Riley, H. D., 183
RS-70, 178, 182, 220, 222-225, 226-
    227
Rusk, Dean, 150
Russell, Richard B., 1-2, 280
Russia, *see* Soviet Union

SAC, 9, 35, 36, 37, 38, 42, 50, 53-54,
    127, 140, 143, 152, 271, 302, 304
SACEUR, 127
SAM, 270
SEATO Alliance, 313
second strike, 52, 92-95, 148
Shrike missile, 287
single-threat countries, 61-62
Skybolt missile, 121, 124-125, 182,
    216, 217-220, 222, 242
Smith, Margaret Chase, 68
Sokolovskii, V. D., 97
South Vietnam, 61, 65, 261 ff., 294,
    313
Soviet Union, armed forces, 214, 215,
    282, 302, 303, 307-309
  air defenses, 218

Soviet Union (*continued*)
  conventional capabilities, 72, 84, 88, 103, 107, 108, 119–121, 133, 214, 215, 261, 289
  force make-up, 21, 65, 82–84, 130
  missiles, 93, 94, 152, 217, 304, 305
  strategy, 89, 97
  See also Khrushchev, Nikita S.
Sprint missile, 230
sputniks, 28, 38, 207
Stahr, Elvis J., 258
"stalemate," 210, 211, 212
Stennis, John C., 31
stockpiling, 37, 119, 151–152, 163, 165, 208–209, 254, 280, 306
Strategic Air Command, *see* SAC
Strategic Army Corps, 70
strategic concepts, 6–7, 8–26, 33–42, 47, 50–53, 71, 77, 88, 130, 139, 166, 278, 293, 302, 303
strategic hamlet program, 263–265
strategic nuclear warfare, 10
Strategic Retaliatory Forces, 149, 173, 182, 208, 227
STRICOM, 191
Strike Command, 191
Symington, Stuart, 212, 227
systems analysis, 179–188, 243–245

TAC, 70, 191, 248
Tactical Air Command, 70, 191, 248
tactical nuclear weapons, 97
Talos missiles, 30
Taylor, Maxwell D., 22, 24–25, 34, 39, 262–263
test ban, 43–44, 149, 152–153, 156, 158 ff., 209, 276, 278
TFX, 245–246, 249, 250, 295–296
Thailand, 99, 317
Thor missiles, 30, 149, 213, 242
Titan missiles, 78, 152, 195, 225–226, 304
Titan II, 153
Titan III, 188, 233, 234
Truman, Harry S., 18, 22
Turkey, 99, 213, 311, 317

underground tests, 149, 155, 162, 163, 164
"underkill," 208

unilateral acts, 138–139, 141, 144, 301, 305
United Kingdom, 124–126
United Nations, 4–5
United States
  Air Force, 13, 15, 29, 38, 58, 68, 95, 96, 170, 172, 173, 178, 180, 181, 191
  Armed Forces, 3, 5
  force make-up, 34, 35, 41, 42, 48, 52, 53, 58, 59, 63, 64, 67, 69, 70, 71, 78–83, 87, 97, 98, 119, 139, 166, 172, 215, 281–285, 290, 293
  Army, 13, 14, 29, 34, 58, 63, 67, 81, 96–98, 150, 172, 178, 191, 192, 271, 272, 287, 306
  Marine Corps, 58, 71, 79, 98, 271
  Navy, 13, 15, 68, 71, 78, 79, 98, 170, 172, 173, 180, 181, 183–185, 202, 271, 285, 307
United States Strategic Bombing Survey, 5–6
USSR, *see* Soviet Union

Vance, Cyrus R., 86, 214
Venezuela, 90
Vienna Conference, 1961, 60, 65
Viet Cong, 262 ff.
Vietnam, 62, 99, 260 ff., 317
Vinson, Carl, 205–206, 235–236, 240
Voice of America, 317
Vulcan bombers, 124

war by accident, 139
war by miscalculation, 139, 143
Warsaw Pact, 86, 132, 307–308
weapons-effects tests, 160–161
weapons systems, 170, 171, 173, 175
Webb, James, 233
West Berlin, 91, 113, 257, 258
West Germany, 308
Wheeler, Earle G., 271–273
White, Thomas D., 51
"whiz kids," 2, 32–33, 292–293
Wilson, Charles E., 25, 31, 44
Wilson, Robert (Bob), 240

XB-70, 227

yield-to-weight ratios, 150–151, 153–154, 157